WEST SURREY
Walks into History

ALSO BY THE LAIRD PRESS

WEST SURREY
Walks into History

David McDowall

THE LAIRD PRESS

COVER:
The Countryside in Autumn, Edward McKnight Kauffer, 1938.
© TfL Reproduced courtesy of London's Transport Museum

First published by The Laird Press
31 Cambrian Road, Richmond, Surrey TW10 6JQ
www.thelairdpress.com

© David McDowall 2013

British Library Cataloguing in Publication Data
A catalogue record for this book is available from the British Library

ISBN 978-095278478-4

Designed and typeset in Monotype Plantin & Formata
by Peter Moore

Printed in China
The Hanway Press Ltd, London & Lion Production Ltd

' *Believe me, for I know, you will find something far greater in the woods than in books. Stones and trees will teach that which you cannot learn from masters.* '

St Bernard of Clairvaux, c.1130.

' *A true conservationist is a man who knows that the world is not given by his fathers, but borrowed from his children.* '

John James Audubon, 1785-1851.

Contents

Maps

West Surrey walks overview, pp. 10-11.
Overview sketch maps at the outset of each walk.

Acknowledgements

I am extremely grateful to the following, who have gone out of their way to help me: Handa Bray, Graham Hadley, Peter James, Leo Jenning, Elizabeth Rich, Briony Thomas, and Patrick Yarnold. I am also greatly indebted to the following institutions which have allowed me to use their resources: the Guildford Institute, Haslemere Museum, the London Library, the National Library of Scotland; and the Surrey Wildlife Trust.

The illustrations are by kind permission of the following: the Guildford Institute, p.20, p.28, p.217; Peter James, p.52; London's Transport Museum, cover; Valerie Martin, p.169; Puttenham and Wanborough History Society, p.140, p.142; Ockley Parish Archives, p.57, p.59; Thursley History Society, p.63; Shere Museum, p.171, p.188; Deborah Wolton, p.35. To the best of my knowledge the remainder are all out of copyright, including photographs in Gertrude Jekyll's *Old West Surrey* (1904), but excepting possibly those of the late Mr M.W. Inman (p.111), whose estate I have been unable to trace. Mapping is based on Ordnance Survey on behalf of HMSO.

This is the seventh walker's guidebook I have written. Each one of them has been laid out and designed by Peter Moore, and I am in his debt for the consistently high quality of his work which readers find so instantly attractive. It is also the seventh that my dear wife, Elizabeth, has edited. She still has to correct the same grammatical infelicities that beset my first guidebook 17 years ago. On that score I am forever flat-lining. I am so grateful for her patience as well as her skill and her love.

David McDowall
Richmond, April 2013

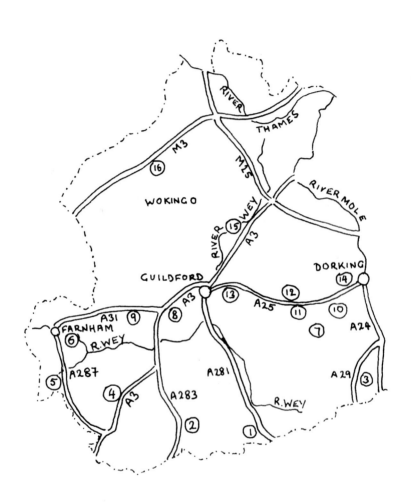

Overview of West Surrey walks

WALKS

1. ALFOLD & THE WEY-ARUN JUNCTION CANAL
2. CHIDDINGFOLD & DUNSFOLD CHURCH
3. OCKLEY
4. THURSLEY & THE DEVIL'S PUNCH BOWL
5. FRENSHAM GREAT POND & RIVER WEY
6. WAVERLEY & TILFORD
7. LEITH HILL & HOLMBURY CAMP
8. THE HOG'S BACK: COMPTON TO GUILDFORD
9. PUTTENHAM VILLAGE & COMMON
10. THE WOTTON ESTATE
11. SHERE & ITS HINTERLAND
12. SHERE'S DOWNS, NEWLANDS CORNER & ALBURY
13. St MARTHA'S HILL & CHILWORTH POWDER MILLS
14. RANMORE & POLESDEN LACEY
15. THE RIVER WEY NAVIGATION & NEWARK PRIORY
16. CHOBHAM COMMON

Introduction

I have defined West Surrey as that part which lies west of a line following the River Mole from the Thames (opposite Hampton Court Palace)
southwards to Dorking and thence southwards west of the A24.

Many people are disparaging about the Surrey countryside. Walking is
severely limited by the heavy suburbanisation of the northern part of the
county, which once included the entire south bank of London's Thames.
There are still many small patches of open land good enough for a short
stroll, but hardly any of them sufficient for a properly rewarding walk.
Further south, an intense network of arterial routes interrupts the landscape, and even minor roads are busy because of population density.
They are a jarring presence for walkers. As a result almost all the walks in
this book lie beyond the bounds of suburbia and main roads.

Despite all the above, Surrey has a higher proportion of common land
than any other English lowland county save Hampshire, which has the
New Forest. There is public access to 36,000 acres of the county. It is
proportionately the most heavily wooded county in England. The Surrey
Hills, 160 square miles, are protected as an area of outstanding natural
beauty. Green Belt legislation covers virtually everywhere else. Of the
whole county, 38 per cent is open field, 24 per cent woodland and 20 per
cent is heath, downland or heath-woodland.

All the walks in this guide are circuits, and most are between 5-10km
in length, between two and four hours in duration. I have tried to cherry-
pick walks (and those who know Surrey well will think I have missed all
sorts of delights) which are not only visually rewarding but which also
reveal the elements that shaped the western part of the county before the
railway and tarmac roads transformed it. I have deliberately designed
some walks to cross the geological boundaries, so that one may note
with pleasure the sudden sharp differences beneath one's feet and in the
foliage.

Every landscape tells a story, based upon the geology which deter-
mines the ecology, historic land use and even architecture. That is why
this walker's guide is subtitled 'Walks into History.' I hope that every walk
completed will reward you not simply by the beauty of the countryside,
but by contributing to your picture of Surrey past.

We are fortunate to have some remarkable witnesses dating back to 1650, and I have had no hesitation in calling upon them to give their own impressions. These are:

1 John Evelyn (1620-1706), an outstanding diarist, writer and gardener who spent his childhood and old age at Wotton. He pioneered new forms of garden at Wotton and at Albury, the latter now sadly disappeared. And he wrote about trees and soils. He is described more fully on page 148.

2 John Aubrey (1626-97) was a 'riches to rags' antiquary and biographer. His *Monumenta Britannica* (absurdly not published until 1982) is a foundation text of English archaeology, recording sites which have subsequently been erased. In 1673 he was licensed to produce a survey of Surrey, and so began his 'perambulation', published in five volumes in 1718-19.

3 William Cobbett (1763-1835), the son of a Surrey labourer, became an essayist, politician and agriculturalist. He farmed at Barnes on the Thames, and later at Normandy, north of the Hog's Back. He was a radical of fierce opinions, some of them appalling, but also a doughty champion of the rural poor. His *Rural Rides* and autobiographical writings provide an extraordinary and impassioned insight into Surrey as it entered a period of radical change. Here is a foretaste about his childhood:

> I was bred at the plough-tail, and in the Hop Gardens of Farnham in Surrey... I do not remember the time when I did not earn my living. My first occupation was, driving the small birds from the turnip seed, and the rooks from the peas. When I trudged further afield, with my wooden bottle and my satchel over my shoulders, I was hardly able to climb the gates and stiles, and, at the close of the day, to reach home was a task of infinite labour. My next employment was weeding wheat, and leading a single horse at harrowing barley. Hoeing peas followed, and hence I arrived at the honour of joining the reapers in harvest, driving the team and holding the plough.

4 Gertrude Jekyll (1843-1932) grew up at Bramley, just east of Godalming, and became famous for her skill as a garden designer. She learnt photography in the 1880s and recorded the vanishing traces of the rural world in which she had grown up. *Old West Surrey* was

published in 1904, based on 'notes and memories' of her early life: both a paean to the scene of her youth, and a lamentation at its passing. As you travel through the Surrey Hills it is impossible not to be struck by the dramatic sunken lanes, some of them still very narrow, despite the tarmac surfacing. Jekyll recalls driving her trap down one such narrow lane:

> Two labourers stood at the edge of a field, some ten feet above a hollow lane, where I was driving, and passing a farm cart, with barely an inch to spare. The cart had stopped and had one wheel already a little way up the steep bank.
>
> 'Lane's ter narrer.'
>
> 'Yus' (long pause, and then this profound remark); 'it ain't wide enough.'

5   George Sturt (1863-1927) was a Farnham-born writer and wheelwright. A grammar school teacher, he was compelled to take over the family wheelwright shop on the death of his father in 1884. His respect for the ordinary working people among whom he lived in Bourne, then a hamlet, now part of Farnham, was never clouded by romanticism or caricature. He wrote with the eye of love about people's lives, their triumphs, tribulations and qualities, both good and bad. Like Jekyll, he lamented the end of an intimacy with and close understanding of the land, brought about by modern technology and suburbanisation. He was a prolific writer, his most notable classic works being *Change in the Village* (1912) under a pseudonym, George Bourne, and *The Wheelwright's Shop* (1923). Easily available second-hand, if you do nothing else, read these books. I promise you will not regret it.

Like Jekyll, Sturt knew Surrey when it still had its own distinctive dialect, when ordinary folk, for example, pronounced 'plough' as 'ploo', and 'put' as a golfing 'putt', and used words that were incomprehensible to the incoming settlers from London. Who, coming from the City, would guess that *bever* was elevenses, or that *bait* was the afternoon snack? You listen to your native neighbour complaining he's *beazled* [tired out] carrying *bavins* [bundles of faggots] for the *gaffer* [master], who treats him as a *runagate* [good-for-nothing]; with a *shimper* [a glance in passing] *caterways* [diagonally] across the green he sees a notorious *blobtit* [prattler] who likes to *gamack* [gossip]; and while he *shimpers*, he should take care not to trip on the *clivers* [surface roots] of trees which might be *sproddies* [stag-headed oaks] and mind that *dorling* [the runt of the pig litter] which loves rolling in the *slub* [thick slimy mud of the Weald], and so on.

At the end of this book there are a few pages of background notes, a compilation of things learnt and kept in mind while writing this book. Virtually all the illustrations are old, many of poor original quality. They have been enhanced for clarity as far as possible.

Finally, I regret there is some repetition of information, from one walk to another, but it will only become really noticeable if you do all the walks, in which case I shall happily look forward to your complaints.

How to use this book & practical points

I have tried to make every walk accessible by both car and public transport. Every walk is a circuit, and if you are car-less and use public transport you sometimes start the walk at a different point on the circuit from car users, as indicated in the introduction to each walk. It is hardly surprising that if you wish to walk well away from population centres, getting there by public transport can be a challenge. The most challenging are Ockley which is almost impossible to access by bus; Ranmore Common is not served by bus, one must either walk or take a taxi from Dorking Station, and Chobham Common must be reached from Chobham village. Always check the public transport for yourself.

ROADS: I have sought to avoid roads as much as possible. Occasionally there is no choice. Please bear in mind the potential danger: as a general rule, walk in single file on the right hand side, facing the oncoming traffic (which makes you far more noticeable), and make sure the leader is wearing something bright.

MAPS: Even though the written directions are meticulous, with sketch maps where there might still be doubt, some prefer to use an OS map to follow the lie of the land. The appropriate 1:25,000 OS Explorer map is listed at the outset of each walk and periodic 8-figure grid references provided, which take you to the nearest 10-20 metres of where you should be standing. (If you normally only use 6-figure references, you are used to locating a position to the nearest 100 metres. The fourth and eighth figures of an 8-figure GR theoretically indicate within 10-metre accuracy, helpful if you need to be sure of a small footpath.) Even if you are using a 1:50,000 Landranger map or, like me, often use a battered old one-inch (1:63,360) map, the grid references remain the same. You may like to plot the walk on your map beforehand, but fail to read the text and you may miss out on the significance of the landscape.

MAKE A DAY OF IT: where there are other obvious attractions reasonably close to a walk, I have flagged these up, and also given a summary list of these on p.255.

Alfold and the Wey-Arun Junction Canal

Distance 9km/5 miles: 2½ hours
OS Explorer Map No.134

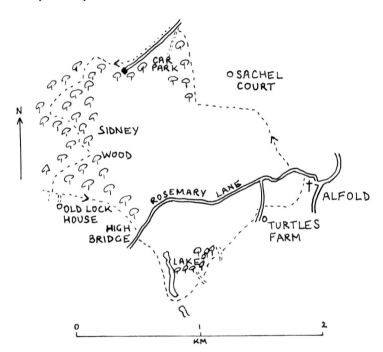

BEFORE YOU WALK

The themes of this walk are the economic life of the Weald, based on an iron industry which consumed plenty of local wood, and the attempt to create access to external markets for trade. Almost half the walk follows the Wey-Arun Junction Canal, which sought to address the deep economic isolation of the Surrey Low Weald at the outset of the nineteenth century. The stretch to be walked is the most technically difficult section of the canal construction through hilly country before its descent towards the coast. There is something heroic and beautiful about the empty canal bed now. You may wish to read over the descriptive section (p.22) before embarking on the walk.

Starting from Alfold church, be brief with this visual treat at the outset and relish it on your return, before repairing to the Crown Inn (at the time of writing up for sale), Alfold Barn or The Sun in nearby Dunsfold.

You will be wondering about the name, Alfold. Its origin is very simple, meaning 'old fold', clearly a reference to the early, in fact Saxon, stock-herding of Wealden life.

If you are looking for any other themes, try thinking about the Weald's notorious mud, glorious mud, particularly if you undertake the walk after rainfall, and be shod accordingly.

If car-less: No. 24 and No. 42 bus to Alfold Crossways, 1½ km walk into Alfold to start.

Refreshment: Alfold Barn (tel. 01403 752 288) www.alfoldbarn.co.uk. Two km north at Alfold Crossways, turn right onto Horsham Road, Alfold Barn is shortly on the left.

Start: at the heart of Alfold village, in front of the church [GR 0380 3400].
For the time being, just enjoy the words of Nairn & Pevsner: 'the tiny place formed by two tile-hung cottages beside the footway to the church, [is] another of the picturesque cameos in which Surrey excels.' Investigating the church can come at the end of the walk.

Follow the path through the churchyard, and on reaching the road turn left. Ignoring the footpath next to Linden Farm, after 100m take the footpath to the right (just after Dover Cottage), where the road curves to the left [GR 0355 3410]. Follow it over three stiles. After the third, walk straight across the open field, making for the barns, their roofs just visible on the skyline straight ahead. Go through the metal gate, across the tarmac and through the second metal gate, following the path towards the red brick house, which after about 100m takes you to a stile on the fence on the left [GR 0330 3455]. Cross the stile, and make for the metal gate on the far side of the field.
On your right stands the red brick house, Sachel Court, a late Victorian pile, already with an Edwardian look. It is the headquarters of the Merchant Seamen's War Memorial Society, founded in 1920 and which

came here in 1947. It continues to give succour to retired seafarers of the Merchant and Royal Navies, and fisheries, through sheltered accommodation and holiday homes for

> *Those that go down to the sea in ships, that do business in great waters;*
> *these see the works of the Lord, and his wonders in the deep.*
>
> Psalm 107.23

And next time you tuck into haddock, plaice or some other seafood, raise a glass to the fishermen whose lives involve peril on the sea, and be thankful.

On reaching the metal gate (just beyond a stile), walk to the woodland, and continue through it for just over 100m until reaching a larger cross track. Turn right and almost immediately left, then after a few paces, turn right just beyond the sign 'Riding by Permit only', towards the open field visible through the trees. Before following the path just inside the woodland with the field on your right, take a quick look at the landscape straight ahead [GR 0280 3475].

In the distance there is a view of the Lower Greensand Hills, as they appear from the Weald. This is, indeed, classic Low Weald territory: plenty of lapsed hazel coppice (see p.172) under a canopy of standard oaks. Coppice is very widespread here and is the principal flora characteristic of this walk. Every open field here was once 'assarted', or cut, from the ancient natural woodland, probably in the late Middle Ages or even in the seventeenth or eighteenth century, much later than the rest of England. Much of the underwood would have been taken for iron foundries, the principal Wealden industry, while much of the oak timber went to build houses.

Now take that path on your left which shadows the field, just inside the woodland, for about 400m.

Underwood rather than timber was always the principal woodland crop of Surrey. Duly coppiced, it fulfilled a wide variety of tasks. One of the important ones was for conversion into charcoal. Charcoal can achieve far higher temperatures than wood.

Charcoal was produced in significant quantities to fuel the iron working industry in its hey-day in the sixteenth and seventeenth centuries (see below). It is widely believed that the iron industry destroyed the oak woodland of the Weald. This is a myth. Neglectful landlords did indeed deplete their stock, but most landlords were constantly replenishing by

Joseph Kingshott, woodman and collier, aged about 60, standing in front of a heap of ash, presumably after a successful burn in about 1900. He was born just over the Sussex border in Ludgersall, and was a familiar sight, charcoal-burning in the Alfold and Plaistow woods.

sowing new stands and new coppice, if anything increasing the acreage of woodland.

After the decline of the iron industry, those who made charcoal in the Weald, found new and growing demand in the hop business. Hop driers liked to use charcoal for their small kilns. By 1900, however, hop production was itself in decline around Farnham, and the charcoal industry of the Surrey Weald was in its death throes.

After 400m the path veers to the left. Cross the hardcore road (leading to a car park) and after 15m on reaching the tarmac road [GR 0262 3519], turn left along it. (After 400m a house should be visible ahead.)

Like many woodland floors in Surrey, if you are here in early May, you will see bluebells. Bluebell drifts are a quintessentially British sight from Cape Wrath to Land's End. They are indicators of 'ancient woodland', in other words woodland that has existed for at least 400 years, and in their own right they are objects of wonder. They burst forth in song at the selfsame time as the cuckoo:

And azuring-over greybell makes
Wood banks and brakes wash wet like lake
And magic cuckoocall
Caps, clears, and clinches all –

G.M. Hopkins, *The May Magnificat*

Wood is heavy and charcoal light. It made sense to convert wood to charcoal on site before transporting it. Colliers worked on location, and lived in rudimentary turf or canvas-covered huts while working (p. 251). They would prepare the wood, by cutting it to one metre lengths, stacking it in bundles, or 'cords', to season, before being laid around a hearth of some four or five metres diameter, stacked in layers sloping inwards. At the centre of the 'dome' would be a 'chimney' of split logs, about 2 metres in height. Layers of straw, leaves or turves were laid on top, and finally a layer of earth to shut out almost all oxygen. The pyre would be lit on a windless day, and canvas screens kept in readiness (as below) to protect against any draught. A perfect burn will result in the wooden logs emerging carbonised but virtually unbroken, but the size now greatly diminished, as below.

Look out, too, for the wood anemone, another indicator of ancient wood-land. It flowers early to catch sufficient light before the full shade of the tree canopy. Where bluebells spread rapidly, the wood anemone moves with slow deliberation underground, no more than two metres in a century, so when you see a swathe, you may rightly wonder at its antiquity. There are also yellow pimpernel, dog's mercury, enchanter's nightshade, wood speedwell, pignut, lily of the valley and wild daffodil.

When you can see the house, with its access gate, about 100m ahead at the end of the road, slip onto a path on your right [GR 0220 3490]. A wooden post a few paces along it very discreetly marked 'Wey-South Path', takes you along the right fork. Follow this path for about 200m till you pass a metal gate. A few paces beyond, turn left, with the bed of the Wey-Arun Junction Canal on your left [GR02003495]. Walk beside the canal for almost 2km (till you reach a formal hardcore cross-track with a house beyond it).
But first read the following.
The Wey-Arun Junction Canal formally closed in 1871. What you now see is the canal bed, progressively cleared of over a century's tree and shrub growth during the past 30 or so years. It is all the work of volunteer passion. Parts, for example at Loxwood, have been fully restored, but the intention is to complete the whole canal to achieve a through route to the coast. (Inspired? Visit www.weyandarun.co.uk.)

The canal was a bright idea to link London's principal waterway, the Thames, with the south coast, via the River Arun which reaches across the Sussex Weald, and at the south end would lead to Portsmouth, via the Portsmouth and Arundel Canal. Arun navigation had been improved in the sixteenth century to make Arundel, six miles inland, a viable port, and an Arun Canal progressively extended northwards to reach Newbridge, near Billingshurst, in 1787.

It was during the Napoleonic War in 1810 that the Earl of Egremont, who lived at Petworth, thought it a compellingly sensible thing to have a route to the south coast that did not involve running the gauntlet of hostile warships in the Channel. He persuaded others that a junction canal would do the trick. In 1813 the Royal Assent was obtained. The initiators convinced investors that about 30,000 tons of local freight, and up to 100,000 tons, or one twelfth of the London-Portsmouth trade would be carried by the new canal, to run from the Wey at Shalford, just south of Guildford, to Newbridge.

The route had to cross a watershed between the Wey at Godalming and the descent from the Surrey-Sussex border to the coast. That watershed occurred near Cranleigh, but shortly thereafter work near Alfold was substantially delayed by the discovery that 2,000 yards had to be cut through friable sand and required lining with clay. Along this stretch, right here, the canal had to negotiate very difficult terrain to maintain its altitude as it negotiated the hillside.

As you walk, you will notice how the canal at one point clings to the hillside with a steep slope falling away to the right. You will also note (after about 1½ km) a sudden widening of the canal to form a 'pool', where barges could be assembled before beginning their descent through Lock No.16. The lock has long since gone, but it is marked by a section of still overgrown canal bed at a visibly lower level. It is unclear who actually carried out the manual labour, but it probably involved French prisoners of war, underfed and grossly overworked.

The canal was completed with no fewer that 26 locks in 1816, but not before the contractor had gone bankrupt. The ensuing trade was profoundly disappointing and the canal turned out to be a poor investment. Even in its best year, 1839, when it carried 23,000 tons of freight, it was totally eclipsed when compared with, for example, the Kennet & Avon Canal's 300,000 tons. One of the reasons for the poor level of usage may have been the huge problems in keeping the summit levels along this stretch navigable during periods of drought. In the 1840s the canal received its commercial deathblow: the laying of railway lines to various population centres along the south coast. By the mid-1860s the canal was derelict and weed-filled.

Turn left on reaching the cross track (with a house opposite) [GR 0163 3390]. After 50m pass a gate on your right (to Old Lock House) and soon after pass a sign marked 'Sydney Wood'.
The Old Lock House is now private but once was for the keeper operating Lock No.15, where the canal began a steeper descent, with another three locks at roughly 200 metre intervals.

The woodlands nearby were the site of a revival of Surrey glassmaking in the second half of the sixteenth century, when a team of skilled French Huguenots from Lorraine procured a licence to make 'glass for glazing such as is made in France, Burgundy and Lorraine.' Their product must have been much more sophisticated than the earlier glass making

The late seventeenth century Ashburnham long case clock depicts the work of the iron foundry and its cannon production. The inside of the face: at 11 o'clock iron ore is extracted and transported; at 1 a tree is felled and the wood cut; at 2 it is turned to charcoal. At 3 the hammer driven by the millrace is at work beating sheet metal; at 4 a cannon, which would have been cast, is weighed, and at 6 one can see the mill wheel driven by the millrace. On the outside of the face: at 4 and 5 a man works the bellows to produce molten iron for a fireback; at 1 and 2 a man wheels more fuel into the furnace, while underneath molten iron is collected; at 10 and 11 a cannon is calibrated by target practice, and at 7 and 8 a cannon weighed and registered.

at Chiddingfold (p.42). Production ceased after 1615, when James I prohibited the use of charcoal for glass-making, insisting on coal instead.

Follow the track till you reach a white house and beyond it the tarmac road, Rosemary Lane.

The white house is relatively modern. There used to be a 'High Bridge' across the canal here, which is now simply a name on the map.

Long before the existence of the canal and its high bridge, Sidney Wood had been a thoroughfare for smugglers. A local woman, 'Dame Tickner' (it is hard to be sure of her identity as there were several Tickners in the village), who was supposedly born in 1764 and who in her youth had lived on Rosemary Lane, remembered in her old age in about 1850:

> When in bed she would hear them splashing down the lane on their powerful horses laden with spirit kegs…. The smugglers' kegs were hidden in farm houses in Sidney Wood, where recesses in the great chimneys received them, and if a farmer allowed smuggled goods to be hidden in his farm, he would always find a present of spirits left behind for him.

The smugglers must have been on their way to London, perhaps using one of the large heaths to the north, for example Bagshot or Hounslow Heath, as a final hide before making for their destination in the city.

Turn right and almost immediately turn left along the footpath once again [GR 0231 3359] shadowing the canal on its right side for 500m.

While walking you may care to contemplate all that coppicing, and how it once fuelled the Surrey-Sussex iron industry. Before the late fifteenth century iron was produced by 'bloomeries', circular floors of sandstone with alternate floors of charcoal and ore built into a conical heap, and covered with clay. Bellows were used to obtain maximum heat. The molten metal collected in a sump, or 'bloom', and was beaten into sheets by hammering at a forge. Blast furnaces were introduced to the Weald by Walloons from the Low Countries in the late fifteenth century. These required waterpower for the bellows and for hammering, hence hammer ponds to give adequate 'head' to drive a waterwheel to power the hammer. The only traces today are a few surviving ponds and 'Hammer' remembered in place names. William Camden, whose *Britannia* was published in 1586, reminds us what a noisy and noisome industry it was:

> Full of iron mines it [Surrey] is in sundry places, where for the mak-
> ing and fining whereof there bee furnaces on every side, and a huge
> deale of wood is yearely spent, to which purpose divers brookes in
> many places are brought to runne in one chanell, and sundry me-
> dowes turned into pooles and waters, that they might bee of power
> sufficient to drive the hammer milles, which beating upon the iron,
> resound all over places adjoyning.

Sussex was England's principal centre for iron working up to around
1600, and the land around Alfold would have been a charcoal supplier
to iron working in the neighbourhood. The increasing cost of producing
charcoal, and competing demand for the hop industry, seriously reduced
the iron industry in the Weald. The coup de grâce came with the discovery in Durham that coal could be turned into coke, but the end was
greatly hastened by acute droughts between 1737 and 1750. For example,
in 1744 it was reported at one works:

> Mr Crowley's furnaces are blown out for want of water.... They
> tread the wheel at Waldron, Robertsbridge and Beckly [all in Sussex],
> which is an excessive charge... as if men should walk in one of your
> Capstans, night and day for a quarter of the year together.

The very last forge to close was at Ashburnham in Sussex in 1820.

Turn left over the first bridge.
On your left is a scenic lake. It looks as if it has been here a long time. In
fact it is modern landscaping, formed by stopping up a stream.

Follow the path to cross the foot of the lake [GR 0263 3309], and up through the gate on the far side. Follow the path straight across the field, and through the gate on the far side, this time keeping to the left side of the field, against the woodland except for the last few paces.
Alfold was unlike most other parishes in Surrey, because out of over
2,000 acres, it had no more than twenty deemed to be 'waste', unfit for arable, pasture or meadow. However, the clay was heavy and unsuitable for
either wheat or barley, so it could only produce oats. As in so many parts
of the Weald, where the pattern was of small-holding farmers, oxen were
still being used to draw their ploughs in 1800, long after most of England
had shifted to horse-drawn ploughing. The unavoidable truth was that by
1800 Surrey was still noticeably backward compared with its neighbours,
as a report on the state of Surrey in 1794 acidly confirmed:

Upon these very small farms, every species of bad husbandry is practised; foulness of the land, the want of ability to manure the soil, a poverty of produce, the occupation in a state little better than that of wretchedness and misery and, too strongly evinced by their more wretched habitation.

Much parish land was set aside for coppice grown for various purposes but principally for charcoal production. Coppice now constitutes an important habitat nature conservation.

Cross the track and continue through the next gate in the same direction to the far side. Again, ignore the cross track, but on entering the field through the wide metal field gate, walk diagonally to the opposite corner where it should be possible to see a stile and gate.

As you approach you will see the smart ordered gardens and buildings of the seriously horsey Turtles Farm [**GR 0334 3370**].

Cross the stile to the left of the gate and follow the edge of the field beside the horse track until signposted after about 100m across a stile on your right. With your back to this stile, look across the two tarmac tracks for another stile and signpost slightly to your right, a bit nearer the buildings, and follow its direction along the edge of two fields. Cross the stile and stream in the gully, climb uphill still following the signs. Cross another stile and after a few paces pass the small village cemetery on your left.

Unlike the old tombs of the village churchyard, most of which are safely in the more distant past, this cemetery of the recently departed is a gentle *memento mori* whispered in our ear while we are still fit and healthy. Like taxation, it inescapably comes to all of us. Across the landscape, in the fields, woodland, farmsteads and churches we see the traces of how others have lived their lives.

On reaching the road turn right and shortly thereafter turn right again into the village churchyard.

THE CHURCH OF ST NICHOLAS

THE EXTERIOR. The structure is more typical of Sussex than Surrey, with its immense and elegant cat-slide roof sweeping almost to the ground, partly covered with Horsham slates. The walls are Bargate stone, rendered with plaster. The fifteenth century bell tower is dressed in small shingles. If you have time to kill, wander around the churchyard, almost always a rewarding exercise. One of those buried here was Mary Woods, in April 1683. She was interred wrapped in cloth, a legal requirement between the years 1678 and 1815 in order to provide demand for the ailing wool trade. Scotland made a similar demand at about this time, in its case, with linen.

THE INTERIOR. The nave and chancel were probably built around 1100, and the south aisle (on the right) about a century later, when the rounded Norman pillars must have replaced the outer wall. The north aisle (on the left) was built about 80 years later. Stand at the back of the central nave, beneath the bell tower under the massive fifteenth century timber frame which

The Rev. R. J. Sparkes, vicar of Alfold in the middle years of the nineteenth century. One would never guess from this portrait that he sired no fewer than 22 children, a fact of which his magnificently fertile wife was immensely proud.

holds it up. Fashioned with axe and adze, this frame is a real joy to behold. You will notice that the pulley for the bells has been locked – clearly following too many instances of youthful roistering. Standing here one may also envisage the original structure before the south aisle was added. The arches supporting the south aisle were removed at some stage and the whole aisle removed. They were only replaced when the building was restored in 1842, and the pier bases for the south arcade discovered, which is why the round piers lack capitals. The addition of these two side aisles is an indicator of population growth that was happening all over England, in part brought on by the prosperity resulting from the stability following the political disorders of the war between Stephen and Matilda, 1135-54. Population growth, however, faltered and then reversed due to climate change with years of failed harvests and famine in the early fourteenth century, leading up to the massive population collapse over a few short months in the Black Death of 1348-9.

THE FURNISHINGS. There are several features worthy of your admiration.

- The baptismal font carved from Bargate stone, decorated with modified Maltese crosses, is one of the oldest and best preserved in all Surrey. It is probably eleventh century, perhaps installed when the church was first built. It still has the staple inserted in 1236 for a lockable lid, to prevent the theft of holy water for magical rites.
- The pulpit is Jacobean, one of elegant simplicity with a sounding board behind to help the congregation hear more clearly.
- Just beside the door stands a chest bearing the names of the two churchwardens of 1687.
- As you leave, admire the wrought-ironwork of the door.

ON LEAVING THE CHURCH

Note the stocks, apparently one of only two complete sets in Surrey, information that implies that while almost all Surrey is now utterly unprepared, Alfold remains ready for any collapse of social discipline. There was a schoolhouse adjacent to the graveyard in the 1870s, filled with 43 'exceedingly backward' children. Any of these children, apparently, who dared to laugh in church was thrashed, committed to the stocks, and given time to regret his or her zest for the funny side of life. This three-part treatment must have been a great success at instilling respect for authority but a dead loss at teaching love, which one might innocently have thought to be the real mission of the Church.

Walk down into the village, noticing that the heart of the village lurks in a dell, and take a good look back at the view of the church with its neighbouring cottages.

You will recall the words of Nairn & Pevsner: 'the tiny *place* formed by two tile-hung cottages beside the footway to the church, [is] another of the picturesque cameos in which Surrey excels.' They continue:

> However accidentally or unconsciously arrived at, this group provides an experience on the same level as a good Lutyens house. It is worth while seeing how it is obtained – chiefly by the repeating small-scale rhythm of the scallop-edged tiles (plain tile-hanging would not have the same effect at all), but also the contrast given by the plain white-painted ground-floor, brick in one cottage, brick and half-timber in the other.

So delight in it.

WALK

2

Chiddingfold to Dunsfold Church

Distance 10km/6miles: 3 hours
OS Explorer Map No.133

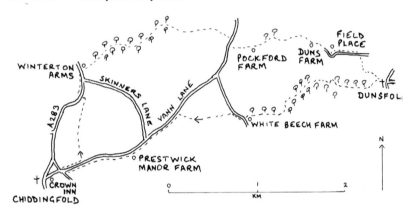

BEFORE YOU WALK

Chiddingfold lies in the heart of the Low Weald, with deep tenacious clay underfoot and oak, 'the weed of the Weald', the most common inhabitant of the extensive Wealden woodlands. So this walk is devoted principally to native trees and in particular to the English or Common oak (*Quercus robur* or *pedunculata*), the principal material from which England's houses and ships were built over many centuries.

Quite as much as the Rose, the Oak embodies a profound idea of England, associated with the idea of liberty in the greenwood. Think of Herne's Oak, and of Robin Hood. Most of all, however, the oak has entered the national imagination as a trusty bulwark against its enemies, never more so than with regard to the Royal Navy, given voice in its eighteenth century anthem, 'Hearts of oak are our ships/Hearts of oak are our men.' By then, however, the oak had been consciously lodged in the national imagination for at least a century, with Charles II seeking refuge in an oak in 1650, and with John Evelyn lamenting the 'the notorious depletion of England's "wooden walls'", and claiming there was 'nothing which seems more fatally to threaten a Weakning, if not a Dissolution of the strength of this famous and flourishing Nation.' There was no doubt about the importance of oak in reality as well as the imagination, but perhaps his ear had been bent a little too much by Samuel Pepys who, like other members of the Admiralty, wailed of a critical oak shortage every time they had to purchase oak at commercial rates, while merchant shipping found oak procurement no problem. In any case, Evelyn later admitted that most landowners assiduously replanted after felling oak and in truth probably extended their woodland. Oak made our fleets and in Surrey it made our dwellings. Until the nineteenth century virtually every house was timber-framed. Finally, it is no accident that the National Trust chose a sprig of oak leaves as its symbol. It taps straight into our beloved countryside and into the idea of who we are.

If car-less: Bus No.71, Guildford (to Haslemere) to the Crown Inn, Chiddingfold

Refreshment: The Crown Inn (tel. 01428 682 255) on Chiddingfold Green.

Start: at the Village Green near the Crown Inn (one of your rewards at the end of the walk) [GR 9620 3545]. Walk uphill on the east side of the Green (along the quiet side with the shops). At the top, cross the intersecting (Pickhurst) road to proceed straight up Pockford Road, past the village post office.

Immediately on your right, admire a couple of old timber-frame cottages, with a tile-hung flank wall. One can see the beauty of the aged silver-grey oak frame (the old Surrey style) but traditionally the brickwork would have been left bare.

After 150 metres watch out for and turn left at the footpath sign (beside a lone sycamore tree just beyond Rose Cottage) [GR 9645 3555]. Continue straight across the field with hedgerow at first on your right side, then later with a field edge on your left. Approaching the corner, ignore the turning off to the right, and walk straight through the gap in the hedgerow. Ignore the path to your left and continue straight, crossing two stiles, until you descend to reach the A283 [GR 9645 3620]. Turn right proceeding downhill along the A283 footpath for 250 metres (sorry!) to the Winterton Arms [GR 9648 3649], turning right along the marked bridleway (currently through a builders' yard) just before it.

Follow the path for just over 1km through woodland along the valley bottom, deviating neither to the right nor the left. The stream immediately on the right is one of the many feeders to the river Arun. After about 250m, when the stream almost oxbows into the path, pause to read the following.

The streams of the Weald often cut very deeply through the clay, which easily erodes with the water, while holding its banks pretty much vertical.

The theme of this walk is meant to be the oak of the Weald, but perversely you will see that this valley floor has few oaks but plenty of ash. Ash loves the dampness, and, as any gardener knows, can be surreptitiously prolific. Enjoy it while you can. Ash dieback (*Chalara fraxinea*) threatens to efface it from the British landscape, one third of our tree cover.

Ash was highly valued in the past, as John Evelyn confirms:

> The use of ash is (next to that of oak it self) one of the most universal... In sum, the husbandman cannot be without the ash for his carts ladders and other tackling, from the pike to the plow, spear, and bow. For of ash were they formerly made, and therefore reckon'd among those woods, which after long tension, has a natural spring, and recovers its position... In short, so useful and profitable is this tree, (next to the oak) that every prudent lord of a mannor, should employ one acre of ground, with ash or acorns, to every 20 acres of other land, since in as many years, it would be more worth than the land itself.

One purpose, however, which Evelyn omits and which you may now be missing is an ash walking stick. Sixty years ago, out of the whole of England, Chiddingfold was exactly the right place to come. Alas, you are now too late. 'The best walking sticks,' wrote one wood expert in the 1950s, 'are specially grown in West Surrey nurseries.' And nowhere more so than at Chiddingfold of which it was still possible to write in 1967, 'throughout the parish may be seen copses of sweet chestnut and ash trees which are especially grown for the making of walking sticks and umbrella handles – a rural industry which is almost entirely confined to this part of Surrey.' Before the mid-nineteenth century, Chiddingfold grew the material, but despatched it to London to be made into walking sticks. From about 1850 the villagers began to make the finished sticks themselves before despatching them for sale in London and elsewhere.

Walking sticks were widely known as the Chiddingfold speciality. Some were curved under pressure and moist heat. But there was another method: ash seeds would be sown in nurseries and after about eighteen months transplanted, but at an angle slanting into the ground. The terminal bud would be cut off so that the shoot resumed growth from a side bud by its cut tip. The new shoot would rise over the next eight or so years at virtually a right-angle with the old stem, ready when the shoot was thick enough to become a walking stick, the original stem forming the handle. As the grain of the wood follows the sharp bend, such sticks are far stronger than they look.

Sweet chestnut sticks were cut from coppice after two or three years, when they were a little more than one metre in length. The handle end was inserted into a pile of hot damp sand, and then curved around a wooden ring held in a vice. The hot handle was held in place by tying it to the stick's shank, until it had cooled and accepted being bent. The same process was also used with ash and even oak. A century ago Chiddingfold had several stick factories. Today they have vanished. Few of us use sticks and those who do often go for Nordic sticks, made of modern materials. Lapsed ash and sweet chestnut coppices are reminders of the way things were.

Pause at the wooden bridge on your right, but do not take it. You will notice that it has replaced a stone and brick bridge, its remains now merely detritus in the stream bed.

Here, deep into the Low Weald, is as good a place as any to contemplate wood and timber and their uses. Most of the trees on this walk are oak standards, but beneath them is the ubiquitous hazel coppice, with a few other tree species: ash, alder and birch. Just under half of all Surrey's woodland is coppice or lapsed coppice, and most of it would have been hazel, cut every seven to ten years. Wherever there is a lack of good stone for drystone walls – which means all Surrey – hazel was a greatly favoured coppice species, since it is the best material for making hurdles for folding livestock, or enclosing arable, or indeed coppice, to protect it from grazing.

Hurdlers would work out in the coppices, rather than carry their cuttings back home. There was a good reason for this: the rods were at their most workable within the first hour or two of being cut, when they could still be easily twisted and woven without snapping, thus 'not a nail or wire in a wattle hurdle.'

The heyday of hurdle manufacture was in the days of 'arable sheep farming', when sheep were folded on root crops on downland to manure

A hurdle-maker, c.1900. He could make 10 hurdles a day, roughly one hurdle per hour. He used a base-frame, a beam with vertical holes in it, into which to slot the upright poles of the hurdle before weaving the horizontal split hazel rods. The space in the centre of the hurdle allowed the shepherd to put his hand through it to carry a couple of hurdles, or to slot a stake through several to carry on his shoulder. The man is wearing a leather pad on his midriff and another on his knee to protect his clothing from the rub of loose split rods which would otherwise tear his clothing.

the land. But hazel was also widely used for barrel hoops and crates, both vital before the days of mass-produced metalware and plastics.

Some hurdlers also used young oak stems like hazel, and to the south the Sussex trug was made of oak. Yet by the nineteenth century this was a subsidiary purpose of growing oak. Until the introduction of tropical barks and chemical treatments in the second half of the nineteenth century, oak bark was the principal source of tannin for curing leather. With the importation of massive quantities of pine and other conifer timbers from the New World, from around 1800 onwards, the value of bark for tannin eclipsed the value of oak timber. Trees would be felled in the spring when it was easier to strip, or 'flaw' to use the Surrey expression, the bark off the wood. It was the bast, the inner part of the bark, which yielded the best tannin, and to remove it, the leg-bone of a horse was the favoured flawing tool, better than anything, apparently, made of iron. (What happened to the outer bark is told on p.187.)

SESSILE OAK   PEDUNCULATE OAK

The sessile (or 'stalk-less') oak bears its acorns without a stalk, while its leaves have long stalks. By contrast, the acorn of the common oak bears its acorns on a long stalk (or peduncle), while its leaves are virtually stalk-less. However, the two species frequently hybridise.

After about 1km of walking through valley bottom, you emerge from woodland [GR 9748 3690], to continue with open fields on either side.

The English pedunculate, or common, oak is the predominant species in the clay of the south and east of England while another native species, the sessile or durmast oak, is often found on the poorer sandy and heathland soils and is dominant in north and western Britain.

Across the centuries oak had defined the economy of the Weald. Nothing native compares with oak as load-bearing timber, be it for houses or for ships. John Evelyn knew the value of English oak: 'The land and the sea do sufficiently speak for the improvement of this excellent material; houses and ships, cities and navies are built with it; and there is a kind of it so tough, and extreamly compact, that our sharpest tools will hardly enter it.' Evelyn was not one for nationalist bombast. Nevertheless, having used French and Spanish oak timbers he reckoned that English oak was better.

Writing about the Weald in 1798, William Marshall, one of a growing band of agricultural commentators, described the Wealden oak culture:

> When a wood of timber is fallen, the shoots from the stools are protected, as coppice wood. And at the fall of this, every seedling plant of oak that has sprung up in the interspaces is sedulously left, to rise to another crop of timber, it being an invariable principle of management.... to reject all sapling shoots from the stools of fallen trees as standards for timber. At the next fall of coppice wood, the timberlings, or "tellers" left at the first, are thinned where they are too numerous.... until the whole ground be occupied by seminal trees.

The reason for thinning was that the trees might grow too straight in their bid for light, and there would be 'scarcely a strong knee or sharp crook' in a hundred acres. With sufficient space, oaks will grow with great angularity, because it is in the nature of the common oak for the terminal bud to abort and the branch to continue through a lateral bud. The consequent 'angularity' is not only beautiful in a Rackhamesque kind of way but, more importantly, was exactly what carpenters looked for, the natural angle being many times stronger than the best carpentered joint. Today we have lost this sense for the timber's own strength.

After another 700m following the path ahead, you will reach a cottage and 50m beyond it a tarmac road. Turn right and after 50m turn left (just before a large Victorian tile-hung house), over a stile along a marked footpath. Walk across the field, making for the white cupola to the left of the barn buildings.
Ahead lies Pockford Farm **[GR 9835 3671]**, which has existed at least since the twelfth century, quite an early date for the Weald. It must have been one of the early 'assarts', or clearings in the Weald woodland. Its name origin is 'goblin's ford', pock being the same as 'puck'.

Pass through the two gates. Follow the track, passing the farm buildings on your right. Shortly after, continue straight through the gate ahead when the main track turns right. With hedge and woodland on your left for about 150m, watch out for the footpath sign tucked into the woodland on your left, and turn half right across the field, following the path. Once across the field, follow the path with the fence on your right, till you reach farm buildings (Duns Farm) [GR 9901 3675].

Walk through the middle of the Duns Farm complex, down the vehicle track. After 200m as the path rises you will see Field Place, up on your left. Pause at the stile on the left of the road.
Although it is difficult to get a good view (however, there is more to see at the front), Field Place is a fine example of a large isolated Wealden farmstead, a tile-hung stone and brick building with adjacent tarred weatherboard barns: a classic. Although the present buildings are much younger, it was the home of a Walter de la Felde in 1255, clear evidence of Norman penetration and possession in the Weald.

It was, perhaps, at such a Wealden farmhouse near the river Mole, inhabited by a man named Charrington, that William Cobbett stopped during one of his rural rides, in the mid-1820s. He was horrified by the recent change in social mores associated with the enclosures, with farmers ceasing to host their workforce during the working day, but now aspiring to be 'a species of mock gentlefolk':

> This Squire Charrington's father used, I daresay, to sit at the head of the oak table along with his men, say grace to them, and cut up the meat and the pudding. He might have taken a cup of *strong beer* to himself, when they had none; but, that was pretty nearly all the difference in their manner of living. So that *all* lived well… Everything about this farm-house was formerly the scene of *plain manners* and *plentiful living*. Oak clothes-chests, oak bedsteads, oak chest of drawers, and oak tables to eat on, long, strong, and well supplied with joint stools. Some of the things were many hundreds of years old… There appeared to be hardly any *family* in the house, where formerly there had been, in all probability, from ten to fifteen men, boys, and maids: and, which was the worst of all, there was a *parlour*! Aye, and a *carpet* and *bell-pull* too! One end of the front of this once plain and substantial house had been moulded into a '*parlour*'; and there was a mahogany table, and the fine chairs and the fine glass, and all as barefaced upstart as any stock-jobber in the kingdom.

Going up-market, with wine decanters, glasses and so forth, rendered the long oak table redundant:

> … the labourers retreated to hovels, called cottages; and, instead of board and lodging, they got money; so little of it as would enable the employer to drink wine; but, then, that he might not reduce them to *quite starvation*, they were enabled to come to him, in the *king's name*, and demand food as *paupers*.

Cobbett found italics essential to express his trenchant views.

Cross the stile and walk across the field with Field Place on your left. Cross the stile at the top of the field and continue along the road, past its pond and duck house, but pausing to admire the frontage of the house. Having passed Field Place, after 200m look out for the gate on your right, just before the hedgerow, and take the stile just after it. Follow the edges of the field until you reach the gate in the diagonally opposite corner, and continue diagonally across the next field making for the stile with the church just beyond it. Turn left.

Immediately to the left stands a revived weather-boarded barn, with sawn oak boarding. The building has been redeemed from years of gentle decay only just in time, which is wonderful.

Traditionally oak timbers would be hewn, to get down to the heartwood, or cloven in the case of smaller pieces. Unlike sawing, which cuts through the cellular structure, both hewing and cleaving splits the wood leaving the cells intact, thus denying weak points for the entry of water or fungi. Consequently sawn oak lasts far less well than hewn or cloven oak, be it coppiced underwood for posts, weatherboarding or more substantial timbers.

In northern Surrey the architectural habit was for weatherboard, or clapboard (a corruption of 'cleft-board'), houses and these would be cleft from Wealden oak. In the Weald clapboard characterised barns, as here, not houses. Such boards could last a century or more, even when cloven thin, unlike water-absorbent modern sawn weatherboarding. Smaller pieces were made into shingles, used for so many Surrey church steeples. Those oak shingles have now all gone, displaced by imported Red Cedar from the New World. Cleft oak was also used to uphold heavy Horsham slates on any number of church roofs, the slates themselves held in place by cleft oak pegs.

Building his wagons, George Sturt learnt the importance of understanding the material:

> Under the plane (it is little used now) or under the axe (it is all but obsolete) timber disclosed qualities hardly to be found otherwise. My own eyes know because of what my hands have felt, but I cannot

A timber waggon for carrying felled tree trunks. The length of the chassis is adjustable, depending on the length of the logs. The draught-horse shafts are on the right. Trunks could be loaded from lying on the ground parallel with the waggon: a couple of draught horses on the far side of the waggon would pull chains over the top of the waggon to drag each trunk up a couple of ramps over the wheels and onto the transoms (the beams above the axle-trees). Or, with more sophistication, trunks could be lifted by a pulley mounted on a 'gin' (see p. 111).

teach an outsider, the difference between ash that is 'tough as whip-cord,' and ash that is 'frow as a carrot,' or 'dowty,' or 'biscuity.' In oak, in beech, these differences are equally plain, yet only to those who have been initiated by practical work... With axe or chisel or draw-shave they learn to distinguish between the heart of a plank and the 'sap', ... what shakes [the fissures in the grain] are good and what bad.... In my shop we bought trees 'in the round' – as they lay in the wood or the hedgerow where they had been felled or 'thrown.' And, immediately, the season of throwing came into question. Some oak, cut down in the dead of the winter, was called 'winter-cut.' It dried into excellent material, the sap almost as hard, though nothing like so durable, as the heart.

This deep knowledge about timber began to disappear in the second half of the nineteenth century when iron, steel and imported pine replaced oak timbers for construction. Writing in 1924, Sturt lamented the demise of such knowledge:

...what could never be recovered, because in fact War had found it already all but dead, was the earlier English understanding of timber, the local knowledge of it, the patriarchal traditions of handling it. Of old there had been a close relationship between the tree-clad country-side and the English who dwelt there... A sort of greedy prostitution desecrated the ancient woods... I resented it; resented seeing the fair timber callously felled at the wrong time of year, cut up too soon, not 'seasoned' at all.

At what time of year were the trees felled from which these new weather-boards were sawn?

Turn right to enter the grounds of the church of St Mary and All Saints, Dunsfold [GR 9982 3637].

The place name Dunsfold originates in an unusual Saxon personal name, 'Dunt': Dunt's fold. Before the Second World War Dunsfold was about the remotest village in Surrey, standing above one of the tributaries of the river Arun.

ST MARY AND ALL SAINTS

St Mary and All Saints is a real rarity. It was built in about 1270, prob-ably by royal masons since its clerical appointments were at that time in the gift of the Crown. If that is so, the building represents an official view of what was reckoned appropriate for a small settlement, shortly after the completion of Westminster Abbey. The church is wonderfully simple, with no surplus ornament. It has survived the centuries with only a very few changes, few enough that it might be worth noting them in order to relish so much that is original. The west window dates from the early fourteenth century; the bell-turret is probably fifteenth century (judging by the four-post timber cage on which it sits). In the nineteenth century the chancel arch was widened and raised, a new north east vestry was added, and the tracery in the east window (above the altar) was renewed. Otherwise, what you see is original.

THE EXTERIOR. The outer walls are of Bargate stone, and the mortar has been galletted (studded with ironstone, or carstone, chips), originally intended to stabilise undressed fragments of Bargate stone. By the seventeenth century, however, galletting was simply a decorative feature. Ironstone, or carstone (see p.236), is used for galletting, its dark colour making it distinctive. Looking at the foot of the walls, holes have been cut, presumably for sluicing the church floor. Three ducts can be seen externally (blocked up inside), with the old wooden plugs on chains still in place.

The yew outside the south door is worthy of admiration. To say that it was here at the time of Domesday is probably a considerable understatement. It will always be impossible to date, since by the time of death much of the inner part will have rotted away, thus thwarting a count of the rings. Alone among trees, the yew has retained its Celtic name in English speech (in Welsh *yw*, in Scots Gaelic, *iubhar*, pronounced 'ewer'). Along with Scots pine and juniper, it is Britain's only native conifer. The association of the yew with churchyards is a mystery, perhaps connected to the pre-Christian use of these sites. It was, of course, the wood of preference for the Welsh longbow. It was also used for axletrees, steps in ladders and for turnery.

THE INTERIOR. There are several points of interest.
- The massive four-post cage for the fifteenth century bell turret.
- In the chancel on the south side: the three sedilia seats for the priests are separated by colonettes of Sussex marble.
- The *pièces de résistance*, however, are the pews (according to a pedantic reproof in 1810, they are definitely 'old oak seats, not pews'). They were probably installed when the church was built, but they are certainly thirteenth century and reputedly the oldest anywhere in all England. They have been widened for our ever-broadening

fundaments but remain reassuringly uncomfortable, so no chance of dozing off during the sermon. But how could one doze, anyway, conscious that one sits on the most ancient extant Wealden oak furniture, hewn by craftsmen who knew their material so intimately?

Leave by the lych gate.

Lych is Saxon for corpse, the gate being the traditional resting place for coffin bearers to lay down their load while awaiting arrival of the priest.

(If you are interested in a site for sore eyes, **turn right down the hill for 150m to the Holy Well**. It says little for the alleged curative powers of the water for eye diseases that the well is plastered with warnings not to touch the stuff. Health & Safety, it seems, are both of very little faith. **Retrace your steps to St Mary's.**)

Turn left out of the lych gate and left again, past the redeemed barn. Instead of retracing your way towards Field Place, follow the footpath straight ahead. It descends, and in due course doglegs into the field on the valley bottom.

This is one of the many classic valley bottom meadows in the Weald, a stream running on the far left side of the field. In the past it would have been an important provider of hay.

One man went to mow…And he is, indeed, carrying his oak bottle of pop – well, beer or cider actually. He would take pride in his scythe, the shaft tailored to his size, strength and 'swing'. His bag would contain bread and cheese for his breaks, and a steel or whetstone to keep his blade keen. Usually he would not have mowed alone. It was convivial work, as several labourers moved slowly forwards in a line. Gertrude Jekyll writes, 'Often they began work at daylight, and on some farms it was the custom that the man who arrived first got a pint of ale. The mowers' regular meals were breakfast at six, lunch at half-past nine, dinner at noon, afternoon lunch at four, supper at seven, when the farmer generally gave each man a bottle of beer or cider. A man would mow an acre of hay a day for half-a-crown or three shillings.'

After 250m, where the field narrows, look out on your right for a small metal gate into the woodland [GR 9928 3634]. Do not take it, but turn left across the field to the small footbridge, and follow the path for ¾ km to a second footbridge.

Not far from here may be found traces of quartz sand. This made Chiddingfold the centre of English glass making between the fourteenth and seventeenth centuries, the oldest documented glass workings in England. A Chiddingfold furnace supplied the glass for St Stephen's Chapel, Westminster, in 1350. Even at its peak, glass production was confined to an area only 10 miles square in the extreme north west of the Weald Clay. John Aubrey hints at the reason for its demise: 'In Queen Elizabeth's Time here were 11 Glass-houses, which, as Nusances, and in [this] regard there were others at Hindhead, were put down by a Petition of Part of this County.' The pungent and pervasive smell of the glass works must have been terrible. Only the richest would have had glazed windows. Most people just had wooden mullion bars in their window openings (you may see one for yourself at Shere, p.188), but lived with the appalling stench of a luxury industry beyond their reach.

Glasshouse sites have proved hard to find. The great searcher was a retired clergyman, the Revd. T. S. Cooper, who lived at Chiddingfold from 1875 to 1918. He had such poor health that he was himself unable to excavate. He relied on six daughters who seem to have taken to his hobby even more enthusiastically than he did. One has the impression that competition was sufficiently fierce between the girls that each would keep her own counsel regarding fragmentary evidence until sure she had located an actual site. The first glasshouse was found in 1911, and since then nine other probable sites have been found near the village.

Continue, after 150m the ground beginning to climb. After a small gap, continue through woodland until you reach the attractively restored barn, and beyond it, White Beech Farm [GR 9831 3600]. Turn right and after 50m turn left along a small bridleway.

This bridleway is clearly an old track, as one can tell from its high banks and sculpted feel. The oak trees lining this end of the old track, however, are not native oaks. Their leaves betray them as Turkey oaks, first introduced to England in 1735, which spread rapidly across southern England, mainly because of their vigorous growth and natural propagation. Here, incomprehensibly, they seem to have been deliberately planted. Ornamental they may be, yet the timber is of little value, being far inferior to the native common oak. Native oaks line the bridleway further on.

Turn left [GR 9756 3601] and walk 1½km along the lane back to Chiddingfold.
How many farm wagons once took this route from outlying steadings, from Field Place, Duns and Pockford farms? The chassis of such wagons was often made with ash, but oak was always used for wheel spokes. It was the only wood that could be trusted. It was even used for the driving wheels of Stevenson's *Rocket*. George Sturt, responsible for the family wheelwright shop in Farnham, knew a thing or two about wheel spokes. Spokes, he said,

> were invariably oak, chiefly because oak alone, of the suitable English hard-woods, could be cleft instead of sawn. It mattered with spokes. A cut across the grain, on a saw-bench, might have produced a cross-grained spoke that would be liable to snap shamefully. Therefore spokes were never sawn…. But the cleaving had to be done in the summer, while the oak was full of sap and would "run" from end to end. Cleaving was a job for the woods therefore; woodmen with beetle

One of George Sturt's waggons, with its oak spokes. The chassis would have been built mainly of ash, its springy quality capable of absorbing the shock of uneven ruts. If looked after, a waggon like this would easily outlast a farmer's working life, unlike today's farm vehicles.

(pronounced bittle) and wedges usually had first handling of the beautiful yellowish parallel grain for spokes, that split easily yet was tough as wire the other way. So the spokes were bought, by the hundred or the long hundred [120 or more short spokes], in their native woods.

One may imagine, then, the sound of the beetle cleaving oak echoing through the coppice and woodland around Chiddingfold.

Soon after passing Skinners Lane on your right, pass Prestwick Manor Farm on your left.

This manor dates back to the mid-thirteenth century, and probably earlier. But it is the two end-to-end barns you should admire. They belong to the seventeenth and eighteenth centuries, though their weatherboard will be more recent. This is what Gertrude Jekyll had to say of similar West Surrey barns in 1904:

> Early in the nineteenth century, when corn was at a high price at the end of the great [Napoleonic] war, these barns were reckoned to hold £1,000 worth [probably well in excess of £50,000 in today's money] of grain, to be threshed as required on the floors between the bays... Now, alas! these fine old barns stand empty. With much else that is gone of the beauty and poetry of agricultural life, the measured beat of the flail is no longer heard. Its cheerful, rhythmical sound is silenced; for the corn is now threshed in the field by steam machinery instead of being garnered and beaten out by hand, and the grand old barns no longer justify their existence.

We cannot bring back the threshers. Who, in their right mind, would wish to stand all day threshing in a barn, and taking home a pittance at sunset? Yet Jekyll might have been somewhat mollified to learn that these wonderful old barns are usually not allowed simply to fall down, but are redeemed, sometimes very skilfully, as dwellings or for the storage of farm equipment.

As you enter the village, turn left down the side of the Green to savour the houses.

Chiddingfold possibly means 'the fold of the dwellers in the hollow,' a name that certainly makes sense in that the village lies in a hollow or dell.

Cross the Green and the main road to visit the church of St Mary.

ST MARY'S CHURCH

St Mary's was badly restored in 1869 by Henry Woodyer, castigated by Nairn & Pevsner as an architect, 'who should have known better'. He could not resist tarting the church up, including heightening the tower as one can immediately see. The main buildings are thirteenth and fifteenth century.

THE EXTERIOR. The church is approached through a lych-gate roofed with Horsham slate, presumably held up on cloven oak, and dated 1888. The porch is fourteenth century but with a thirteenth century doorway. The chief external attraction, however, lies in the dell beyond the church, the new church hall. Denied permission to add to the existing church, necessity proved the mother of this delightfully self-effacing invention, designed by Jim Garland and completed in 2010. Its roof covered by grass provides the perfectly understated but elegant solution to parish needs.

THE INTERIOR. The roof has been raised, as evidenced in the elongated shafts, originally thirteenth century but lengthened in the fifteenth, to the four-bay arcades of the central nave. The thirteenth century chancel arch has also been heightened. The chancel itself has a crown-post roof, allegedly of chestnut, but be suspicious: most 'chestnut' timbers in churches turn out to be sessile oak. Carpenters hated the unreliability of shakes, or fissures, in chestnut trunks. At the west end look out for the window made up of fragments of stained glass. These are pieces of glass picked up from Chiddingfold's various factory sites.

There once was a gallery across the west end of the church, for the use of musicians and singers, but this was removed in 1860, part of the growing divide between the sacred and the profane in village life. Until then, the more musical villagers would have sung in both pub and church, songs earthy or divine as the occasion demanded. But across the Church of England there was a growing movement towards 'pure' choirs, unsullied by suspect music from the world outside – a regrettable trend that must have contributed to the progressive emptying of churches across the land. It marked a breach in village communities, between the world of the hostelry and that of the church and unwittingly a contradiction of what Christianity claimed to be about. It should never have been like that. When we think we are improving things we so often fall victim to the surreptitious law of unintended consequences.

Cross the main road to the Crown Inn.

Whether you seek refreshment or not, the Crown Inn (tel. 01428 682255) is well worth looking at. It is fifteenth century, possibly earlier, perhaps the village building referred to as an inn and documented in 1383. Until the 1940s it was tile-hung, but the tiles seem to have been removed to appeal to the fashion for exposing the timber-frame. Mercifully the timbers have not been blackened. The left corner of the first storey is upheld by an upended tree or branch. You can bet it is an oak.

Ockley

Distance 6km/4 miles: 3 hours
OS Explorer Map No.134
(and, hardly necessary, No.146)

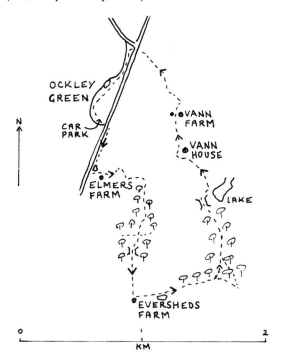

BEFORE YOU WALK

Stane Street is the Roman road running through Ockley, heavily disguised as the A29. Regrettably this is the only substantial and accessible stretch of this Roman road in West Surrey, but at least the traffic through Ockley is limited to 30mph and your exposure to its traffic will, I promise, be slight. Apart from the A29, Ockley (Occa's Clearing) is a delight, even though, aside from the Green, it is really the product of ribbon development along the ancient street. Ockley Green stands out as one of Surrey's beauty spots, with its inspired western border, a combination of old cottages, oak trees and infiltrating countryside. You have probably driven past it often enough and thought how nice it would be to stroll along the far side of it. This treat lies at the end of this walk.

In the meantime most of this walk gives an idea of the extent of Wealden woodland, much of it only cleared since the thirteenth century. For centuries it was used for summer livestock grazing, and only began to be seriously settled after the Norman Conquest. Even then, the Weald population remained thin. It was still thinly populated in 1800, one visitor observing, 'In travelling over the Vale [Weald] lands nothing strikes a person more than the extreme fewness of the inhabitants.' The Weald was one of the last tracts of English woodland to be opened, patch by patch, by cutting out clearings, or 'assarts', in the Middle Ages and even later. And here is a fact to stop you in your tracks. England had a smaller proportion of woodland by 1066 than France has today. Most of it had been cut down much earlier. The Weald remains typified by many strips of woodland, to give the landscape an intimate character, a countryside of scattered farmsteads and old barns.

Today the Weald enjoys a prosperity unknown until almost within living memory. It was receiving adverse comment from improvers from the late eighteenth century onwards: 'What an ill managed district. How much unproductive land it contains', exclaimed William Marshall in 1798. Nor had he a good word for those that tended it, 'the tenantry, in general, notwithstanding the lowness of rents, are as poor, weak, and spiritless, as their lands...' Marshall was struck by the 'extreme fewness of its inhabitants, the villages are not only few but small, and a man may travel for miles without seeing a hamlet, or scarcely a roadside cottage.' The next expert to have a go at the Weald and its people was William Stevenson in 1813:

> In passing into the Vale or Weald of Surrey, the eye is not more struck with the appearance of inferiority in the management of the lands, the badness of the crop, the uncouthness and want of intelligence among the farmers and the general circumstances attending inadequate skill and capital than it is with the ruinous and mean appearance of farm houses and offices.

Half a century later there seems to have been little change as a report in the 1850s made clear:

> .... hardly any stock worth mentioning is kept on these farms. The implements used are of the rudest kind; the barn implements in an especial degree, the use of the common barn winnowing machine being frequently unknown. Its place is supplied by sacks nailed to four horizontal spares, which are fixed on a pivot at both ends and when turned briskly round get up a breeze of wind, in which the corn is riddled by hand, and the chaff blown away.

Weald farming practice comprehensively ignored the proximity of London with its enormous appetite for fresh food. Partly this was due to the extreme conservatism of the population. It was easy for experts to berate local farmers' reluctance to innovate. Those who have spent time in extremely poor parts of the world will know that conservatism is a hallmark of poverty. Without any reserves, the failure of an experiment means starvation. So one simply does not initiate anything new. 'Green revolutions' are normally taken up by rich or middle class farmers, who are then able to brush their poorer neighbours aside. Agricultural revolution almost invariably implies cruelty for those unable to join in.

Yet the failure to serve the London market was also the result of poor communications. One might have imagined that the arrival of good rail connections would have changed everything. They did, but in a contradictory and unexpected way. Across the Atlantic, railroads laid across the prairies led to European markets being flooded with cheap grain and cheap meat on refrigerated ships. British agriculture suffered depression on and off from the1870s until the 1930s. But by then Surrey was already enjoying a different kind of prosperity as a dormitory area, a state of affairs that continues to this today.

If car-less: currently there is an insufficient bus service.

Refreshment: One is spoilt for choice: facing Ockley Green is the Inn on the Green (www.inn-onthegreen.co.uk). At the south end is the Cricketers' Arms (tel. 0871 9511000) and the Old School House (aka Bryce's (tel. 01306 627430, www.bryces.co.uk.).

Start at the south end of Ockley Green, by the cricket pavilion (there is parking space) [GR 1455 3985]. Walk back up to Stane Street (A29).

Admire The Tuns on the corner, an uncharacteristic house for the Weald. It has an eighteenth century weather-boarded front, a rarity here and more typical of north Surrey's London basin. Its original weatherboarding would have been of oak, cloven to ensure that the cellular structure remained intact (see p.37). The Tuns was a public house until the licence was transferred to the Cricketers, down the road, in about 1828. Opposite, on the far side of the road stands the Old Nursery, previously the Old School House, and originally Ockley Academy, a boarding school for fifty or so boys, from 1810 to 1860. Banish any thought of Dotheboys Hall. The outlook onto the Green forbids such dark thoughts. It then became a meeting house for Dissenters, or non-conformists as they became more politely known, then a guest house and had a brief career in 1965 as a public house, catering presumably to those in Morris Minors, newly equipped with the Surrey volume of the Shell Countryside guide, and exploring the delights of the new-found outdoors.

Turn right (southwards) along Stane Street.

Your sanity is saved by the speed restriction, even if for every observant driver there is at least one speeding.

Stane Street (literally 'stone street', because it was metalled) is the most significant Roman road running through Surrey. (Two other arterial routes ran from London towards Brighton and Lewes respectively.) Originally Stane Street ran from London Bridge to the east gate of Chichester, the Roman regional capital. It was probably built by c.70 AD, within 20 years of the Roman invasion, and demonstrates the skill of Roman engineers. Dismiss the idea that Roman roads are relentlessly straight. They are only straight where that is best. The engineers quickly understood the principal geographical features along the route, and selected the optimum, adjusting 'straightness' accordingly. A straight line from Chichester to London would necessitate two sharp ascents, rather than one, to cross the South Downs, and later require an even steeper climb across Leith Hill, and would then miss the Mole Gap at Dorking. Having carefully re-aligned the departure from Chichester to a gentler more easterly route, the road was laid in a series of shorter alignments, to avoid obstacles. North of Ockley adjustments were made to avoid the shoulder of Leith Hill, and again at Dorking to use the Mole Gap rather than going over Box Hill. The road was constructed for the most part as an embankment, an 'agger', about 4-6 metres wide, with wide hollows dug either side for drainage. Most roads were strongly metalled with locally available material, gravel, flints, broken stone or iron slag or cinder where close to iron workings. These materials were laid in cambered layers and tamped down, about 25cm thick.

It is unlikely that Stane Street was built primarily for military purposes but rather for commercial and industrial ones, above all, for getting iron out of the Weald. Iron, incidentally, was being exploited in the Weald long before the arrival of the Romans. The exportation of a heavy material like iron or iron ore demanded good roads. The likelihood is that there were many Roman access tracks either side of Stane Street to iron working sites, but these are now lost.

The Ockley stretch was already known as the best surviving trace in the seventeenth century, John Aubrey noting, 'this causeway is eminent in Ockley parish (Surrey) which in winter is extremely wet.... The common people do say it was made by the Devil.' (If your appetite is whetted for finding other traces of Stane Street, your best guide (with useful maps) is still not too difficult to find second hand, S.E. Winbolt, *With a Spade on Stane Street* (1936)).

Cross the road when there is a gap in the traffic and continue. Turn left through the pedestrian gate marked to Elmer's Farm [GR 1448 3950], passing the duck pond on the left, and Elmer's Farmhouse on your right.

Elmer is a corruption of a Saxon, Aylmer, a man who seems to have held much of Ockley, just before the Conquest swept away Saxon landholders.

Follow the path up the slope, passing Elmer's Windmill on your right.

Apart from its base, Elmer's Mill is the loving restoration of an octagonal smock mill which was originally erected here in 1803 for the sum of £735 5s 9¼d. The 'smock' refers to the resemblance between a farmhand's traditional smock (p.229) and the shape of this type of wooden windmill tower, in this case weatherboarded, with eight sides and a revolving cap. Wind technology for milling is far younger than waterpower, which had been in use since before the Conquest and in East Mediterranean lands for at least two millennia. Windmill technology made very slow progress until the late Middle Ages when construction skills and gearing were more developed.

MILL FARM OCKLEY MARCH 5th 1909

Elmer's mill, 1909, its sail frames still intact. It was a corn mill, originally painted olive green, and it plied its trade for a century before ceasing to function around 1912, rendered obsolete by fossil fuel-powered mills. Indeed, the days of Elmer's Mill were already numbered when it was built, for the industrial revolution was in full swing. It lasted as long as it did because of the remoteness of this part of Surrey from industrial centres. It slowly decayed, its sails dropping off one by one, while the weatherboards began to peel away, allowing the rain to rot the timbers within. It collapsed on a still day in 1944. Only the brick base survived. Today it stands again, faithfully restored as a dwelling by a windmill enthusiast, at the time of writing still awaiting sails.

Skirting to the left of the mill enclosure, you are immediately confronted by one of those open spaces, 'assarts', cut out of the Weald. Cross the first stile, and fork right to the metal gate and stile in the far right corner of the field. Cross the stile and follow the path through the woodland [GR 1495 3937].

At first you pass a patch of conifer on you right, planted exotics that strike a false note here on the Wealden clay. After 150 metres there is young planted mixed woodland on your left, an attempt to regain the variety of Wealden woodland, but bear in mind that oak is 'the weed of the Weald'. If the landowner defers to nature, it will eventually predominate.

About 400m after entering the woodland, the footpath begins to swing right as it meets a cross track [GR 1490 3898]. Resist the temptation to turn right. Looking carefully ahead, you will see a wooden signpost, almost hidden in the tree line on the far side of the track, just to the left of the prominent beech tree

in front of you. Cross the track and follow the path descending steeply through the trees into the gully, crossing the footbridge.

Here is a classic Wealden stream, cutting deeply into the clay. It is running due south here to join the North River, a tributary of the River Arun, which it joins in Sussex.

Follow the path from the bridge, winding up to the left.

As you come out of the gully note the banks on either side of the path, indicators that this path is probably old.

Continue walking straight, cross the stile and before you turn left, admire Eversheds Farm [GR 1480 3856].

Eversheds derives from the name of the thirteenth century landholder, Thomas de Everesheved, itself a corruption of the Old English for boar's head. So one is tempted to imagine that Eversheds might once have referred to an armorial bearing. If so, by the end of the seventeenth century, they had no time for such fripperies, for John Aubrey, gives us the words spoken by one of the Eversheds of Ockley when offered a coat of arms by the heralds [from the College of Heralds] on their visitation: 'He told them that he knew no difference between gentlemen and yeomen...' He reminds us that, as in Kent also, there were few large estate holders and that gentry and yeomen tended to think of themselves as of the same social rank.

Eversheds is probably the oldest surviving house in Ockley, originally built in 1450. What you see, however, is a seventeenth century front equipped with tall, elegant sash-windows which let in plenty of light, a complete change from the penumbra of Tudor interiors. Sash windows made their appearance in England after 1650. Despite a later addition on the left, it remains an impressive building, known locally for many years simply as 'The Great House'. The Evershed family was still here in the eighteenth century. Ephraim Figg, later publican of the Red Lion on Stane Street, started his working career as a carter's boy at the Great House in 1891, when he would take corn to be ground at Elmer's Mill.

Turn left along the track, passing a small pond on your right. Follow it straight, disregarding the track that swings to the right just after the pond. On your left you will pass a young mixed native plantation of oak and ash.

Fresh plantations are always to be welcomed, but ecologically they do not compare with natural regeneration. Natural regeneration maintains continuity, allowing existing accretions of plant and animal species harboured within woodland to continue to thrive uninterrupted. It takes very many years for a fresh plantation to acquire even a shadow of its biodiversity.

After 350m the path enters woodland, with an open field on the right. After another 180m (almost exactly 200 paces), and having ignored two unmarked small paths to the left, keep a sharp lookout for the signpost in the trees on the right side of the path, directing you to fork left [GR 1540 3863]. This signpost is difficult to spot. (It comes as the path ahead veers to the right, about 50 paces before the end of the open field and the beginning of woodland on your right). Having forked left, after another 150m follow the path as it swings left with another path coming in from the right.

The heavy clay of this path can become a quagmire in wet weather, but that is the classic Wealden terrain we so easily forget. Much of the clay of the Weald is like this, making it extremely difficult to get timber, or anything else, out. It was for that reason that the Weald was peopled so very late in history. In the ninth century the Venerable Bede, who must have written from hearsay, described the Weald as 'thick and inaccessible, the abode of deer, swine and wolves.' Because of it heavy clay and huge trees people could not entertain the idea of cultivation, but they could use it in the summer months as a place to which to drive their livestock. At first, this was probably limited to pigs, which lived off acorns and beech mast, and were slaughtered and salted to provide for the winter. The medieval pig was a smaller, thinner, blacker and more bristly creature than the modern pig, with a longer snout ideal for searching for mast.

At the time of Domesday (1086), when the Weald was still viewed as an impoverished and largely empty region, pig herding is what the Weald was chiefly used for. The Normans used a special term, 'pannage', for oak woodland which could sustain a pig herd. Yet by 1300 that was changing. The Normans embarked upon vigorous colonisation. Although woodland still predominated, settlements and wood clearance changed the Weald to an area of mixed farming, with the emphasis on livestock, with cattle beginning to displace pigs as the principal product.

Pigs were still raised, as meat which could easily be cured for winter consumption. Indeed, the attics of most fifteenth and sixteenth century cottages in Wealden Surrey are often conversions from chambers where

A plough team, comprising six oxen, c.1900, by which time they were confined to a few places in the High Weald and on the South Downs. Imagine the skill required to turn such a team at the end of the furrow.

bacon was customarily hung to be cured by the smoke of the household hearth. Cattle were much more easily herded, they yielded milk as well as meat and leather, and they could also be used for traction and ploughing. It is an indication of the intractability of the soil that oxen remained the draught beasts of the Weald well into the nineteenth century.

Because it was mostly made of stiff wet clay, the Weald remained as described in the walk introduction, extraordinarily remote and backward, inviting sharp criticism from outsiders. A history of Surrey published in 1900 illustrated the trackless morass of much of the Weald with an astonishing statement: 'In the memory of living men fat pigs, sold at a farm in the Weald of Surrey, had to be killed on the spot because it was impossible to remove them alive, either on their own feet or on wheels.'

This may not have been true here, so close to Ockley and Stane Street, but even well established routes were very slow going after rainfall. In Queen Anne's reign at the beginning of the eighteenth century, Prince George of Denmark tried to visit Petworth, but in west Surrey his progress by coach proved far slower than walking: nine miles covered in six hours, with several attendant carriages overturned.

Even a century ago, the Weald could still be an unwelcoming place, as one writer reported, 'As a rule, I never go to the door of one of these lonely cottages unless I am actually compelled to ask the way. ...The people who are scattered here and there seem to belong to a different race from ours and speak a dialect peculiar to themselves.'

Keep walking straight ahead, over a cross-track, and past a sign marking Candy's Copse on your left.

Candy's Copse is a nature reserve and part of a Site of Special Scientific Interest (SSSI). It is home to nightingales and warblers, but among mammals notably to dormice, which are associated with honeysuckle. They strip off its bark for their nests. Apart from oak, there are ash, beech, birch, hazel and lime trees. The floor of this woodland supports bluebells, snowdrops, primroses, and varieties of orchid. Yet its principal claim on your attention is that it is home to a substantial variety of invertebrates, most famously the rare purple hairstreak butterfly. If you are here at the right time of year you might just see one, or a purple emperor, a white admiral or a silver-washed fritillary.

Ignore a more substantial cross track and walk straight on past a sign for Vann Lake Reserve on your right. After another 150m or so, join another track coming in from the right, descend steeply into the gully and cross the footbridge [GR 1540 3925].

On your right, invisibly, lies Vann Lake. It was probably created in the eighteenth century, possibly to power a flax mill, though there is no evidence that one was ever built. Or was it simply decorative? We are unlikely ever to know. The whole area is now a nature reserve: ancient Wealden woodland allowed to be its natural self: alder predominant in the wetter areas, oak on the drier soils. It has been known for some time that trees and fungi enjoy a vital symbiotic relationship. Mycologists from Kew have counted well over 750 different fungi species here.

Turn right at the first opportunity after the bridge, but before doing so:

Note the rhododendrons that warn that one is back with gardens. Rhododendrons are, of course, exotics. They prevent natural ground cover. They are also shunned by birds, probably because they offer too much cover for predators.

Follow the path; turn left after 100m. You should find yourself walking with an open field on your right, and with a belt of trees hiding another field on the left. After 250m Vann House, a red brick and tile house of about 1850 (albeit its north end, on the right, dating from the eighteenth century), will come into view on the right hand side.

On emerging onto tarmac, turn right past the entrance to Vann House, and along Vann Farm Road. Dogleg through the farmyard (between the farmhouse and the converted barns on the right) of Vann Farm at the end of the road, and take the path half left up the hillside [Explorer Map 134: GR1520 4005], making for the corner of the wood (and gate) on the skyline. Pass the stile or gate and immediately turn right. Keep a distance of about 20m from the fence (now on your right), and after 100m it will be possible to see the stile ahead, among the trees [GR 1510 4021].

   Cross the stile. Ahead is an open field. Strike off diagonally half left, making straight for the playground and green bin you can see in the distance (just on the right of the red-brick building, the Village Hall, on the A29). This is an unmarked right of way. Pass between village hall and playground onto the A29.

The A29 as it once was. This picture, probably taken c.1905, conjures up a more gentle, slower world. The Inn-on-the Green, opposite the pump, was previously known as The Red Lion pub which Ephraim Figg took over as publican. He retired in 1946, and died in 1970, aged 89.

Cross Stane Street (A29) just left of its junction with Lake Road (B2126). Follow the line of houses on the far (west) side of the Green back to the south end and the cricket pavilion.

Part of the pleasure of the cottages on the green is that the majority of them belong to a single coherent period of building, the seventeenth century, a time when the quality of building and the size of domestic dwelling greatly improved (which explains why so little of an earlier date has survived). Virtually each building is a delight. Look out for those that betray the signs of Prince Albert's German influence in the 1840s and '50s: heavy bargeboards on the gables and other wood trimmings that would make Hansel and Gretel feel pretty much at home.

The pump in the middle of the Green is mid-nineteenth century. Restored recently, it tells of the incoming benefactor who made it possible. It is also a reminder of the extraordinary changes that have happened over the past century, in particular the provision of piped water and electricity. Only 50 years ago I would stay with my godmother at her farm just outside Denbigh in North Wales. She managed with candles, coal and water piped from a nearby stream. She still sheared her sheep by hand when her petrol motor refused to work. It was hard work, but she loved her way of life. Writing a century ago, George Sturt recalled the vortex of change in Surrey villages, incomers living cheek-by-jowl with the old country folk, as must have happened here:

> A lath-and-plaster partition may separate people who are half a century asunder in civilisation, and on the same bench at school may be found side by side two children who come from homes, the one worthy of King George III's time, the other not unworthy of King George V's.

JANE SCOTT SCHOOL at the south end of the Green was built in 1871 and named after its benefactor, the governess to a local family who had died in 1838. Whereas her pump became redundant in the first half of the twentieth century, the school remains miraculously in service. But all her schoolchildren today, without fail, belong not to King George V's time, but to Queen Elizabeth's. The cricket pitch was already well established a century ago, but cattle grazed around the pitch except for summer Saturdays, when they were gently persuaded to yield to England's national sport.

The pond, Weaver's Pond, is named after 'Weaver' Knight a basket-maker who lived in a cottage west of the pond and who used the pond to soak withies (willow wands stripped of their bark) for his trade. The end of his basketry came in 1912, presumably as a result of the mass production of cheap metal wares and textiles.

THE BATTLE OF OCKLEY   Finally, according to legend, the Green is the site of the battle of Ockley in 851. Æthelwulf, King of Wessex, and his trusty son Æthelbald, marched northwards along Stane Street to confront a major Danish attack on southern England. They rightly believed that the Danes' objective was Winchester, and that they would take Stane Street as the best available route southwards. In the words of the Anglo-Saxon Chronicle, 'Æthelwulf and his [second] son Æthelbald with the West Saxon levies fought against them at *Acleah* and there made the greatest slaughter of a heathen host that we have heard tell of up to this present day.' According to another account, 'the blood stood ankle deep.' If the battle had indeed been fought on the site of the present Green, the Saxons would indeed have stood ankle deep but in mud, not blood. The place was a quagmire in those days, quite unfit for a battle. It is much more likely that the Saxons chose more advantageous and dryer ground overlooking Stane Street, a couple of miles further north. In 1882 human remains were found at Etherley Farm on the slopes of Leith Hill, two miles north west of Ockley, which may indicate the approximate site of the battle. King Æthelwulf may have thought himself now secure on his throne. Attack, however, is most successful when it comes from a completely unexpected quarter. It was five years later that he was suddenly overthrown by his no longer trusty son Æthelbald, who then had the bad manners to marry his father's young widow. So much for the richness of Saxon family life.

Thursley and the Devil's Punch Bowl

Distance 10km/6 miles: 3 hours
OS Explorer Map No.133

BEFORE YOU WALK

There are three themes to this walk, the principal one being the geology which produced the Devil's Punch Bowl, the largest such formation in Britain. The other two are the flora which dominate the landscape, and at the beginning and end of the walk some truly lovely examples of the domestic architecture of West Surrey.

Thursley is a pre-Christian settlement name. The temptation is to associate it with the Scandinavian god Thor, a likely enough proposition in parts of the country that fell under Scandinavian rule. Yet Surrey remained firmly Saxon. It seems to be one of four pre-Christian religious place names (along with Tuesley, Peper Harrow and Willey) in the area. The most plausible interpretation is that it refers to a god of Saxon

Ⓐ	CAR PARK
Ⓑ	SMALLBROOK
Ⓒ	HEDGE FARM
Ⓓ	RIDGEWAY FARM
Ⓔ	MEMORIAL
Ⓕ	VIEWING POINT
Ⓖ	NT CAR PARK & CAFE

cosmology and means 'the grove, or clearing, where Thunor, god of (and hence) thunder, was worshipped'. A 'ley' is a clearing.

Thursley boasts fine dwellings, to be savoured at the beginning and end of this walk. Edwin Lutyens (1869-1944) was born and grew up here. Indeed, it is the scene of his very first commission, to convert a row of cottages into a single dwelling (to be viewed at the end of the walk). The old houses of the village informed his eye, and one sees just the first inkling of how he would use the architecture of humble dwellings to give them both dignity and intimacy when applied to the large country houses he designed for well-heeled members of the professional classes.

If car-less: Take the No.19 bus from Farnham and alight at Hindhead, walk up London Road 300m to the NT Devil's Punch Bowl car park, and walk across to the viewing point with the bronze sculpture, then take up the walk at ➲ on p.67.

Refreshment: The Three Horseshoes, Thursley (tel. 01252 703268) offers first class food.

Start: Park on the field by the cricket pitch north of the road through Thursley [GR 9000 3980]. (Alternatively, start at the NT Devil's Punch Bowl car park on the London Road above Hindhead and follow the circuit from ➲ on p.67.) Start walking down The Lane next to The Street.

The Lane offers a feast of delightful cottages on either side, of which the most notable is on the left, Olde Hall, built in the sixteenth century. Its timber framing has been properly left to weather, rather than blacked, and the rubble stonework has nice galleting (the small pieces of ironstone placed in the mortar, see p.236). Opposite stand Rose Cottage and Pax Cottage, both tile-hung cottages. At the end of the lane on the right is Badgers, an elegantly simple eighteenth century country house. On the left, Shepherd's Cottage, is late sixteenth century.

Continue along the footpath at the end of The Lane; follow it until you emerge onto the road. Turn left and after 100m, just past Horn Cottage on the left, turn left again, up the private road (marked to Smallbrook Farm) [GR 8968 3977].

After ½km pass Smallbrook Farm on your right.

Smallbrook Farm was originally built in the early fifteenth century, and probably inhabited by a yeoman farmer.

Benjamin and Hannah Parker in their retirement in the 1860s outside the early seventeenth century Horn Cottage. Benjamin had been born in Essex at the end of the eighteenth century. Hannah was local, from Churt, born in 1804. They had spent their lives in service, he as footman to John Chandler, vicar of Witley, she as the vicarage cook, both startling notions judging by the photograph. One would rightly expect no pomp when arriving for dinner, but perhaps be a little apprehensive as to the fate of the crème brûlée. *They had married in February 1839, he for the second time. That they had a daughter the following August indicates an urgency over the marriage, particularly since* flagrante delicto *must have occurred under the vicarage roof. You would never guess such larks from the photograph.*

After another 250m keep walking straight ahead (where the tarmac turns right to a private dwelling). Follow the path [GR 8953 3920], which doglegs twice before reaching another tarmac lane after ½km.

Note the brambles growing in the bank. Brambles love the Lower Greensand soil. If you search for 'bramble' on the internet you are at risk of being directed to a nursing home, or to some thornless heavy fruiting variety, or indeed to instructions on how to eradicate this vigorous plant. You are certainly not invited to celebrate brambles in their native habitat. Yet they demand our admiration, as skilful colonisers, with no fewer than 400 micro-species in Britain. Their tentacles venture forth in wide arcs, systematically to prospect for land to colonise, using their recurved spines to assist through obstacles, and putting their tips into the ground to take root. Indeed, the tentacles were sometimes called lawyers, so hard is it to extricate oneself. So successful are they that they often dominate woodland, scrub and fringe-heathland floors. Apart from their fruit, brambles were valued for their usefulness. Once stripped of their spines, they were used for binding, for example for thatch, rushes, straw baskets and skeps. (On bracken, see below.)

The fields on either side are now the abode of horses, stabled at Hedge Farm. If you are lucky you will see beautiful horses grazing. They are a lovely sight here, as in other parts of the Surrey countryside. Horses a century ago, were an essential feature of the Surrey landscape, but they were mainly working draught horses. Today the sight of horses should also give one pause for thought. The economics of indifferent farmland in a particularly wealthy part of England has determined the keeping of horses for pleasure rather than the production of food. If the world were well enough fed one could be perfectly content. Yet it isn't. As a society we use our capital power to purchase food from all over the world, setting aside some of our poorer agricultural land for other purposes, as here. It is easy to become hair-shirt minded about this, but on the other hand we would be wrong not to feel some unease at this situation even if a resolution of the economic conundrum continues to elude us. In the meantime, enjoy the horses.

Turn right, and immediately past the first building (Hedge Farm) where the lane turns sharp left, walk straight ahead down the very narrow footpath [GR 8970 3876], marked by a yellow hydrant sign, between a field gate on its left and the side entrance to Hedge Farm on the right.

Here I owe you a fulsome apology for more barbed wire fence threatening you on your left. Unfortunately there is no avoiding it, but you will be rewarded.

Follow the path down the wooded slope, and around to the left when compelled, meeting an old sunken lane running in from the left. Cross the stream and follow the track up the opposite side of the gully.

The stream, out of the Devil's Punch Bowl, runs northwards, joining the north branch of the River Wey at Elstead. The large pieces of sandstone lying in the stream are indicative of what lies beneath the topsoil here.

Pass Ridgeway Farm on your right.

Ridgeway Farm contains medieval timbers, an indicator of its origins in the mid-fifteenth century. What you see on the exterior is principally sixteenth and seventeenth century refurbishment, using the same kind of sandstone as was lying in the stream. As for the 'farm', like Hedge Farm it is seriously horsey.

After another 140m or so, turn sharp left at the intersection with a tarmac road [GR 8897 3860], and walk straight up the footpath in the apparently overgrown gully, resisting the track to its left.
As you walk the silence is very noticeable: a reminder of how quiet the countryside was before the advent of the internal combustion engine. The footpath is initially lined with holly. Holly loves acid soil and so is common in Surrey. Because of its prickles it makes excellent hedgerows, and there are plenty of lapsed hedgerows elsewhere to note as one walks. Its spiny leaves are there to protect it against grazing, the leaves becoming progressively less spiny above the browse line. Nevertheless, the spines are a notable failure, for sheep and deer will happily graze holly. Traditionally holly was often coppiced or pollarded in order to produce winter fodder for livestock. Its two other key virtues are that it can grow in the shade of taller trees, and that its roots stabilise banks, so it is perfect as a woodland boundary hedge.

Apart from its willingness to grow on Surrey sandy soils, there are other reasons for holly having been welcome. Unlike conifers, holly actually contributes to the humus and helps counteract 'podsolization', the process whereby minerals like iron and aluminium leach down as a result of acid action, to form concentrations at deeper levels – hence, for example, the creation of impermeable 'iron pan'. Its wood is close grained and was used for such things as cogs and other artefacts like spindles that had to be hard. The bark yields bird-lime, the glutinous substance used for catching birds in the Middle Ages. Its key disadvantage is that it is difficult to eradicate, and individual trees can live for 250 years or more.

The path narrows, as many a sunken lane narrowed until tarmac was laid and erosion ceased. It was the impact of human and animal feet, and water run-off which created sunken lanes and most of these must have been like this. There is a story from about 1840 of villagers at Coldharbour, less than four miles south of Dorking, being unable to carry a coffin to town because the lane from the village was so narrow that there was leaving insufficient room for a man either side of the coffin. The burial had to take place in Coldharbour itself. Here one can see the credibility of that story.

Continue walking on the main path ahead and after just over ½km enter the NT estate. At choices keep walking straight ahead, opting for the higher ground.

As the landscape begins to open out, there is an increasing amount of bracken, and among it, bilberries or hurts (p.113). Bracken is a sure sign of nutrient-poor acidic soil. It is often seen as a threat, engulfing acid grassland. Bracken and ferns, along with lichens and mosses, are more or less the oldest forms of flora extant. Ferns emerged 400 million years ago, 40 million years before seed bearing (angiosperm) plants. Bracken, like most ferns, spreads through its root structure or rhizomes, and is a rapidly coloniser difficult to eradicate.

Yet bracken was greatly valued by our predecessors for its usefulness. It served as litter for both animals and humans, and as a floor covering. It was dried for use as tinder and kindling. And within the last 200 years its ash was still being widely used with mutton or pork fat to make soap. For the poor there was no alternative. Commercial soap, made from wood ash and tallow, was an expensive item because of the duty placed on it. In the eighteenth century soap-boiling pans were fitted with lids, locked by tax collectors nightly, to prevent unmonitored production. The tax was only abolished in 1853. Without bracken, poor people would have been much worse off. It demands our respect.

After just over 1km, the view opens out to the Devil's Punch Bowl on the left. At the top, about 200m further on, look out for the concrete memorial ahead, half hidden in a cluster of trees [GR 8880 3698] just to the left of the main path.

The signage may tell you as much as you wish to know about the 1937 bequest to enlarge the National Trust's estate here by William Robertson, in memory of his two brothers who died in the First World War. But you may like to know a few more personal details. Norman was, like William, a lawyer. But he was distinctly elderly for military service, aged 38 when he volunteered in October 1914, and only just eligible. He must have been inspired by the brilliantly skilful retreat from Mons in late August, when it looked as if the small British expeditionary force would be overwhelmed by swiftly advancing German forces. This was followed by the critical Battle of the Marne in September, in which British and French forces repelled the German army just when the latter expected to enter Paris. After basic training in the Inns of Court Regiment, Norman was commissioned in February 1915. He survived for over two years and with the rank of captain was posted missing on 23 April 1917. 'Missing' usually meant 'dead', but he had been captured during a German counter-attack in the trench system four miles east of Arras. In May William received a postcard from Norman with the good news that he was alive and well. In June Norman suffered acute appendicitis. His captors operated without delay but, after initially appearing to recover, he died of blood poisoning on 20 June, aged 41.

Laurence, a year younger than Norman, volunteered in 1915. He was a chartered accountant and district auditor. He fell in one of the terrible but fruitless contests in or near Delville Wood on 30 July 1916. His personal effects were returned to William: a cigarette case and a pocketknife, the poignant remains of a life prematurely cut down.

Was it for this the clay grew tall? The serenity of the landscape makes this not a bad place to think about warfare and what it represents: a collapse, indeed a denial, of the human spirit and its potential for good, and how it sucks decent men (and now women) into a collective act of darkness.

Continue following the path along the edge of the escarpment.
Remarkably, the top of Hindhead Heath boasts one of the thickest layers of heathland surface peat (30cm) in southern Britain. Peat forms because of the chemical qualities of acidic soil, which inhibit the breakdown of vegetable matter into humus, the result of podsolization. Beneath lies acidic sand and sandstone rock.

Pass through the NT exit gate. After 75m or so, fork left off the vehicle track and continue along the wooded footpath near the edge of the escarpment without deviation. After just over ½ km the land opens up to the right revealing the NT car park (and café for refreshment) beyond.

⟳ A short way ahead is a viewing point [GR 8910 3590].
The bronze sculpture's text cites the mixed-up myth concerning the Devil's Punch Bowl. Only in a pick-and-mix folkloric *smorgasbröd* is it possible to conflate the misplaced pre-Christian Nordic Thor with the Devil of Christianity.

Now to the landscape. 'Surrey,' as one writer has observed, 'may come in like a lamb at the Thameside meadows of Runnymede, but she goes out like a lion at Hindhead.' It was always hazardous country here. Samuel Pepys crossed the heath here in August 1668, 'having an old man

Gibbet Hill, on the Portsmouth Road, about one km south of here, showing three ruffians, hanging from the gibbet in 1786 as a warning to others. They had murdered and robbed a sailor who had befriended them. The story may be found on his tombstone (p.73). The original picture had hung in the Royal Huts Hotel in Hindhead.

a guide in the coach with us; but got thither [Liphook] with great fear of being out of our way, it being ten at night.' Hindhead Heath was never a place to get benighted. The most notorious case was in 1786, when three footpads murdered a sailor. (You will come to his grave in Thursley churchyard.)

On one of his rides in 1822, William Cobbett called Hindhead Heath 'certainly the most villainous spot that God ever made. Our ancestors do, indeed, seem to have ascribed its formation to another power, for the most celebrated part of it is called "the Devil's Punch Bowl."' The name is a piece of nineteenth century whimsy. Before then, local people knew the Punch Bowl as 'The Pit'.

You will be wondering how the Devil's Punch Bowl was made. It owes its origin to a stream flowing northwards (to be crossed again later on). This stream has cut a valley through the sandy rocks. The steepness of the sides is explained by springs created when water draining through the sandy stratum hits the impermeable Wealden clay bed beneath to spring out of the hillside, sapping the sandy sides of the valley. The undermining action of the springs has made the head of the valley larger than the rest of the valley, hence the 'punchbowl' effect. It is the largest such formation in Britain. Descending into the valley bottom the flora changes, with an increase of clay-loving plants, and boggy patches where the water has difficulty draining away.

A broom squire making brooms, out of heath sprays. The sprays were 'bundled' out of bavins (faggots), often by women, the bond left loose for the broom squire to push onto the end of the stick, when he would tighten the two hazel or withy [willow wand] bonds. Besoms made from birch sprays were more expensive, for they were harder to bind effectively and required three hazel bonds. Finally a hole was bored through the spray and stick, and a peg driven through to ensure a long lasting broom. This broom squire seems to have roofed his shed with iron, but Gertrude Jekyll says they used heather thatch: 'In old days it was usual to keep their money in some hole in the thatch inside; they considered it safer than keeping it in cottages…An old friend, who knew their ways well, told me he had known of a sum of between three and four hundred pounds [in today's money at least £16,000] being kept in this way.'

Behind you is the edge of Hindhead, which had its fashionable moment in the late nineteenth century, when many members of the late Victorian literary and intellectual community settled in the area. One contemporary remarked that Hindhead was, 'the literary Olympus, the abode of so many cultured notables that some wag felicitously suggested that the name should be altered to Mind Head.' George Bernard Shaw came to stay in 1898, and in a public address upset the local schoolteacher by encouraging the children to disobey their elders.

By the mid-nineteenth century Hindhead Heath was known for its economic life. Over the previous centuries poor folk had squatted along its fringes, and erected hovels to inhabit, and thus become freeholders. Many were known as 'broom squires' (a corruption of 'broom squarers'), their principal living made by making brooms from broom, from heather (for which the generic term 'broom' was also used) and besoms (now ludicrously only thought of as witches' brooms. On the real witch's broom, see p. 225). Besoms were made from birch twigs bound onto the end of an ash pole.

When the National Trust took over the Devil's Punch Bowl in 1906, it prohibited the cutting of birch and charged for cutting the heath, a measure that outraged local folk who had been harvesting the heath, birch and bracken for generations. Some set fire to the heath in revenge. Broommaking here did not die out until around 1930. One old Surrey woman told Gertrude Jekyll,

> Best place I ever lived in was at Mr Woods's at Hambledon. Quietist and best master I ever lived with. There was a redbrick kitchen-floor. I used to flow he [sic] down with a green broom; best of brooms for bricks; make the floors red. You makes 'em of the green broom as grows on the common.

With our petrochemical plastic brooms we are, sadly, on another planet.

Continue walking in the same direction for 150m and fork left, pass through the wicket gate, and immediately turn left [GR 8923 3580]. Follow the track for 1½ km until fields open up on either side.

You will pass through beech woodland, characterised by 'summer darkness', the intense shade of beech trees, which even holly finds challenging. The soil is too rich and the shade too great here for brambles. As you pass open fields, look out for Exmoor ponies. If you see one you are likely to see more, on account of their herding instinct. They are here to crop seedling trees and thus help recover the heathland landscape.

Where beech is used to line the woodbank beside the track, look out for 'inosculation', the joining together of originally separate plants. Beech inosculates more willingly than most other species, but holly will do it too. There are even better examples further on. It looks as if this habit was the motive for planting beech since it helps to bind and stabilise the bank.

After 350m of fields on either side, watch out for the Broom Squire signage and some magnificent old yew trees and traces of an old wall on your left.

Hindhead, Devil's Punch Bowl, The Broom Squire's Cottage

George Mays, in 1907, the configuration of the track behind him still recognisable. He is carrying his 3½ quart milk pails on a yoke, and walking towards Hindhead. The figure in the doorway must be his mother, Frances, with whom he lived. He never married. He spent his whole life in the valley. For 24 years, until about 1915, he had a daily round, delivering milk to his customers up the hill, in Hindhead. He kept pigs and was a broom squire too. It was Mays or a neighbour in Highcombe Bottom who angrily told a visitor how, on account of new National Trust restrictions, he could no longer forage but had to obtain his materials from Petworth, miles away: 'I have orders right away as far as Dorking, for forty-two dozen, which I shall not be able to supply.' Mays was probably the last of his breed. He came by his trade honestly. His maternal grandfather was a broom-maker and also an hotelier in Hindhead. His great grandfather had built The Royal Huts Hotel at the crossroads in Hindhead, to replace the crude shelters used by broom squires awaiting the wagons to take their wares to market. With Mays' death in 1939 this extraordinary continuity was lost. Where can one find such continuity now?

Look at the photograph on the signage. The buildings of Highcombe Farm have now entirely gone but the track remains recognisable. The farm was possibly built in the eighteenth century when improved live-stock breeding led to increased land reclamation. By the middle of the nineteenth century it was occupied by a Norfolk man, George Mays, who described himself as 'gamekeeper'. His son, also George, was born here in 1859 and took over in about 1891. The farm buildings were empty but still standing in the 1950s.

Continue for almost ½ km until a cottage is visible on the right, at the end of the open field on the right. Turn right [GR 8890 3746] down towards the cottage but follow the path as it turns to the left and over the stream. Through the gate [GR 8905 3770], take the right track uphill for 250m and turn left on reaching the cross-track. Follow the track which after about 250m curves to the right uphill. As it descends look out for gates simultaneously to the left and the right and pause.

The view to the left is quintessentially English: a beautifully sculptured valley leading the eye down to Punch Bowl (once Pitlands) Farm. This is Highcombe Bottom, the original name for the whole valley. The name meant 'hay valley bottom', a tribute to the rich meadow on the floor of the north end of the combe. In the far distance lies the Hog's Back.

Continue, following the track around to the left (another track soon coming in from the right [GR 8952 3774]).

After 1km just before the tarmac, the first house on the right is Upper Highfield Farm, built in 1554.

On joining the tarmac at the junction, turn right along the village road. Continue for another 1km along the tarmac lane, past some of the outlying dwellings of Thursley, passing Hedge Farm.

There are still surviving parts of Hedge Farm that date back to the mid fifteenth century.

On entering the centre of Thursley, walking down The Street, watch out for:

1. HILL FARM on the left, first visible with the church steeple just behind. Its rear and flank are hung with hand-made warm reddish-orange tiles, to protect the building from the prevailing south-west weather. This must be one of the most beautiful examples in Surrey. The front is a delight too: strait-laced plain red brick. The original building dates from around 1500, but the frontage dates from the early eighteenth century.

2. ST MICHAEL AND ALL ANGELS (the Archangel Michael, it seems, can seldom evade his subordinates) was Saxon until the Victorian restorers got their hands on it. Alas, they really pulled the place about. Yet, like so many Surrey churches, in spite of the dreadful things done by restorers, the spirit of community devotion to this building over the centuries is palpable and compelling.

THE EXTERIOR is almost all nineteenth century. At least the late fifteenth century belfry survived. The sundial mounted on the wall reminds us not only of the time of day, but its measurement of our lifespan. The most notable grave in the churchyard is a tall stone, 25 paces from the north west corner of the church marking the interment of the nameless sailor, who 'fell a Victim to three Ruffians' rage' on the Portsmouth road to Hindhead one September evening in 1786. He had generously entertained them at the Red Lion (see below), before they decided to rob him of his earnings and his life. The murderers were duly apprehended and hanged, their bodies then hung up to rot on Gibbet Hill in iron gibbets specially forged for them in Thursley's smithy. Someone clearly felt very strongly indeed, to stump up the money for such a gravestone. George Mays is also buried here, as well as members of the Lutyens family.

THE INTERIOR is dominated by the wonderful great timber cage on which the belfry rests. Forget that it is probably much larger than necessary. It is simply a joy to behold, an interloper at the time that the belfry was planned, but one that successfully defied those restorers. The four corner posts are oak tree trunks, each over 700 centimetres (2ft 6ins) thick, held together by tie-beams at the top. It is beautifully made.

Other features to look out for: in the chancel on the north (left) side: two small Saxon double splayed windows, still retaining wooden frames to hold oiled linen or panes of translucent horn. The restorers missed these, for they only came to light in 1927. Beneath them is a Saxon oven recess, for baking the wafer used in the Mass. A Norman window has survived above the arcade on the north side, while on the south chancel wall there are two lancet windows and a sedilia or priest's seat also discovered in 1927.

THE FURNISHINGS. On the right side, the Tracey Sheppard glass engraved doors to the vestry on the right (organ pipes above) were installed in 2010, a real delight, poetry in glass. There should be an information sheet on the pew beside the doors to tell you more. At the rear, the Bargate stone font decorated with a wavy band is pre-1100 and probably Saxon. There is a locally made chest, dated 1622. On the wall are the Royal Arms of 1783, handsome but clearly propaganda to remind those inclined to seditious views that while they might be there to worship God, when it came to obedience the boss was definitely King George.

3. Just past the church on the left stands THE OLD PARSONAGE, the centre half-timbered, the oldest parts dating to 1411.

The rest of The Street is filled with delights, mainly ranging from the sixteenth to the first half of the nineteenth century, but look out on the right for the tell-tale buttresses of the Lutyens-designed Prospect Cottage. It was built as a very modest village hall in 1900, and subsequently converted into a cottage.

At the end and facing The Street and The Lane is Edwin Lutyens' very first essay in architecture, THE CORNER, a row of three early eighteenth century cottages which he converted into a single house in 1888-90, with a big tile-hung addition at the back. He was only nineteen.

Finally, to the right, the Three Horseshoes merits close inspection, particularly for its fine food.

The Red Lion, Thursley's original hostelry, stood on the old Portsmouth Road. The old building still stands, on the slip road from the A3, its role rendered redundant with the motor car. It was here that our nameless sailor on his way to Portsmouth had generously and unsuspectingly treated his assassins.

Frensham Great Pond and the River Wey

Distance 7½km/4 miles: 2 hours
OS Explorer Map No.145

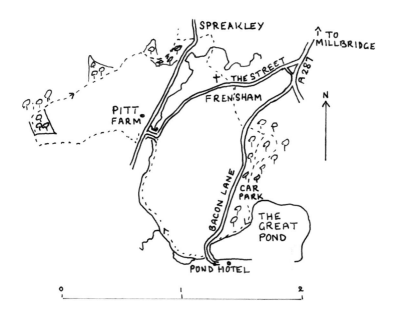

BEFORE YOU WALK

If you are looking for the theme to this walk, 'the answer,' in the immortal words of the classic radio comedy show, *Round the Horne*, 'lies in the soil.' Almost the whole of Frensham lies on the lower greensand. This walk from the edge of the Great Pond contrasts the astonishing pure but highly acidic sands of Frensham Common with the rich silt of the Wey valley and the fertile soils of the hills to the west.

First things first, however. It is important to get one's pronunciation right. Almost a century ago a local writer recalled that in his youth the

If you wish to pass for a real aboriginal, your best authority is Will Hammond, who was born here in 1842. He was the blacksmith in George Sturt's wheelwright shop in Farnham (see p.14). He always called his birthplace 'Fruns'm', and nearby Churt he pronounced 'Cheert'. So now you know.

village 'was known to all indigenous inhabitants as Frens-ham. The alteration [eliding *s* and *h*] was brought by "outlander" immigrants.'

If car-less: Bus No.19 from Farnham, alight at Millbridge and walk into
Frensham village to take up the walk at ➲ on p.84.
Refreshment: Frensham Pond Hotel (tel. 01252 795161) to the left out
of the car park.
Make a day of it: Explore Farnham and the Farnham Museum,
38 West St, Farnham, open Tues-Sat, 1000-1700 (tel. 01252 715094,
www.farnham.museum@waverley.gov.uk).

**Start at Frensham Great Pond car park [GR 8440 4060] on Bacon Lane (the west
turn off the A287 immediately south of the turning to Frensham parish church).
Approach the lake, turn right and proceed alongside the wooden railings until
these allow close proximity with the pond.**
If you have not been here before, the most astonishing thing is the pure
sand, bereft even of gravel, as on the seashore. As soon as you are close
to the pond's shoreline, look across to the high ground beyond the main
road. Today the hillside is covered in trees and shrub, but three thousand years ago it was almost certainly stripped of most of its tree cover
by the local community. Eight thousand years ago the area was inhabited by Mesolithic people, who were hunter-gatherers, and 5,000 years
ago by people with a Neolithic culture. It was the Neolithic people, our

ancestors, who introduced the first farming, keeping penned and herded livestock (which thus became domesticated), and later began growing basic crops. By 3,500 years ago, the Neolithic way of life began to be slowly displaced by the Bronze Age culture, with the first use of metal. Along the skyline there are at least four Bronze Age barrows, or burial mounds. Today they are covered in bracken, shrub and trees. They would have been highly visible when constructed about 3,000 years ago. We cannot know what these funerary barrows really represent. They look westwards, to the setting sun as do, for example, a similar chain of late Bronze Age barrows in Richmond Park. Why were they set in a line along the ridge? What did they signify? We can only speculate that they have formed some kind of boundary, between one kindred group's territory and another's, or perhaps between land set aside for the sacred and that for the profane, or perhaps related to some form of astronomy. We will probably never know.

Now to the pond, which is natural and fed from the Silverbeck, near Churt. It has at some stage – perhaps in the Middle Ages – been doubled in size, to almost 3km in circumference. This western side is the enlargement, the original pond being east of the present centre. The presence of a Mesolithic site either side of the pond strongly suggests that it has been here at least 8,000 years and probably for several millennia more.

How, one might ask, can such sandy soil hold water? Water retention here is the result of 'iron pan' formed when ferruginous content in the sand precipitates into a hard crust a metre or more beneath the ground surface.

The pond is first mentioned in 1208, during the reign of King John, as belonging to the Bishop of Winchester but looked after by 'Walter the Fisherman'. Fish were supplied to the bishop's table at Farnham Castle, and even to the market in London. With Friday designated as a day of fasting by the Church, fish was an essential part of the Friday menu for richer people before the Reformation. At the beginning of the eighteenth century John Aubrey noted that the pond was 'well known for its Carps to the London Fishmongers.'

Frensham Great Pond used to be frequented by birds which are now rare. In 1779 Gilbert White, living just over the county border at Selborne, reported three brace of 'long-legged plover', an old name for the Black Winged Stilt (an infrequent visitor to Britain, with currently four or five sightings a year). Of these, five birds were shot by the pond

The first seaplane trial.

keeper and only one, rather pointlessly, was spared. There were ospreys infrequently here also, but the pond keeper could not resist shooting them too to protect his fish-stock. The last recorded one to be shot here was in about 1890. You might have forgiven ospreys for never returning. Now that we have learnt not to kill such magnificent creatures, the occasional osprey and hen harrier have started to make a miraculous return. A century ago, however, having extirpated such natural masters of flight, humans arranged their own aerial amusements. In 1913 the world's first seaplane was tested here.

As one veers left on joining the road, Frensham Pond Hotel is in view to the left. After 100m stop by the metal railing around the culvert on the right of the road. Generations of the family Marden rented both the White Horse Inn (where the Pond Hotel which you are approaching now stands) and the Great Pond from the lord of the manor. From the eighteenth century and possibly earlier there used to be a five-yearly fishing exercise, finally abandoned in 1885 when the last of the Marden tenants died. First, the ditch below the pond penstock, in fact probably exactly where you are standing, was fitted with gratings and then the penstock was opened. The pond took six weeks to drain down to a small pool in the deepest part of the pond, in which seethed a mass of fish. Men provided with landing nets and baskets waded into the mud, scooped out the floundering fish and sorted them: 'Many tons of fish were taken out on these occasions, and by the end of the day the stewponds [temporary holding ponds] were a squirming mass of Pike, Perch, Roach, Dace, Tench and Carp, many of them of great size.' Harvesting was such a major spectacle that local children enjoyed a day's holiday to watch the fishing. The heavier fish were sold to London's Jewish traders to supply East European immigrant communities with a fondness for coarse fish. There was also a mill here in the mid-sixteenth century.

Follow the bridleway on the right of the culvert [GR 8407 4006], through the woodland.
Unsurprisingly, the dominant trees here are all wet-loving: predominantly alder and, much later on, a small plantation of poplar. Almost immediately the stream flows into a pretty pond. Shortly thereafter it is joined by the South Branch of the River Wey (which rises on the Sussex-Hampshire border) and becomes much larger. You will pass a metal foot bridge to your left, and later pass an Arts & Crafts period house above on the right, one of the outhouses of Frensham Manor, a large Tudor timber-framed house, which stands on the site of predecessors from at least two centuries earlier. It was held as a sub-manor of Farnham from the twelfth century. Sadly, one is denied a view. Just before reaching the road you will see a neo-Georgian house on the left, which is barely 50 years old. It replaces a corn mill which was still here in the mid-twentieth century. An old mill outhouse survives on the right of the track.

On reaching the road, turn left across the bridge [GR 8365 4101], then follow the road around to the left.
To your right is Pitt Farm, with its characteristic hop kilns (never oast houses in Surrey, but always kilns). If you wish to see Surrey's last hop field, go to Puttenham (see p.139).

After 200m turn right up a footpath, just before a stone dwelling (Mill Cottage). [GR 8350 4092]. Follow the path for about 1km.
On the right of the path is a relatively modern hedgerow, almost exclusively planted with hawthorn, or 'quickthorn', used from the early

eighteenth century for enclosing previously open fields. Very old hedge-rows tend to have a variety of hardwood species. This one is probably not much more than a century old. The ditch and the oak trees are likely to be old. On the left of the path are ash and hazel coppice, perhaps still cropped as fuel.

When about 100m from the tile-hung house ahead, turn right over a stile [GR 8265 4094], and follow the path across the field into the corner of the wood. After about 200m when you come to a cross-track, turn right and follow the track, without deviation, to emerge onto the crest of the hill and continue with open fields [GR 8280 4129] and good views on either side.

To your left on the distant hillside stands the very extensive Alice Holt. Think of George Sturt, a grammar school teacher compelled to take over the family wheelwright shop in 1884 when his father fell ill. He went out one day to Alice Holt to buy standing oak for use in the shop. He bought a tree in a particular clay hollow, sound at the butt (base), but which 'began to be "foxy" two feet up.' He did not easily forgive himself his poor judgement: 'I don't think my father or grandfather would have bought timber from that hollow. They knew "England" in a more intimate way.' Sturt had enormous respect for those who knew the land so minutely, but he was unnecessarily hard on himself. Buying live oak is notoriously difficult. John Evelyn (p.148), who knew a thing or two about timber, wrote two centuries earlier in *Sylva*:

> There is not a thing more obnoxious [liable] to deceit, than buying of [oak] trees standing, upon the reputation of their appearance to the eye, unless the chapman [customer] be extraordinarily judicious, so various are their hidden and conceal'd infirmities, till they be fell'd and sawn out.... A timber-tree is a merchant-adventurer, you shall never know what he is worth till he be dead.

However, on another timber-buying venture in Alice Holt, Sturt witnessed the skill of a true countryman:

> I pushed through some brambles in "Alice Holt" and came to a patch of spurge (or it may have been a mist of blue-bells), the tall young forester who was showing me the oak-trees suddenly dropped forward his full length without bending: and when he stood up he had got a rabbit in his hands.

Continue through another patch of woodland, or 'shaw', to use the proper local word.

Shaws are surviving groves of woodland, frequently only belts still edging fields cut out of woodland long ago. The word is ancient and still common in Surrey and Kent.

On emerging, turn left to follow the edge of the field to the corner.

Pitt Farm lies in the valley down to the right.

Cross the style into the next shaw [GR 8352 4167] from which one emerges to turn right, with the woodland on your right. Follow the edge of the field.

On your right you may note the stand of sweet chestnuts (in winter one can tell which they are by their characteristic leaves on the ground). There is a direct link between this stand and Pitt Farm in the valley below, for it must have been originally planted to provide hop poles. Just over a century ago they would have been felled every ten years, when 4-5m tall (14-16ft), the tip of the pole only about 3cm/1inch in diameter. Two poles were required for each vine, working out at roughly two thousand poles for every acre of hops. So in the heyday of hop-growing, tens of thousands of poles were required.

Why was chestnut so greatly favoured? Chestnut grows with unusually narrow sapwood behind the bark. Its heartwood forms at an early age and has great resistance to decay, better, for example, than ash, which until about 1800 had been the favoured species, and even better than oak when set into the ground. Even so, there was constant demand for replacement poles, which explains why everywhere one goes in old hop country in Surrey and even more so in Kent, one finds plentiful stands of lapsed chestnut coppice. Indeed, because of hop-growing, the chestnut became a highly common tree on the clay-with-flints soil of the North Downs. From about 1900 the old system was replaced by 'wirework', with hops trained up lengths of twine suspended from overhead wires, held up by 'king poles', larger, stouter chestnut poles, grown on a sixteen year rotation.

The chestnut is an 'honorary native', having probably been introduced by the Romans. Because they twist with age, and develop 'shakes', or splits, along the grain, they produce unreliable timber. So they were always felled young or coppiced. Indeed, by the 1950s it was the only wood species still deemed profitable to coppice, grown for stake fencing. John Evelyn knew this well enough, 'the chesnut [*sic*] affords the best stakes and poles for palisades.' Today such coppiced shoots are cloven into three segments and bound on galvanised wire to form durable fencing, each cleft cut to the heart of the stem to ensure each stave has its share of the most durable heartwood.

To the left, once it has come into view, stands an enormous mock Tudor pile, Frensham Heights School, on the far side of the valley. Its Victorian architect was ominously described as a 'builder of institutions'.

Follow the path around the edge of the field and, turning right, through a gate and another shaw [GR 8380 4175], when you start to descend, soon on tarmac, through the purlieus of Spreakley.

After all the woodland through which one has walked, it is satisfying to learn that Spreakley derives from Old English meaning 'a woodland clearing marked by young shoots'.

Go straight across the road and pause before going along Hammondswood Road.

Is this road named after Will Hammond, George Sturt's blacksmith, who was born in Frensham? It would be nice to think so. Hammond worked alongside George Cook, the master carpenter in the wheelwright's shop. Neither had any education, yet both were master craftsmen in their own trade, with the skill to provide elegant solutions to the problems they encountered. They took enormous pride in the quality of their work, oblivious to the cost of their time. It was of these two craftsmen that Sturt wrote: 'These men, I knew, would sooner have been discharged than work badly, against their own conscience.' How many in one's own field of work could one name today with such standards?

Such was their care that, speaking of this team, Sturt recalled,

> … we got curiously intimate with the peculiar needs of the neighbourhood. In farm-waggon or dung cart, barley roller, plough, water barrel, or what not, the dimensions we chose, the curves we followed (and almost every piece of timber was curved) were imposed upon us by the nature of the soil in this or that farm, the gradient of this or that hill, the temper of this or that customer or his choice perhaps

in horseflesh. The carters told us their needs. To satisfy the carter, we gave another half-inch of curve to the waggon-bottom, altered the hooks for harness on the shafts, hung the water barrel an inch nearer to the horse or an inch farther away, according to requirements…. One important point… was to make the wheels of waggon or dung cart "take the routs." as we said. (See one of their waggons, p.43)

The 'routs', or ruts, varied in depth from place to place, and the width would also vary from one county, or indeed district, to another, an indication of how little contact there was between districts, until macadamised surfaces changed all that.

Pass St Austin's and The Malt House on your right. Turn right down the marked footpath just afterwards [GR 8410 4180], opposite a lime tree bearing great swags of mistletoe.

Mistletoe loves to colonise lime trees, since the latter has such fibrous stringy bark to which mistletoe can easily adhere. (On the virtues of the lime, see p.153.) Apple is another favourite, because of the flaky surface of the bark.

Continue over the footbridge across the Wey, and follow it up to the Street in Frensham.

You may wish to visit the parish church on your right:

ST MARY'S CHURCH

St Mary's Church was an outlying chapel of Farnham in the early middle ages.

THE EXTERIOR. The original church site was abandoned in 1239 shortly after the nearby bridge over the Wey was destroyed by flood, and a new building erected here, on higher ground. The lower part of the tower is 'Decorated' (fourteenth century). The sanctuary walls at the opposite end of the church date from the original 1239 construction. The churchyard is a real treasure, when so many churchyards no longer possess visual harmony.

THE INTERIOR. Something of disappointment, as a result of heavy-handed restoration in 1868. Its charm lies, as in so many village churches, in what it says about the community. Churches may be temples to God, but they are also shrines of the community, where villagers for countless generations have tried to make some sense of their own lives and also done what they can to cherish the lives of their neighbours. If you wish to look around, St Mary's produces its own pamphlet about the history, but the notices of what goes on today are of more interest.

LOOK OUT FOR a great copper cauldron sitting on its iron trivet (currently in the sanctuary). This belonged to Old Mother Ludlam and supposedly lived with her in the cave near Waverley Abbey (p.89). It is probably seventeenth century, so one must suppose that Old Mother Ludlam (if she was a genuine person) dates from that time too, but it is probably safer to suppose absolutely nothing about her as a real person. The font is probably Norman, made of Purbeck marble.

On leaving the church turn left along the Street and after less than 100m turn right just beyond the (currently pink) rough-cast cottage, up the footpath 'Lover's Lane' [GR 8430 4140].

(⮌ Car-less walkers come into the village from the main road, and turn left up Lover's Lane, at the rough-cast cottage shortly before the church.)

After 300m cross the first road and continue another 200m until reaching Bacon Lane. You can turn right and walk back to the Great Pond car park, but you must endure the unpleasantness of the traffic. Better, turn left and after about 30 paces along the road turn right up a footpath [GR 84404110], taking the right fork thereafter, which climbs to the crest of a mainly wooded ridge of sand.

This is the edge of Frensham Common, which almost completely surrounds the Great Pond. Beyond the pond, but on the same infertile sand, lies Churt, to which David Lloyd George came ostensibly to write his war memoirs. In fact he chose it as a quiet place to keep his mistress. With such sandy soil, he needed huge quantities of manure for his orchards and obtained it from the cavalry barracks in Aldershot, as he drily remarked, 'the only use he had ever found for cavalry.'

Turn right when at the top (there is a narrow belt of open ground) and follow the path which takes you down a slope, forking right (but it does not greatly matter) where the path divides. On reaching a broad and very sandy track shortly after, turn right. After about 500m you will reach the car park.

Two centuries ago the land around the pond was virtually treeless, and as recently as one hundred and fifty years ago the Common was the abode

An old Frensham house as photographed by Gertrude Jekyll. It is a Surrey classic: a tall chimney, long 'catslide' pitches, lean-to additions, the exterior apparently unpainted, brick or plaster and structural timbers. The garden is complete with skep.

of wild ponies, red and fallow deer, but was also:

> the resort of broken men and desperate characters of every kind. No man's property was safe from their depredations. Sheep were stolen from their folds, pigs from their sties, and slaughtered hogs from farm-houses, before they could be converted into bacon.... Not one house in Churt but had its windows strengthened against attack in similar fashion.

Today's desperadoes are unlikely to be out on the Common. More probably at this very moment they are trying to pick the lock of your car.

Waverley and Tilford

Distance 9km/5 miles: 2½-3 hours
OS Explorer Map No.145

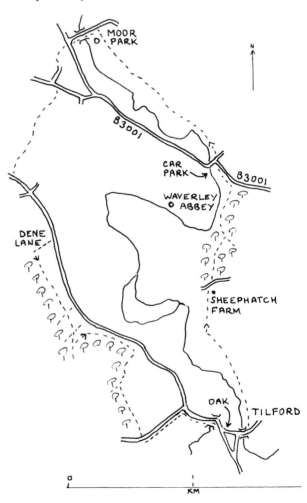

BEFORE YOU WALK

The principal theme of this walk is the way that the landscape along the Wey has been used and valued across the centuries. For example, 800 years ago, the monks of Waverley Abbey were engaged in experimental agriculture, alongside their search for spiritual renewal. Later, at the end of the seventeenth century one of the great formal gardens of England was laid out at Moor Park by a renowned gardener, Sir William Temple. It marked the suddenly growing taste in landscape for pleasure. The garden has gone, but the grounds and house remain. Later still, after Dunkirk, the Wey valley was prepared as a barrier against enemy invasion, which has left its own dismally ugly remains. In complete contrast to Temple's formalism and these military defences, there are the examples of nature unrestrained: the morass of alder carr, or bog, in the Wey valley and, later, a tract of sandy acid land in Bourne Wood. In recent years both have become nature conservation areas reflecting our present concern with the progressive erosion of our environment: tiny bastions where, it is to be hoped, the diversity of nature will be redeemed. All these things, and it is not difficult to identify other indications of our response to the landscape through the ages, are noticeable on this walk. There is plenty of signage on this walk to provide fuller information.

Warning: I owe you a major apology for an unpleasant but unavoidable stretch of road walking, about ¾km, on Tilford Road. Please bear in mind that it is safest to walk facing the traffic, and it helps if at least one (lead) walker wears a bright colour.

If car-less: Bus No.46 from Farnham (15 mins), or longer from Guildford, to Waverley Abbey car park.

Refreshment: after two-thirds of the walk, at the Barley Mow in Tilford (tel. 01252 792205).

Make a day of it: visit the Rural Life Centre, Reeds Road, Tilford, open Wed to Sun, mid-March–end October, 1000-1700, in winter Weds & Suns only, 1100-1600 (tel. 01252 795571, www.rural-life.org.uk), or explore Farnham and the Farnham Museum, 38 West St, Farnham, open Tues-Sat, 1000-1700 (tel. 01252 715094, www.farnham.museum@waverley.gov.uk).

Start at Waverley Abbey Car Park (on the B3001 between Elstead and Farnham) [GR 8700 4550].

THE PILLBOX

Resist the temptation to look at the ruins of the abbey now, and keep it as the reward on completion of your walk. But you may wish to examine an uglier feature, the Second World War pillbox, first of at least four to be found on this walk. Pillboxes were rapidly thrown up when invasion seemed inevitable after Dunkirk in May 1940. By October 18,000 pillboxes had been constructed, mainly across the southern approaches to London and the industrial heartlands. The idea was defence in depth, to slow the enemy down. The one you are looking was part of the GHQ line, the most important line of the fifty defence lines intended to protect the heartlands of Britain. The purpose here was to delay an advance across the River Wey valley and prevent capture of the Hog's Back, an immensely important tactical vantage point from where enemy observers could direct artillery fire and air attack on targets up to the Thames, which could have inhibited London's contact with south-west England. This one is sited with a wide field of fire across the valley bottom.

Made up of both brick and reinforced concrete, this pillbox housed an anti-tank gun but would probably not have stood up to tank fire for long. It is immediately noticeable that there are no fire-apertures at the rear, rendering it indefensible if enemy infantry was able to work their way around it. Who would dream of staying inside, once they knew they had been outflanked? It is doubtful that its accompanying small arms pillbox (to the left) could have afforded it much protection from the flank and rear.

By October a crucial battle had been won in the air. Had the Germans invaded, they would have needed to capture a port in order to land tanks, heavy guns and supplies in adequate quantities. The Royal Navy remained significantly stronger than the German fleet and would have interrupted attempts at supply across the Channel, and it is now believed that for this reason an invasion would have failed. Had, however, German tanks reached the GHQ line, the likelihood is that they would have breached it.

Return to the main road and turn right, over the bridge (noticing the old bridge on your right), cross to the left side of the road and walk straight ahead where the main road turns right. Turn left a few paces later, immediately after Stella Cottage (named after Jonathan Swift's 'Stella', with whom it has no real connection), along the marked footpath [GR 8715 4560].

After about 200m you will reach Old Mother Ludlam's cave. The signage tells you all you probably wish to know. The 'Ludwell' once provided spring water for Waverley Abbey. 'Lud' may be from the Celtic word, meaning 'loud', a reference to the gurgling of the spring. 'Old Mother Lud', an eccentric, apparently lived in the cave, possibly in the seventeenth century, but she has come down to us as an undocumented legend. William Cobbett lamented that in his maturity the cave had lost the charm it held in his childhood:

> It is not the enchanting place that I knew it... The semi-circular paling is gone; the basins to catch the never-ceasing little stream are gone; the iron cups, fastened by chains, for people to drink out of, are gone; the pavement all broken to pieces; the seats for people to sit on, on both sides of the cave, torn up and gone; the stream that ran down a clean paved channel, now making a dirty gutter; and the ground opposite which was a grove, chiefly of laurels, intersected by closed mowed grass walks, now become a poor ragged-looking Alder-Coppice.

In this, Cobbett may not have been entirely accurate, since the alder-carr, or alder bog, somewhere along this stretch of the Wey was the scene of an early personal triumph (see below). Today the cave is home to various bat species.

Continue walking.

Down below in the valley bottom is a swamp, in fact an 'alder carr', hotching with wild life and a real rarity in this part of the world. It is the only deep water alder swamp in Surrey and has been re-developed over the past 20 years. However, it must have been here in all its miry glory two centuries ago, that William Cobbett recalled a childhood experience:

> A huntsman, named George Bradley, who was a huntsman to Mr Smither, of Hale, very wantonly gave me a cut with his whip, because I jumped in amongst the dogs, pulled a hare from them and got her scut, upon a little common, called Seal Common, near Waverley Abbey.

Young Cobbett would not have been so treated had he been a gentleman's son. He knew it and resolved to repay Bradley. The next time the hunt was out on Seal Common, he was ready with a red herring, which he dragged over the place:

> I clapped down my herring, went off at a right angle towards the west, climbed up a steep bank very soon, where the horsemen, such as they were, could not follow; then on I went over the roughest part of the common that I could find, till I got to the pales of Moor Park, over which I went, there being holes at the bottom for the letting-in of hares. That part of the park was covered with short heath; and I gave some twirls about to amuse Mr Bradley for half an hour. Then off I went, and down a hanger at last, to the bottom of which no horseman could get without riding round a quarter of a mile. At the bottom of the hanger was an aldermoor, in a swamp. There my herring ceased to perform its service…. [Thus] amidst conjectures, disputations, mutual blamings, and swearings a plenty, they concluded, some of them half-leg deep in dirt, and going soaking home.

Continue for about 1km, passing two pillboxes, one for an anti-tank gun, the other for supporting infantry, until you reach Moor Park on your left [GR 8620 4656].

MOOR PARK

Look out for the helpful signage. William Temple (1628-1699) and his wife, Dorothy Osborne (1626-1695) were the most celebrated owners of the house. Their claim to fame is that theirs is *the* great love story of the English seventeenth century. They had met almost by chance, on the Isle of Wight in 1648, during the huge unrest of the Civil War. Both felt an instant attraction but knew that their respective families would be desperately opposed and therefore prevent their marriage. Over the next four years they barely saw each other. In December 1652, just returned from abroad, William, now a diplomat, could keep silent no longer. He wrote asking Dorothy whether he must settle his wager of £10 [about £1,000 in today's currency] that she would by now be married. Dorothy wrote back swiftly 'the ten poundes hee claims, it is not yett due…. For I am where I was, still the same, and alwayes Your Humble Servant.' It was the beginning of an intense correspondence, both agreeing to destroy each letter after it was received to prevent discovery. Dorothy strong-mindedly did so. William, weaker, could not bear to part with hers, and they survived, undiscovered: 77 love letters of great tenderness, living proof that love can vanquish reason. Dorothy was introduced to one suitable suitor after another. She refused them all and William, in receipt of her stream of clandestine letters, dared to hope. In October 1653 Dorothy fell into a depression and, thinking their situation hopeless, broke off their understanding. William had to wait until January before her jealous brother was absent and it was safe to visit her. He persuaded her that love should triumph over pragmatism and rational argument.

As the first rumour led to widening gossip, William and Dorothy finally decided to declare openly their love and their determination to marry. The two families sulked, but eventually and very reluctantly acquiesced. William and Dorothy embarked upon a profoundly happy marriage. They took a house in Sheen, but moved to Moor Park in 1686, as a result of a row with a neighbour.

The house was a (now rare) 1630s 'Dutch style' house, which the Temples renamed Moor Park after a country seat in Hertfordshire which Temple admired. (If you wish to know roughly what it once looked like, visit Kew Palace in Kew Gardens, George III's home, which was built by a merchant in the same style in about 1630.) The house, as you see it, is essentially late eighteenth century, and whatever is left of the original is now encased in subsequent building. It was here that Jonathan Swift stayed as a guest, took a shine to young Esther Johnson, the daughter of the estate steward, tutored her and provided for her education. Esther became 'Stella' in one of Swift's novels. Temple laid out extensive gardens here to exemplify his ideas in his essay, *On Gardening*. Sadly they are gone, except for the brick fragments of a Baroque summerhouse.

In the nineteenth century Moor Park became a hydropathic institute. Charles Darwin used to come here for treatment in the 1850s. It cannot have been much fun, nor can it have done much good, but he greatly enjoyed rambling in the nearby countryside, noting in 1858, 'it was as pleasant and rural a scene as ever I saw and did not care one penny how the beasts or birds had been formed.' The timing of his comment was significant. He had just finished writing *On the Origin of Species*, to be published the following year. Another celebrity to resort to hydropathy was Lord Tennyson, who commented in 1844, 'Of all the uncomfortable ways of living surely an hydropathical is the worst; no reading by candle-light, no going near a fire, no tea, no coffee, perpetual wet sheet and cold bath, and alternation from hot to cold.' Yet he thought it did him good, as did many others.

After Moor Park, turn left down the road and cross the bridge. Cross the T-junction to climb the footpath. On reaching the next tarmac road turn left, and follow it uphill. On reaching another T-junction (Waverley Lane) [GR 8580 4620] cross over and take the footpath almost opposite, leading left. Follow the footpath along the side of the fields for almost a 1km.

The fields fall away into the valley to the left. On the right of the path is lapsed hazel coppice, once a valuable resource (see p.172). Later there is an increasing amount of rhododendron, escapees from the many gardens of Surrey where this species flourishes in the acid soil. Rhododendron, imported from Asia became popular in the mid-nineteenth century. In fact it is a menace. Birds dislike it, and it now seems to be a key vehicle for the spread of the tree-killing virus, *Phytophthora ramorum*, that causes Sudden Oak Death but also attacks other tree species, notably larch. It is very difficult to eradicate rhododendron, yet this is precisely what should happen wherever it grows wild.

When you reach the (Tilford) Road [GR 8550 4555], turn left for about ¾ km. (I regret there is no avoiding this stretch of unpleasant road. Keep on the right hand side of the road, in single file and facing the traffic, passing Bourne Grove and Lodge Hill Road on your right.)

This road was here one hundred and fifty years ago, possibly metalled but certainly without the tarmac. More probably, however, it was simply a track, used by farm wagons, pony-and-trap, and other local vehicles that plied their way out between Farnham and Tilford. On either side of the road, as now, there was extensive pine plantation, an attempt to render such poor land productive.

After ¾ km look out for Dene Lane Unadopted Road [GR 8582 4495] on your right and take it (a ploy to avoid more road walking). After about 200m note the first wooden fence on your left (opposite No.59 'Bouverley' and No.55 on your right). At the end of this short fence turn hard left and follow the path, with

back gardens and paddocks on its left, and higher ground topped with conifers on your right. (You will now be walking parallel with the Tilford Road, through the edge of Bourne Wood.)

This is classic heathland, composed of nutrient poor sand, with limited flora such as birch, gorse, conifer, bracken. Amazingly, some people managed to live in this kind of environment, pushed off better lands by enclosures, by population growth or by circumstance.

Off to your right lies Bourne, now a suburb of Farnham, but in the 1880s it was the hamlet where George Sturt lived, situated on sandy soil like this. His neighbours were labouring folk, who eked what they could from poor soil. It was a time and place 'where the names of famous sorts of potatoes – red-nosed kidneys, magnum bonums, and so on – were better known than the names of politicians or of newspapers, where spades or reap-hooks of well-proved quality were treasured as friends by their owners and coveted by other connoisseurs.' It was a place of seasonal work,

> In August, though one did not see, one heard about the gangs of men trudging off at night for the Sussex harvest. In September the days went very silent in the valley, because the cottages were shut up and the people were all away at the hop-picking.
>
> George Bourne (Sturt), *Change in the Village* (1912)

Sturt was no dewy-eyed romantic. He was well aware of the quarrels, drunkenness, poverty and violence that blighted life in Bourne, '…. there is no room for sentimentality about village life. Could its annals be written they would make no idyll, they would be too much stained by tragedy and vice and misery.'

Women bore at least as heavy a load as men. Well into the twentieth century women's work was extremely hard. They were required to clothe and feed up to five or six children in a two-up-two-down cottage, fetch all the water from the well, gather wood or turf fuel or purchase faggots, or possibly obtain coal. And they had to cook on a range or with a crane, or 'swee', over a fire, and heat the copper for the laundry over a fire too. Sturt remembered the huge physical effort required of them:

> I have often met women bent nearly double under them [loads of faggots, or 'bavins' in Surrey parlance], of dead wood or sacks of fir cones picked up in fir woods a mile away or more … toiling painfully along, with hats or bonnets pushed awry and skirts dragging.

A Surrey cottage interior, c.1890, a tired old couple sitting in the ingle-nook, getting what heat they can from the fire. A kettle hangs on a chimney-crane, or swee, over the fire. All the water would have been drawn from a well. A cooking pot, probably containing potatoes with a little smoked pork to give it taste, sits on the hearth. Life for ordinary folk was no picnic. By our standards, in physical terms it was extremely rudimentary. We are separated from them by only a century.

And yet, 'As a general rule the village character was genial, steadfast, self-respecting; one could not but recognise in it a great fund of strength, a great stability.' These villagers stood in desperate need of such qualities. Sturt noted in his journal in 1898,

> I was counting up last night the elemental tragedy stuff that has oc-curred in the cottages within 100 yards from here, since I came here [Bourne] seven years ago. Here's the bald catalogue: 4 deaths of old men; 2 deaths of young men, leaving families; 1 death of a mother; 1 death of an infant; 1 case of sunstroke with delirium; 1 case of haem-orrhage: fits (the man still lying between life and death); 1 girl home "in trouble". The ingenious – almost devilish – torture of poverty is going [on] more or less all the time.

For us cold weather is a mere inconvenience. A century ago for Sturt's poorer neighbours it was a genuine threat, 'Two nights ago there was a warning of snow – a terror to men like Grover [his gardener], who earned their living by work on the ground.' In the terrible winter of 1889-90, Grover had found potatoes that he could get out of the frozen ground, to give to a neighbouring family that was starving. Today, frankly, we do not know we are born.

After about 400m, cross a tarmac track, and after another 200m cross a broad grassy avenue [GR 8600 4428] through the pines. Ahead of you lies ground rising to a knoll. After 20m or so, when the path divides, fork left and do not deviate. The path follows a fence on your right, protection for Bourne Wood heathland (a Surrey Heathland Project).

Inside, ponies and cattle graze the landscape in order to prevent saplings from growing, and thus to regain and maintain its heath-qualities. Heathland attracts certain birds and butterflies that prefer it to other landscapes. Heath must be one of the oldest man-made environments, probably first made by Mesolithic people 7,000 years ago. Over the millennia it evolved its own ecology, of both flora and fauna. Vast tracts of heathland were lost a century ago as livestock ceased to be grazed on it and conifer plantations were established instead. Today Surrey Wildlife is making a major effort to re-establish a heathland ecology where it can, a vital part of the biodiversity we so casually threw away in the twentieth century.

After about ¾ km, you will see green fields ahead through the trees. Follow the path as it curves around to the right but with the fields now close on your left, follow the path as it turns left to shadow the fields, with a thin band of woodland in between. Keep going straight.

Note the lapsed sweet chestnut coppice, once grown for hop poles for the local industry (see p.81). Nearby, efforts are being made to reduce the amount of conifer plantation in favour of areas of native species: blackthorn, birch and hazel, a suitable habitat for heathland fauna.

After another ½km, where the track turns to the right, descend onto the road ahead (The Reeds Road) [GR 8654 4340], and turn left. Walk ½km to the junction and turn right to Tilford.

Tilford, once probably 'Tilla's Ford', has skilfully retained its charm by putting its outlying suburb high up on the hill on the north side of the village. The western approach passes old houses. Look out for Tilford

House, built circa 1727 on the left. It still bears baroque details at a time when these were going out of fashion in favour of Palladianism, for example all the windows have rounded heads, and there is a tiny broken pediment over the central bay, a Doric doorway with a sundial between lintel and hood. A simple brick outbuilding on the right of the House, but close to the road, was built as a Presbyterian chapel in 1776.

Cross the first of two similar medieval bridges. These have pointed cutwaters upstream, rounded ones downstream, probably built by the monks of Waverley Abbey, and in the words of Nairn & Pevsner 'they have something of the unaffected functionalism that one might expect of a Cistercian bridge.'

Take the left side of the triangular green:
The King's, or Tilford, Oak, is about 30 paces along the left hand side of the green. It is worthy of inspection, and may not be with us much longer. It is reckoned to be well in excess of 800 years old. Untampered with, oaks normally live for only about 350 years, as a 'standard' or 'maiden' tree. Such a standard would normally be felled after 30-40 years, to provide good load-bearing timber. Left any longer, medieval man would have found its weight and size difficult to manage, particularly in the absence of hard surface tracks.

Almost all older oaks, ones that exceed 350 years like this one, have been pollarded, that is, cropped above the 'browse line' every ten or fifteen years, the wood being used for fuel, charcoal burning, etc. Pollarding, rather than coppicing at ground level, was the method of cropping above the 'browse line', where livestock might graze around the foot of a tree, as here on the village green. The practice fell into disuse with the easy availability of fossil fuels and increasing labour costs. Coppicing always required fenced-in areas, to prevent destruction by livestock.

An oak pollard can live for well over a thousand years, as long as it is regularly cropped. Once, however, cropping lapses, as in this case, the tree will begin to age. The trunk opens, the heartwood is exposed and rots, but the life of the tree may be sustained through the green wood just below the bark. It runs the risk of becoming top-heavy, thus vulnerable to high winds (this oak has been anchored with a steel hawser).

Along with its beauty and historical significance, there is an ecological reason for valuing a tree like the Tilford Oak. In the words of the

The Tilford Oak, c.1905. What has the Tilford Oak not seen? It remains a silent witness to the passing centuries. It may have been here as a young tree when the Cistercians first established their presence on the Wey.

landscape historian, Oliver Rackham:

> An old tree, especially a pollard, is a world of different habitats each with its special plants and animals: bats roosting in the hollow trunk; hole-nesting birds in smaller cavities; many special beetles and spiders [one might also add fungi] in the red-rotted heartwood of the trunk; peculiar lichens on the ridges and beneath overhangs of old bark. Any old tree should be treasured, for ten thousand young trees do not provide these habitats.

It is difficult to overestimate the value of these venerable ancients.

After the Tilford Oak, note the Institute on the opposite side of the Green.

The Institute (1893) is a typical early exemplar of Edwin Lutyens' style, with its strong references to the local vernacular, its position backing into the hillside, its external staircase and long seat below. After 1918 Lutyens became closely associated with architecture for the nation: the Cenotaph, the war graves, New Delhi, and so on. His work became grand and more austere, while what you see here at the outset of his career remains intimate and imbued with great charm.

Pass the mid-eighteenth century Barley Mow (unless you wish to pause for refreshment), and continue over the second bridge (which, before crossing, merits examination from the downstream parcel of green).

The river here has greatly increased in size since the first bridge, having been joined by the northern tributary from Black Down. It flows eastwards from here to Godalming, thence to Guildford into the Wey Navigation (p.214).

Almost immediately after crossing the bridge, turn left at the pillbox [GR 8740 4346]. Follow the path for almost ½km, veering left on the tarmac, past Tilhill House overlooking the Wey.

The name Tilhill is now associated with forestry and environmental landscaping, taking its name from the house where the 1947 purchaser, Archie Aitkins, established a 20 acre nursery on which to grow trees he was unable to obtain elsewhere. The business has long since outgrown its location and has moved to a 200 acre site at Greenhills, south of Tilford. 'Tilhill' probably derives from 'Tulla's Hill', and was known as Tulehill or Tolehill in the early Middle Ages. The first vowel later became an 'i' in the probably mistaken belief that it had the same name origin as Tilford.

About 200m after Tilhill House, take the path forking right, uphill. After about 400m it will bring you past Sheephatch Farm. Press on to the road.

A 'hatch', you will not be surprised to learn, was a fenced livestock enclosure.

Cross the road and carry on along the footpath. Turn left at the T-junction [GR 8720 4498], and the path will bring you down through woodland to the B3001. Turn left and follow the road back to Waverley Abbey car park and grounds. Follow the signs to Waverley Abbey.

This valley is so lovely that it cannot be that far from Arcadia. William Cobbett remembered his childhood here:

> When I was a little boy, I was, in the barley-sowing season, going along by the side of a field near Waverley Abbey; the primroses and bluebells new spangling the banks on both sides of me; a thousand linnets singing in a spreading oak over my head; while the jingle of the traces and the whistling of the plough-boys saluted my ears from over the hedge; and, as it were to snatch me from the enchantment, the hounds, at that instant, having started a hare in the hanger on the

other side of the field, came scampering over it in full cry, taking me after them many a mile. I was not more than eight years old; but this particular scene presented itself to my mind every year from that day.

WAVERLEY ABBEY HOUSE

On your right is an eighteenth century man-made lake and behind it Waverley Abbey House, built in 1723 by Colen Campbell, the great exponent of Palladian architecture. He plundered dressed stones from the old abbey, but it was rebuilt in the 1760s. In all, it has been a poor exchange for the near total destruction of the abbey buildings. Its chief claim, however, is that Walter Scott is rumoured to have stayed here as a guest of the owner. Some claim, without proof, that it was from here that he took the name for his novels. The house is now a conference centre.

THE ABBEY

The abbey of the Blessed Mary of Waverley was the first Cistercian foundation in England, established in 1128 by a gift of land from William Giffard, bishop of Winchester. Giffard was powerfully placed. He was a cousin of the Conqueror, one of the latter's inner circle of trusted *confidants*, had been his clerk and after the Conqueror's death became chancellor to William II (Rufus). He was a keen supporter of the new monasticism, of which the Cistercian Order was the chief exemplar, founded exactly thirty years before, in 1098 (see below). In its hey-day Waverley was the same size as Fountains, its sister foundation in Yorkshire.

The signage tells you some of the essentials. The twelfth century buildings were entirely demolished in favour of a larger complex in the early thirteenth century. This was not simply aggrandisement. In 1201 a great storm inundated the abbey complex, and almost carried away its walls. It certainly ruined the entire crop of wheat, hay and flax. The structural damage was probably so great as to require virtually complete reconstruction. It is characteristic of the builders' unhurried vision that the new abbey church was commenced in 1203 and, although the choir and high altar were in use by 1231, the nave was not completed until 1278. Even on a fine day, it is obvious how low-lying the abbey is and how liable to flooding. Further inundations occurred in 1215, in 1233 to a depth of 2½ metres inside the buildings, and once more through the church and communal buildings in 1265.

Following Henry VIII's renunciation of Rome and his dissolution of the monasteries in 1536, Waverley was gifted to his childhood friend, William Fitzwilliam. The two shared a passion for sports and martial pursuits.

Fitzwilliam was nothing if not pragmatic. He willingly supported Henry's break with Rome and enthusiastically helped in the dissolution of the monasteries, receiving for his pains not only Waverley but another abbey, a nunnery, two priories and estates in several other shires. He built on the site of the abbey here, which implies that he, too, must have plundered some of the stone.

THE CISTERCIANS

The ruins may not themselves inspire, but the lives of the Cistercian monks who spent their lives here are interesting, even inspirational. The order had been founded in 1098 by monks dissatisfied with lax observance of the Rule of St Benedict in the religious houses to which they belonged. Under the dynamic leadership of Bernard of Clairvaux the new order spread rapidly and by his death in 1153 boasted 338 foundations from Sweden to Portugal, Scotland to the Eastern Mediterranean. The order took its name from Cîteaux, near Dijon, where it had its headquarters.

Whereas the long-established monasteries were preoccupied with community life, theological doctrine, liturgy and the commemoration of each saint's day through the year, Cistercians were primarily concerned with their own individual spiritual journey. In this they formed the vanguard of a changing religious mood at the end of the eleventh century, from community to individual, from the public world to the private one. Introspection had not hitherto been a principal preoccupation, but now it was. As one monk at that time wrote, chiding his fellows, 'See how ignorant you are of your own self; there is no land so distant or so unknown to you; nor one about which you will so easily believe falsehoods.'

In the words of one medievalist, 'The searching of the soul was a programme consciously and systematically undertaken, and transmitted to the whole school of Cistercian writers, so that, in the words of one early Cistercian, "a man may begin perfectly to know himself, and by progress in self-knowledge may ascend to the knowledge of God."'

Introspection called for something more than a study of the Scriptures and other texts. St Bernard told his fellow Cistercians to learn also from

THE NORTH-WEST VIEW OF WAVERLEY-ABBY, IN THE COUNTY OF SURRY.

To Charles Child Esq. This Prospect is humbly Inscrib'd by his most Obedient Servants Saml & Nath.l Buck.

Waverley Abbey in 1737, with Colen Campbell's Palladian house behind. One can see that there was still plenty of the abbey still standing, unlike today. This early illustration reflects the beginning of antiquarian interest in such medieval ruins.

nature: 'Believe me, for I know, you will find something far greater in the woods than in books. Stones and trees will teach you that which you cannot learn from masters.'

Few of us would have stood up to the rigours of Cistercian life. William of Malmesbury tells us that the tonsured monks:

> wear nothing made of fur or linen.... neither breeches, unless they are sent on a journey, which at their return they must wash and restore. They have two tunics with cowls, but no additional garment in winter.... They sleep clad and girded and never, after Matins [just before dawn] return to their beds.... They never leave the cloisters but for the purpose of labour, nor do they ever speak either there or elsewhere, save only to the abbot or prior.

There is another reason for taking interest in the Cistercians and what they might have been up to here at Waverley. They were social and economic revolutionaries. Unlike all the other existing orders, they accepted lay brothers of lowly birth. Furthermore, they rejected feudal agricultural practice. This consisted of setting aside the best, 'demesne', lands for the landlord, who made the subject tenants work it, while allotting the poorer land for use in common by the tenants themselves. The Cistercians, as the landholders, carried out the hard physical labour themselves as a daily routine of monastic life, assisted by the lay brothers who also lived within

The seal of the abbey of the Blessed Mary of Waverley, portraying the Virgin and Child enthroned in glory. She holds a spray of lily, a symbol of purity: 'As the lily among thorns, so is my love among the daughters.' (Song of Songs 2:2).

Beneath her, under the arch, the abbot is at prayer.

the monastery. Instead of 'demesne' and 'common' open fields, they ran consolidated farms, thinking critically from direct experience on how they could improve productivity. By their commitment to experimentation, they became the unrivalled innovators of agricultural practice in twelfth century Europe, reclaiming marginal land and improving livestock quality and production. They were shrewd in choosing or accepting good alluvial sites for their farming, here as, later, more famously at Fountains and Rievaulx in Yorkshire. Here they must have been involved in much reclamation from woodland and shrub. But they knew a good opportunity when they saw it. They might therefore have taken satisfaction in the Saxon meaning of the name 'Waverley': 'a woodland clearing on swampy ground', and in what they had successfully done with it.

Leith Hill and Holmbury Camp, and the slopes of the Weald

WALK

7

Distance 11km/6 miles: 3½ hours
OS Explorer Map No.146

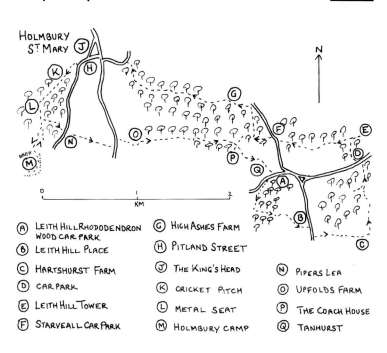

(A) LEITH HILL RHODODENDRON WOOD CAR PARK

(B) LEITH HILL PLACE

(C) HARTSHURST FARM

(D) CAR PARK

(E) LEITH HILL TOWER

(F) STARVEALL CAR PARK

(G) HIGH ASHES FARM

(H) PITLAND STREET

(J) THE KING'S HEAD

(K) CRICKET PITCH

(L) METAL SEAT

(M) HOLMBURY CAMP

(N) PIPERS LEA

(O) UPFOLDS FARM

(P) THE COACH HOUSE

(Q) TANHURST

BEFORE YOU WALK

This walk explores the edge of the Lower Greensand escarpment, typified by infertile sandstone and, beneath it, the fertile slopes descending into the Low Weald. The differences of landscape, its uses and its history are dramatic. It is the most strenuous walk in this guidebook, and takes you to the two highest points of south-east England: Leith Hill (294m/965ft) and the Iron Age site, Holmbury Camp (261m/856ft), one of several Iron Age hill forts which front the escarpment. The lower greensand escarpment shadows the North Downs to its north, stretching from Farnham eastwards across Surrey and deep into Kent.

If car-less: Take the No.32 or No.22 bus from Dorking to Pitland Street in Holmbury St Mary (30 mins), and pick up the walk at ➲ on p.110.
Refreshment: The King's Head in Holmbury St Mary, halfway through this walk (tel. 01306 730282, www.kingsheadholmbury.co.uk).

Start: at the National Trust car park at Leith Hill Rhododendron Wood [GR 1313 4280], near the top of Tanhurst Lane, 50m from the junction with Leith Hill Road and Abinger Road. (If it is full, use the small car park beneath Leith Hill Tower [GR 1397 4290] or Starveall car park [GR 1305 4325] and pick up the walk on p.106 or p.109 respectively.)
Save up the Rhododendron Wood for the end of your walk.

Turn left out of the car park and walk down Tanhurst Lane for 250m, turning left again into the gate with the National Trust mark: 'Leith Hill Place' [GR 1291 4270]. Follow the track downhill, passing an orange-headed marker almost immediately, and turn left after 250m at the second orange marker, to follow what is clearly an old path. Where the track swings to the right, keep straight on along the grassy path, following 'the Woodland Walk' (ignoring the Etherby Farm loop to the right). Go through the gate into the field, and make for the gate on the far side.
All this land lies within the Leith Hill Place Estate, now owned by the National Trust. The parkland rolling away into the Weald, with its wonderful view into the distance, represents the high point of the English landscape tradition, towards the end of the eighteenth century. Above the track, on your left, stands Leith Hill Place. Originally it was a gabled house, built around 1600, but in about 1760, its owner, John Folliatt, had it completely refaced in stone to look more fashionably Palladian.

Folliatt was a recently retired general, distinguished by his rarity value. He must have been almost the only man in the eighteenth century to have risen from the rank of private soldier to that of lieutenant-general. This was extraordinary, even if his membership of a gentry family gave him a huge leg up.

In 1847 Josiah Wedgwood, of the pottery family, bought the estate. His wife, Caroline, created the Rhododendron Wood (at the end of the walk). Caroline's younger brother, Charles Darwin often stayed in the house

Leith Hill Place, a classic Jacobean style mansion before it was refaced in the mid-eighteenth century.

and frequented these slopes where he carried out various experiments, often with the help of his three nieces. The youngest of these nieces, Margaret, married her next-door neighbour, Arthur Vaughan Williams of Tanhurst.

Their son, Ralph (1872-1958) spent part of his childhood here and he gives Leith Hill Place its greatest claim to fame. Ralph Vaughan Williams is a worthy claimant to the accolade of England's finest twentieth century composer. Beginning without much apparent talent, Vaughan Williams doggedly stuck with his musical study in London. In the words of a relative, 'it will simply break his heart if he is told that he is too bad to hope to make anything of it.' In fact Vaughan Williams made so much of it that it is impossible now to think of quintessentially English music without invoking RVW. His passion for folksong was matched by his ability to write works of angry modernism in protest at the evils of the twentieth century.

He had seen service both as a medical orderly and as a gunner in the First World War, the crack of the guns being responsible for his deafness (jocularly known as 'gunner-ear', a condition I share with him) in later life. But it was the bleakness of the post-1945 world which inspired some of his later music: the Holocaust, Hiroshima and totalitarian regimes. He returned to Leith Hill in 1905 as the first director and conductor of the Leith Hill Music Festival, a celebration of amateur music about which he felt passionately, and itself a product of the transformation of this part of Surrey from the habitat of principally poor country people to that of upper middle class professionals escaping the city.

On reaching the road, turn right and after about 100m turn left through a small wicket gate in the hedgerow [GR 1347 4215]. Follow the path straight ahead. Go through the gate into the next field, and pass a cedar of Lebanon on the left.

England's first cedar of Lebanon was imported in 1638, at the dawn of European fascination with the Levant. Extremely handsome with their characteristic layered branches, planting cedars of Lebanon became highly fashionable in parkland. They suggested romantic biblical antiquity, for Hiram, King of Tyre, supplied Solomon with timbers of cedar for the Temple. Cedars symbolised size and strength. In the words of the psalmist, 'The righteous shall flourish like the palm tree: he shall grow like a cedar in Lebanon.' The cedars of Tyre have long since been cut down but one can still find genuinely ancient giants in the Lebanon. However, despite their antique appearance, most extant large specimens in English parks were planted after 1800. Perhaps Caroline Wedgwood planted this one.

On the far side of the field, cross the track and follow the left edge around the next field. After about 200m look out for a stile in the hedgerow on the left. Cross it and the wooden bridge, navigate the boggy ground on the far side and turn right along the track, which will take you to Hartshurst Farm.
Hartshurst, 'the wood of the hart', is mentioned in Domesday, 1086. Hartshurst is a mid-sixteenth century steading, but added to and patched subsequently. The long pitch of the main roof is a lovely 'catslide', while Horsham slates cover the west wing. The old granary, standing on its 'mushrooms' (to thwart rats) is an unusual survivor. Most such granaries disappeared in the early twentieth century.

Cross the stile beyond the granary, and walk straight ahead. Just beyond the trees to the left, stands an almost isolated oak [GR 1410 4220]. On passing it, turn left up the slight gully, straight for Leith Hill Tower, just visible on the skyline. After 150m you will pass woodland on your left. After another 150m you will enter it at the National Trust sign. Follow the path through the trees for about 100m and then turn right up the track to the road.
You will notice the transition of the soil, which is increasingly sandy. Because of its acidic quality, the principal tree growth is conifer, birch, and oak which, unlike many trees, is not choosy where it grows.

On reaching the road turn left and right through the car park and up the steps to Leith Hill Tower.
It was probably of The Landslip Car Park 500m to the east that John Aubrey wrote 300 years ago:
     ... from the Side of thereof [the hill] a great Part of the Brow is slidden

> down into the Grounds below, caused by a Delf [quarry] of Stones
> dug out of the Sides of the Mountain, and the bare Places (from
> whence the Earth is parted) being a reddish Colour, plainly appear
> above forty Miles distant.

Trust me, this is easily the most strenuous part of this walk. Avoid catching a bout of Mountaineer's Foot. Mountaineer's what? As an intrepid rock climber and trekker in East Africa once patiently explained to my wife, it is 'the inability to put one foot in front of another.'

At the top, pause for breath.

An account over a century ago tells us that, 'On July 27, 1876 a tourist walking over the hill trod upon a snake which bit him; he managed to get to Ockley, but died in two days.' Once bitten, walking to Ockley was surely a fatal mistake. Rather than watch where you put your feet, you would do better to watch your back. You are much more likely to be zapped by a mountain biker than by an adder.

The author of a guidebook almost two hundred years ago wrote ecstatically of the view,

> I passed over a hill [Leith Hill] which shewed me a more transporting
> sight than ever the country had shown me before, either in England
> or Italy... a place... in so great obscurity that it is unknown to the very
> frequenters of Epsom and Box-hill.

It is difficult now to credit the fact that so much of Surrey remained largely unknown until the advent of the railway, not only to outsiders but also to relatively local people.

Turn right at the T-junction (where the noticeboards are) to visit Leith Hill Tower.

Leith Hill, like so many places, comes by its name honestly, for 'Leith', or Lalida its earliest recorded rendition in 1166, means a very steep slope. After those steps, one cannot quibble about that. It survives, high above the Weald because it is made of chert, the particularly hard version of Lower Greensand, which once arched like a carapace across the whole Weald.

Leith Hill Tower was built by Richard Hull, a Bristolian who had settled at Leith Hill Place. By the mid-eighteenth century survey skills were sufficiently advanced that one could accurately measure altitude. Hull could not bear the thought that his property was only 35ft short of one thousand. He built the tower in 1766, so that he could be 1000ft above sea level and brag about it. His aim achieved, he expired aged 83, in 1772. Unfortunately, his builders were not up to the job and major structural repairs were necessary by the 1790s to prevent the tower falling down. Rumour has it that he was buried head first, vertically in the floor of the tower. He was still remembered locally in 1822, 'as very liberal to the poor, but an odd sort of gentleman.'

Arthur Young, England's first agricultural journalist, toured here in 1793:

> You command a view of the total range of these hills, from one end of the county to the other, with the whole Weald of Sussex, immediately at your feet – bearing the appearance of one uniform mass of wood [either he was exaggerating or the Weald has lost a lot of trees since then]. At the bottom of this hill is immediately discovered a system of husbandry and soil, the very reverse of the preceding [sandy infertility]. The soil from the sands of Surrey, is become a very stiff, strong loam upon clay – and that upon sand-stone the hardest of which the roads are made, and they are excellent.

William John Evelyn, who did much to expand and rebuild Wotton House (p.148) also repaired the tower in 1864, and added the castellation on top. Perhaps the most remarkable thing about the original tower is that it accurately replicates a Wealden tower of the thirteenth century, a very unusual thing in the eighteenth century before the gothic revival swept the country.

Turn back to follow the Greensand Way (marked by light blue bridlepath signs, and initially by signs to Starveall Corner Car Park) westwards. Stick with the light blue signs or the ones marked 'Greensand Way'. After 1km you will reach Leith Hill Road.

Much of this land was open heath until the late nineteenth century. Livestock would crop tree shoots, so that the predominant flora would have been heather, bracken, bilberry (see later, on p.113), with occasional trees that had escaped the attentions of grazers to reach maturity. With the progressive collapse of livestock grazing from around 1850, birch would have colonised open ground *en masse*. Holly, not minding the shade of birch, would have followed on.

If you are a gardener, look out for salal (*Gaultheria shallon*), ground cover with dark green leaves, pink or white flowers in May and small dark

Leith Hill Tower as it looked in 1910, still bare of trees at the very end of Leith Hill's history as grazed heathland, and the beginning of its mass touristic popularity.

berries in the autumn. It was introduced by that most intrepid and hardy of Scottish collectors, David Douglas, in 1826. (His short life reads like a ripping yarn. He travelled alone with what he could carry on his back, collecting unknown plant species and living off the land in freezing conditions in the Rockies.) He had come across salal the preceding year at the mouth of the Columbia River, not far from Vancouver, having been told about it by his compatriot, Archibald Menzies:

> On stepping on the shore *gaultheria shallon* is the first plant I took in my hands. So pleased was I that I could scarcely see anything but it.

He knew from Menzies that it grew luxuriantly even under thick pine cover. Once in Britain, it was not long before it had escaped from the garden into the countryside, where it rapidly took hold. It was here, on Leith Hill, that it was first recorded as naturalised in 1914. It now covers about 50 hectares of the landscape hereabouts.

(If you parked at Starveall car park, this is where to pick up the walk.)
Cross Leith Hill Road and dogleg to the right, to continue along the Way on the far side [GR 1310 4320]. Ignore the first track to the right, but 100m later turn right as marked, following 'the Greensand Way'. Ignore the first turn to the left (marked to The Coach House) but take the sharp left turn 100m later (also marked) [GR 12854350], taking you past High Ashes Farm.

There are very few ash trees, compared with beeches, to validate this steading's name, but there must have been some once. The predominant tree cover as you walk later, is Scots pine, one of Britain's three native conifer species (along with yew and juniper). The Scots pine is a recent arrival here. These hills were open heathland, and pines were only planted on the Surrey Hills in the 1770s, thus changing the landscape dramatically.

Beech trees were favoured on woodland boundary banks because they hold banks stable, and their roots and lower branches inosculate (grow into each other). There are one or two nice examples as one walks.

Follow the track for 1½ km until it descends to a tarmac road (Pasture Wood Rd), and turn left, past Bulmer Farm.
The name seems to have corrupted. It was known as Bullmoor Farm in 1870.

At the main road turn right and immediately left up Pitland Street.
◗ Pitland Street [GR 1125 4409] is a hamlet, now part of Holmbury St Mary. (Be enticed by the thought of refreshment at the King's Head, on the right, just off Pitland Street.)
Holmbury St Mary is a modern name for two hamlets, Felday and Pitland Street, and dates from the dedication of the church of St Mary in 1879. 'Holmbury', refers to the hillfort, the name deriving from either the 'ham'– settlement – and 'bury' – fort, or holly fort, holm being old English for holly. Felday, in a gully ½km to the north, probably means 'well watered land'. Pitland is 'land in the hollow'.

Holmbury St Mary and its neighbouring village of Peaslake are essentially creations of the past 150 years. With the arrival of rail and metalled roads, the Surrey Hills were rapidly transformed into a playground for London's professional classes. Many of the houses are late Victorian and play up to the ideal of a romantic retreat in the countryside, imitating or even parodying the traditional vernacular architecture. The incomers effected an extraordinary transformation from what this countryside had been. In the words of one historian writing a century ago:

> This neighbourhood was formerly one of the wildest in Surrey. Sheep stealers, smugglers and poachers found a refuge in these remote hills. Some of the cottages have, still existing, very large cellars (excavated easily in the sandy hill) which are far too large for any honest purpose,

Harvesting timber. Even after the introduction of tractors, foresters preferred to use horses for heavy work. They were more skilful on rough terrain.

Tushing, or pulling, a log by chain from where it has been felled to the gin poles.

The horses on the left lift the tree trunk using the gin pulley so that it can be swung onto the pole waggon.

The horses are re-harnessed and the loaded pole waggon moves off.

and were no doubt made for storing smuggled goods till they could be conveniently taken on to London.

Furthermore, he recalled, 'a very old man who told him how as a child he remembered his father holding open a gate so that thirty men on horse-back, with kegs of brandy behind them, might ride through.' There was a heavy through traffic of such illicit goods across the heaths from the south coast up to London. It was also a custom of the Surrey hills that when a villager found a cache of contraband goods hidden on the heath, he or she was entitled to put a chalk mark on a small proportion of the whole, which the smugglers would leave behind, a well understood bargain for the vil-lager's silence.

Pass on your right Ringwood Cottage and Heathcote, and look out for the road name change to Holmbury Hill Road. Take the next track up to the right, which leads up to the village cricket pitch. Pass the pitch on your right (resisting the right fork to the cricket car park), following the path straight ahead for another 250m until a major track intersection [GR 1055 4360].

Turn left along the track _just before_ the metal bench. After about 200m, just before the path divides, note a grassy path (with a couple of pines on its left) to your left, which you will be taking on your return. For now, take the right fork uphill. Follow it without deviating onto any tempting tracks to the right. It will lead progressively up to Holmbury Camp after about 300m.

Look out for the sign, 'The Hurtwood Control', on the right of the path where the path dips. This marks your entry across the double rampart and ditch of the north-east corner of Holmbury Camp. Still keep to the same path, and try to make a mental note of it for your return journey in 15-20 minutes' time. It will take you up the left (east) side of the Camp and up to its southern promontory [GR 1040 4290].

John Aubrey came here in the 1670s and jotted down, 'A very great camp…. From here a noble prospect.' The signage tells you that Reginald Bray formally opened Hurtwood for public access in 1926. Bray, squire of the extensive Manor of Shere, believed that this landscape should be enjoyed by the public. In fact the land had been open to the public for some years but at some cost and inconvenience, principally resulting from fires lit intentionally or by accident. In 1911, for example, sixteen fires destroyed a total of 350 acres of woodland. By 1924 no less than one quarter of the woodland of the Hurtwood area had been lost to fire, including the southern slope below Holmbury Camp. By this stage the culprits were the motoring public, with their campfires and casually abandoned cigarettes.

As for 'The Hurtwood Control', recently renamed 'Friends of the Hurtwood', it strives both to provide the landscape for public enjoyment while conserving it as a nature reserve. (Buy *Around the Hurtwood*, an ideal visitors' guide next time you are in a local newsagent.)

Until just over a century ago, livestock grazing and the harvesting of turf by local people had largely maintained a heathland landscape, one that probably dated back to the Neolithic period, 5,000 years ago. William Bray (see p.179) had planted Scots pine here at the end of the eighteenth century. In rapidly changing economic circumstances in the early twentieth century, Reginald Bray decided that by creating a small timber industry he could help keep the local community viably employed, so he again planted Scots pine and other conifers, much to the upset of conservationists. Bray tried to balance his duty to conserve with his duty to the local community, for which he felt a strong responsibility (for more on this remarkable man, see pp.171, 176).

Hurt Wood was previously known as Churtwood, clearly a reference to the chert, the hard rocky sandstone underfoot which has resisted erosion more effectively than softer sandstones like Bargate stone elsewhere. From the eighteenth century it was increasingly called Hurt Wood, presumably on account of the abundance of hurts, or bilberries which used to cover the ground here.

There can be few plants which have so many different regional names as the hurt. Starting in the north, it is variously called a blaeberry in Scotland, a whinberry and a bilberry in the North and further south variously a whortleberry or hurtleberry, and usually in Surrey just hurts. John Aubrey noted in about 1718:

> Southward of this place [Abinger] the County abounds with Heath and Fern, and is full of Bilberries, which the County People call Whortell-berries.

Aubrey may have thought 'hurt' was a term too Surrey specific, for it was certainly the term in common use here. Much of the hurt 'carpet' has been lost, the result of over-picking, trampling, the decline of heath with the loss of livestock, and the planting of conifers, which cast too much shade. The native hurt has a much more intense taste than any super-market 'blueberry', an imported species. In Yorkshire bilberries are still sometimes baked in pastry, known as 'mucky-mouth pies'.

As you walk, bear in mind that those who squatted on the heath were involved in a variety of nefarious activities apart from assisting the smuggling 'Gentlemen', in order to survive. For only the impoverished would choose to live here. As Cobbett observed, 'Want, horrid want, is the great parent of crime.' These folk also cut fern, peat and stone from the heathland, and made brooms from, well, the broom. Less than 100 years ago, unlike the law-abiding gentlefolk gracing the sylvan glades today, the people hereabouts had a reputation for being taciturn, uncooperative, prone to livestock theft, and a law unto themselves. Some were native, others itinerant Romany.

The Romany had a troublesome reputation. Reginald Bray's father reported to the sublimely named Inspector of Nuisances at Byfleet, 'the gypsies are regarded as a terror and a nuisance.' Even by the 1920s, 'women on their walks were annoyed and frightened by the begging of gangs of men, children lamented that their laboriously filled baskets of hurts were emptied by the gypsies...'

Indeed, there were so many Romany squatting in the hills that the hurt

The first ever school for Romany gypsies, sited on Winterfold.

shrub was ravaged. Parishes sought to expel them over the boundary, to become someone else's problem. In 1923 Bray, minded for compromise not confrontation, allowed up to one hundred Romany to camp at a designated site on the heathland of Winterfold, on the west side of the Hurtwood. In 1926 the Surrey Education Committee (but Bray was surely behind it) established Hurtwood School, especially for Romany children who otherwise remained uneducated. It was the first of its kind. (If you want a moving testimony to this school, search the web for 'Hurtwood school for gypsies', to find the Pathé Newsreel.)

HOLMBURY CAMP

On a clear day the view is magnificent, and the signage will indicate the identity of features in the distance (but beware the map of the fort, which is misleadingly orientated). It is tempting to assume that the Camp gave a commanding view against any approaching threat but one must be doubtful, for the Weald was sufficiently wooded that any enemy could approach from the south entirely unobserved. Holmbury Camp is one of a string of Early Iron Age (150 BC to 50 AD) hill settlements along the lower greensand escarpment. (Another, Anstiebury, is 2km east of Leith Hill Tower, since 1763 wooded and therefore unrewarding to visit). Its purpose is unclear and no evidence of conflict has ever been found, although sling pebbles, collected perhaps from Netley Heath on the Downs, have been found here. Its purpose may have simply been as a large livestock fold and camp. It predates the Roman invasion of Britain, which seems not to have been resisted in Surrey.

The hub of the camp was in the northeast quarter, where the cooking and food depôt seem to have been, and where two springs provide water. Grindstones, or querns, have been found here, made of local chert.

The inner area is divided into two levels by a bank running north-south (but obscured by undergrowth). The lower, easterly portion, appears to have been ploughed, hence the need for querns. One can also reckon that the northern dip-slope towards the Tillingbourne valley (Abinger, Gomshall, Shere, etc) was used for livestock grazing and rearing, while wild boar hunting took place in the heavily wooded Weald to the south.

It is difficult to know when Holmbury Camp was abandoned. A Late Iron Age enclosure has been found on a promontory at Felday, 2km to the north, which may have been a replacement.

With your back to the signage, turn right to retrace your steps from the Camp, along the edge of the escarpment, through the anti-bike barrier, then swing left onto the more established path (the right fork takes you downhill) which will lead you back along the east rampart edge, past the entrance sign for the camp and so back down to the fork. Continue for 30m to find the grassy path off to your right. Take it down to the road.

This road was greatly favoured by rich professionals from the late nineteenth century, using leading architects. The most famous mansion, Philip Webb's Joldwynds, was sadly rebuilt in the 1930s, so there is nothing worth a detour.

Cross the road and take the footpath immediately opposite, next to Pipers Lea. [GR 1085 4330] On reaching the (Horsham) road, turn left and after about 100m turn right down the drive of Upfolds Farm, enjoying the poultry and other animals. Follow the bridleway sign to turn left through the farmyard, and then right with woodland on your left. After ½km the path doglegs to the left over a brook before continuing as a track in the same direction, but now through the woodland.

Much of the woodland on the left seems to have been cut down. Notice how quickly birch, of little value beyond firewood, has colonised the empty patches of woodland. John Evelyn described it as 'this despicable tree... the worst of timber,' because it was unsuitable as a load-bearing wood. If left alone the birches would die after about a century, to be replaced mainly by oak and holly, both of which cast too heavy a shadow for birch regeneration. Instead, birch seeks newly open areas to colonise.

After another ½km, on reaching a cross track (with the Coach House to the right) cross and continue straight up the steep track ahead taking the right fork immediately at the top. Follow it as it winds through the woods.

Look out on your left for sycamore coppice, of all things. Sycamore is a prolific self-seeder and grows rapidly. The coppice here must have been planted for fuel. Once again, John Evelyn would have disapproved, for he hated sycamore (see p.177). Yet sycamore produces the most beautiful veneer, like very pale watered silk. About 50 years ago a large sycamore was sold in North Wales for over £1,000. The purchaser knew he could cut enough veneer to cover five football pitches from it.

The path takes you down steps and up others in order to circumvent the grounds of Tanhurst ('Are the shades of Tanhurst to be thus polluted?'), eventually to reach Tanhurst Lane.

Tanhurst, if you get a backwards glimpse, looks wealthy and comfortable It is a late eighteenth century pile, the home of Samuel Romilly (1757-1818). Few of us have heard of this deeply humane man but perhaps we should have done. Born of Huguenot parents, Romilly was a self-made man who, with some misgiving, undertook a legal career, noting:

> I am soon to enter on a career which … will certainly give me partial and selfish interests, incompatible with the good of others, and which will … compel me to hear the profession of dishonourable sentiments without opposing them, and to be a near spectator of selfish and de-grading conduct…

In 1806 he became the coalition government's solicitor-general. He disliked the fripperies of office and had scant respect for the knighthood that went with his appointment. Temperamentally he was a reformer, persistently concerned to end not only the slave trade, which was achieved in 1807, but also slavery itself, which he did not live to see, nor yet Catholic Emancipation, another cause dear to his heart. Yet he managed to abolish the Elizabethan death penalty for pickpockets and sought unsuccessfully to restrict the use of the gallows more generally. Romilly stood for tolerance and, in the case of criminals, redemption more than retribution. He was a founding father of the nineteenth century liberal tradition in Britain, one of the genuinely Great and Good of the Nation. He had married in 1798. When his wife, Anne, died after a prolonged illness in 1818, he found his grief unendurable and cut his own throat (perhaps I should not have told you that).

On a more carefree note, the Tanhurst tennis court lies plainly in view, a suitable field of combat for Miss Joan Hunter Dunn.

Standing by the Tanhurst gate, one can see in the distance a large white building, Joldwynds, in the shadow of Holmbury Hill.

Leith Hill Rhododendron Wood car park is 50m up hill to the left.

Either now, or on another expedition, the Rhododendron Wood merits a visit, perhaps in May, when most species will be in flower. Caroline Wedgewood created this garden in the first wave of the craze that took

British gardens by storm. Her sense of timing was faultless. Joseph Hooker had just returned from the Himalayas with 43 species of the newly discovered genus, and if she did not actually buy the two illustrated volumes of his great work, *Rhododendrons of Sikkim-Himalaya* (1849 and 1850), she must have thumbed through a copy and gasped at the beauty of the illustrations. Joseph's father, William, then director at Kew introduced the first volume in 1849:

> Perhaps with the exception of the Rose, the queen of flowers, no plants have excited more interest throughout Europe than the several species of the genus *Rhododendron*.

After that, any keen gardener with a large enough garden and the right kind of acidic soil was almost certain to cultivate rhododendrons, which were destined to be immensely popular from 1850 until the mid-twentieth century. The garden here is a monument to that craze.

The Hog's Back between Compton and Guildford

Distance 10km/6 miles: 2½-3 hours, with sites of interest and refreshments, the best part of a day
OS Explorer Map No.145

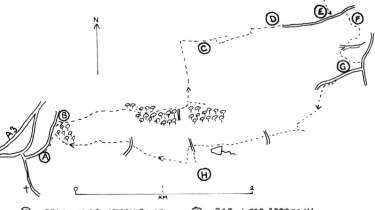

Ⓐ	GF WATTS CEMETERY CHAPEL	Ⓔ	CAR-LESS APPROACH
Ⓑ	WATTS GALLERY	Ⓕ	BOOKER TOWER
Ⓒ	RADIO MAST	Ⓖ	PICCARDS MANOR
Ⓓ	HENLEY FORT	Ⓗ	LOSELEY PARK

BEFORE YOU WALK

This walk takes you on the only stretch of the Hog's Back which is not some kind of hell for the walker, thanks to the cacophony of heavy and speeding traffic. It starts on the lower greensand, with that sudden and satisfying transition from one geological formation (and accompanying flora) to another as you climb the Hog's Back. The route runs eastwards along a greensand section of the North Downs Way, up to the Hog's Back and then doglegs down through the outskirts of Guildford to take a valley route across the Lower Greensand past Loseley Park back to Compton.

There are four attractions at the beginning, middle and end of the walk, depending on your cultural appetite: the strange G. F. Watts Cemetery Chapel at the outset, Loseley Park (the finest Tudor mansion in Surrey) after about two-thirds of the walk, and at the end two attractions: the Watts Gallery and the unique parish church of St Nicholas, Compton, one of Surrey's finest village churches.

If car-less: From Guildford Station, turn right up Farnham Road (A31), and turn right again along Annandale (just after the playing fields and school). At the end, cross Wodeland Avenue to continue along the footpath to its end, ignoring turns to the left, until the T-Junction where the path joins the Hog's Back. Turn left and take up the walk at ⊃ on p.127.

Refreshment: en route at Loseley Park, or at the end at the Watts Gallery Café, which does lunch or tea superbly well.

Make a day of it: Details for the Watts Gallery and of Loseley Park, Surrey's finest sixteenth century house, are at the end of the walk.

Start at the Watts Cemetery Chapel on Down Lane, Compton [GR 9560 4745].

G.F. Watts (1817-1904) was a leading late Victorian painter. His wife built this chapel in 1896. It is unmissable if only because it is so incredibly bizarre. The exterior structure looks like a small Byzantine church, but it is covered with fine terracotta of fanciful pseudo-Celtic art. The interior, dating from 1901, is in the Art Nouveau style but equally strange, heavy and cloying. In Nairn & Pevsner's inimitable phrase, this is 'one of the most soporific rooms in England.' Watts himself painted the piece over the altar: 'The All-Rewarding'. It is very arch, surely the ultimate 'Greenery-Yallery' structure extant. Above the chapel stands another curiosity, the arcade filled with memorial plaques. The terracotta for both the chapel and the memorial plaques was made by the Potters' Arts Guild, an Arts & Crafts venture established by Mary Watts in 1900.

On leaving the Chapel, turn right (northwards) up the road and after 400m turn right again immediately adjacent to the Watts Gallery [GR 9571 4770] up the signposted North Downs Way. Follow the Way for 1½ km.

One is immediately struck by the sandy nature of the sunken track, in places bright orange sand. Lower greensand acquires its name, of course, from its green hue, but you are unlikely ever to see its true colour. Like London clay (which is blue-ish) it turns yellow as soon as it is exposed to the air.

After ¾ km pass iron barns on either side of the track before entering a classic Surrey sunken lane.

On the left are stands of larch and also of sweet chestnut coppice (on the latter, see p.81). Larch is not native, but was introduced in about 1620. John Evelyn knew about it, although still rare in England (see p.152).

It took another century before larch was grown commercially in Britain, initially on the 3rd Duke of Atholl's estate in Perthshire. Like Evelyn, the duke had got it right, for by the beginning of the twentieth century it was reckoned the most valuable tree species to grow. Amongst other things, larch proved salt-water resilient for the strakes of sea-going vessels. Most fishing boats were made of it until displaced by synthetic materials. Today, larch is in acute danger of extinction from a disease that spreads like wildfire, *Phytophthora ramorum.*

After about 1km one passes a cross track, and after another ½ km or so, there is an open gully on your right between the two woods of West and East Warren, with a private vehicle track in it. Pause.

West and East Warren are presumably the old warrens of Loseley Park. Warrens were places set aside for hunting game and falconry, and sometimes where warrens were dug to keep rabbits. Sandy soil is perfect for rabbits, as it drains well, and burrows can be kept dry, so a rabbit warren was probably constructed here. There are still plenty of rabbits about.

Rabbits were probably introduced in the twelfth century from monasteries in northern France. Before the Reformation religious and great houses kept rabbit warrens as the Church did not view rabbit flesh as meat and so it could be eaten on Fridays. It is wonderful how easily any religion can fall into casuistry to circumvent its own irksome rules. Rabbit was also highly valued in a cold climate on account of its fur, a real luxury item. Warrens were usually man-made, dug by warreners (hence the frequency today of the surname Warren and its variants). The rabbit population remained tiny until the nineteenth century but then exploded, thanks to the greatly increased planting of root crops, the proliferation of game keepers (rabbits share the same predatory enemies as pheasants, etc.), and land drainage which rendered much more of the landscape habitable.

UPPER *Hurtmore quarry shows the enormous amount of material removed to access useful doggers.*

LOWER *The unique method of quarrying Bargate stone could hardly be more primitive or hilarious: a 15cm iron block is placed near the doggers to be extracted. A 2m long crowbar is driven under the dogger, but resting on the iron block, which acts as a fulcrum. One end of a wooden plank is rested on the other end of the crowbar. Several men stand on the plank, holding balancing poles. They then jump up and down in unison. As the dogger begins to move, the crowbar is driven further under it, and jumping resumed until it is free. (Shacksted Lane Quarry, Godalming.)*

About 100 metres after this gap turn left [GR 9730 4795] straight uphill past Conduit Farm (one can see the radio masts are just on the right of your path uphill).

Almost immediately one leaves the lower greensand, with its fragments of Bargate stone, rippled millions of years ago by the sea at low water, and crosses onto the more recent chalk. Much Bargate stone for building purposes was extracted nearby, at Hurtmore just south of Compton. Bargate stone occurs in large concretionary blocks known as 'doggers'. Doggers suitable for building are less than one quarter of Bargate beds, so much material must be removed. The old Hurtmore quarry is still there.

Conduit Farm must mark the site of a spring, presumably on the join between the chalk of the Hog's Back and the very narrow layer of gault clay above the lower greensand.

As you ascend, even if you have not noticed underfoot, the hedgerow on your right announces that you have reached the chalk: it has plenty of classic downland flora: the most obviously visible being box, old man's beard and the wayfarer's tree. One can also see that instead of pasture, this chalky soil can sustain arable.

If you are feeling a little puffed on reaching the top, Gertrude Jekyll tells us of a feat up and along the length of the Hog's Back in around 1825 which will leave you gasping:

> A sack-lifter in the Guildford corn-market laid a wager that he would lift a sack of corn in the Guildford market and put it down in Farnham market within five hours. The distance is ten miles. A sack of wheat is four bushels and weighs over two hundred weight [224lb/102kg]. A crowd of people followed him out of Guildford; down the High Street, over the bridge, and up the very steep ascent of the old road on to the Hog's Back. Twice only he… rested for twenty minutes…. He finished well within time, and as he put down his sack in Farnham market he merely said: 'Well, I won it.' Then, looking round he said, 'would any one like to lay me I don't take it back?

You will be dying to know about the wheat he was carrying. Despite Surrey's generally poor soil, wheat grown in the district of Guildford was reckoned the best available, and according to a writer in 1850, 'its prices in the Guildford wheat-market are almost always higher than in any other market in the kingdom.'

The most twisted section of the Hog's Back.

Turn right, but pause before walking along the Hog's Back.

This is an ancient trackway, but how ancient is impossible to say (on pilgrims and other myths, see p.181). Its width, including the overgrown margins on either side of the present track, remind one that the Hog's Back was an important drove road for many centuries.

The Hog's Back is, if not unique, at least a rarity in British geology. Its rarity lies in what happened to the Chalk here. The Chalk had been laid down about 80 million years ago as a horizontal sheet of marine life deposit. Then, between 20 and five million years ago, a series of earth storms (massive geological movements) pressured the Chalk into a dome, of which the North and South Downs are the peripheral remnants. Here, however, the Chalk stratum was twisted violently, almost vertically, and also pulled apart, so that it both folded and faulted, to leave it as the steepest and narrowest part of the North Downs.

This is the only stretch of the Hog's Back where one may walk along the old Guildown trackway, as it was once known, without an inferno of traffic. The width of the trackway runs from the banks demarcating the fields on the north and south hillsides.

It is worth taking a look either side periodically. As Jane Austen wrote to her sister Cassandra in May 1813, 'I never saw the country from the Hogsback so advantageously.'

So, after passing the radio masts on your right, look out after 100m for a chance to slip to the right to enjoy the view from the path along the edge of the field.

ON THE SOUTH SIDE Piccard's Farm stands alone in the valley. The original farmstead of this name comes later on the walk. There was a John Picard farming here in the early fourteenth century. Further off one can see the Wey Valley stretching south from Guildford on one's left, the east branch passing between Chinthurst and Foxborough hills to Bramley, the housing along the valley bottom neatly hidden by tree cover.

Contemplating the Wey Valley between Guildford and Godalming, Cobbett wrote:

> Here are hill and dell in endless variety. Here are Chalk and Sand, vieing [*sic*] with each other in making beautiful scenes. Here are woods and downs. Here is something of everything.

After barely ½ km look out for an opportunity to resume walking along the Hog's Back track itself.

ON THE NORTH SIDE lie the far less attractive flatter sandy soils stretching up to Bagshot and beyond. The land is more heavily built up, there are fewer trees and lapsed heathland is now used for military training.

After another 200m look out on your left (just by the barrier on the track) for the entrance to Henley Fort, now a youth education centre.

If you explore down the tarmac road to your left you will find yourself at the back of the earthworks, hiding the stores and ammunition magazines for which the fort was planned. The earthworks are not that interesting, but their story is.

This fort was one of thirteen planned for the defence of London in the late nineteenth century. It seems almost incredible that Britain, the strongest world power of its day, was fearful of invasion. Ironically, military strength heightens fear rather than alleviating it. (Just look at the United States or, indeed, Israel.) In 1859, a diplomatic incident with France triggered a wave of patriotic paranoia, out of which a volunteer army, the precursor of the Territorial Army, was formed. It was speculated, wildly, that one day France might try to invade, as it had planned to do under Napoleon I in 1803. The growing strength of the French navy was given as evidence of the potential danger.

Even France's shattering defeat at the hands of Prussia in 1870-71 did not allay British fears. In 1889 the London Defence Scheme was approved by Parliament. The idea was that the regular army would confront an invader in the field, but should it be defeated, the North Downs would form a line of defence, manned by the volunteer artillery and infantry units. This strategy was obsolete before the defences were completed, because technical advances gave artillery far greater range and accuracy by the early 1890s than hitherto. A more fundamental objection, however, was that either by a single breach or by outflanking the line, the whole defensive position could become irrelevant (most memorably demonstrated by the failure of the Maginot Line in France in 1940). It made far more sense to rely on defence in depth and for the rapid deployment of reinforcements by rail where they were most needed. Henley Fort was one of the only forts to be constructed.

Once past Henley Fort, look out on the north side for Guildford Cathedral.
This must be one of the best places from which to appreciate the exterior of Guildford Cathedral designed by Edward Maufe, a man virtually unknown outside architectural circles. Nairn & Pevsner damn its outside appearance: 'a rather mealy-mouthed exterior…. it will never be more than a well-mannered postscript to the Gothic revival.'

Maufe had grown up under the influence of the Arts & Crafts Movement, and with a great enthusiasm for the simplicity of Swedish architecture. But that was in the first two decades of the twentieth century. He had won the commission for the cathedral in 1932. A whole generation (and world war) had passed before it was completed in the mid-1960s, by which time tastes had radically changed. Now we have passed beyond the brutalism of reinforced concrete, it is possible to admire the exterior again. However, if you still feel underwhelmed, make sure you see inside the building sometime, where the verdict of even Nairn & Pevsner is a good deal more forgiving: 'a cool interior of real spatial imagination…. The result is a very impressive and sober free-Gothic central 'vessel'…. noble and subtle, and [it] has a queer power of compelling, not reverence, but contemplation.' So if you have not been inside, make a point of doing so.

It is claimed that along the trackway, perhaps near here, Prince Alfred, a pretender to the throne, was kidnapped in 1036. He was the younger son of Æthelred the Unready, whose name means ill-counselled, already a pejorative term by the twelfth century, and acquiring an even more demeaning inference today. Alfred was supposedly enjoying the hospitality of the Earl Godwin, in the words of the *Anglo-Saxon Chronicle*:

> Alfred the blameless atheling [prince], king Æthelred's son came here, and meant to go to his mother in Winchester; but Godwin did not allow it, nor other men who wielded great power, because much was spoken of in favour of Harold [Harefoot, the son of the Danish king Canute], though it was unjust. Godwin intercepted him, set him in captivity and drove away his friends, some killed wretchedly, some were chained, some blinded, some mutilated, some scalped, nor was a more bloody deed done after the Danes came.

Godwin seems to have handed Alfred over to Harold Harefoot, another pretender to the throne, who had him blinded and either accidentally or intentionally killed at Ely.

Harold Harefoot died in 1040. Alfred's older brother, Edward 'the Confessor', ascended the throne peacefully in 1043. Edward and Alfred were Anglo-Normans (their mother was Emma of Normandy) and spent much of their lives in Normandy. It is a persistent popular English view that the Norman triumph at Hastings was a disaster, in which case one should know something of the treacherous Earl Godwin. He was a mountebank, hand in glove with the Danish invaders, most notably King Canute. He played a skilful political game and climbed the hierarchy so that his second son, Harold, was able to seize the throne in 1066. Harold's claim was no stronger than that of his nemesis, William. Whatever you think of the Normans, never reckon the Saxon warlords as nice. They seem to have been just as calculating and brutal.

⮑ **Car-less walkers turn left onto the Hog's Back.**
Continue down the tarmac road, past the first houses on the left and the signs announcing 'Public Bridleway 14' (to those coming uphill). This is the Mount. Pause outside the cemetery on your right (there is a turning place in the road).

The Guildford city gallows stood on the Mount, near the top if we are to believe Daniel Defoe who passed this way in about 1720:

> .... at the top of the ascent from the town stands the gallows, which is so placed respecting the town, that the towns people from the High Street may sit at their shop doors, and see criminals executed.

At some point the gallows seem to have been sited lower down close to the bottom of The Mount, the executioners and citizenry not having the puff of Jekyll's sack lifter.

Turn right (opposite No.86 The Mount) along the marked footpath between the two burial grounds [GR 9907 4900].

At the end of the cemetery on the left stands the Booker Tower. Charles Booker was a corn merchant and thrice town mayor. It was said that he built his tower 'to perpetuate his name after fate had robbed him of his two sons', one to smallpox, the other to drowning in the Wey. The tower was completed in 1839, and its opening made a celebration of the betrothal of Albert to Queen Victoria. At that time the tower stood in open countryside. Elsewhere in the cemetery lies the grave of Charles Dodgson, better known as Lewis Carroll.

Continue following the same direction, along Beech Lane which, after a long curve to the right, takes a steep turn down to the left.

Some of the houses are well worth looking at. Standing on the edge of Guildford, some exude affluence and charm, a few belonging to the burgeoning Arts & Crafts Movement.

At the bottom turn right, and immediately fork left into Chestnut Avenue, which takes you to the main road (A3100 Portsmouth Road).

As you walk, you will pass on your right St Catherine's Village Hall, which serves the local community. It is an old First World War hut, acquired and given to the local Women's Institute with 'the object of improving the conditions of life for the said inhabitants.' Today we feel that phrase uncomfortably patronising, and with too solemn a purpose. We 'enjoy' ourselves in 'amenities'.

Turn right (and grit your teeth against the aggression of traffic)

Before turning right again (first right, up Sandy Lane), you may like to look briefly at The Valley, a small domestic enclave on the far side of the road, under the tile-hung arch covered in creeper. This elegant early Arts & Crafts development was probably designed by Norman Shaw in about 1881. It contains two apparently identical but asymmetric cottage ranges. On the hill above, beside the A1300, half hidden by the trees, stand the ruins of St Catherine's Chapel, which was built in the fourteenth century but fell into disuse in the fifteenth.

Turn first right into Sandy Lane [GR 9928 4835], and walk for 150m until opposite Piccards Manor in the valley on the right.

*St Catherine's
Chapel*

Piccards Manor (the original Piccards Farm) is a sixteenth century farm-stead building with two flanking barns, the one on the right also fronted in Bargate stone, a nice reminder that we have left the chalk of Guildford and the Hog's Back. The barn on the left, however, is in brick but with the most magnificent and typically south Surrey cat-slide roof.

After 200m, as the road rises steeply, take the footpath forking off to the left side of the road, taking you up to the outer compound of Surrey Police HQ, which is on your left. Go straight ahead, through The Firs, with police cars parked on your left and civilian cars on your right, to pick up the footpath straight ahead.

   After about 500m you will emerge into open fields and reach a T-junction [GR 9850 4768]. Turn right and follow the path and tarmac past Orange Grove and Orange Court Farm.

They are named after John Orange, a fourteenth century tenant farmer here.

Cross the tarmac road and continue following the path.

Pillarbox Cottage on the right is sixteenth and seventeenth century, with delightful bulges to alarm any passing structural surveyor unused to old timber-frame houses.

On reaching Loseley Park lake, take a seat to read the following.

Loseley has managed to outstrip its original Saxon meaning: 'pig-sty clearing'. It is reckoned the finest surviving house of its date in Surrey, a picturesque Tudor manor house of restrained simplicity, its 'sobriety and

Loseley Park as it still looked in the mid-eighteenth century.

freedom from fussiness is almost unique.' Its architecture is conservative, looking back to the Gothic age, as one might expect in the depths of the Surrey countryside, whereas the up-and-coming style already drew its inspiration from Renaissance Italy. The house is still occupied by the same family which acquired the estate in 1508, and rebuilt it in the 1560s, plundering Waverley Abbey for its Bargate stone. Was it worth the plunder? Go to Waverley Abbey and see the damage (p.99). Yet much of the dressed stone is chalk, or clunch, quarried from the North Downs.

Loseley is much smaller now than in its hey-day, being only the north wing of a larger structure. As originally planned, the house was to have occupied three sides of a square, a central gatehouse and flank walls possibly with smaller office buildings on its fourth side, thus making a large quadrangle. If you have the time and the energy, it is well worth a visit before continuing to Compton. As for Loseley ice-cream, the business has long since departed.

You may notice a Lombardy Poplar by the lakeside, not so very usual in this part of Surrey, except along the Wey. The species is a hybrid, introduced from Italy in the mid-eighteenth century. It is always planted and has never naturalised itself. Oliver Rackham, the eminent countryside historian, observes that it is always 'male and incapable of looking after itself.' Now where have I heard that before?

Look out for swags of mistletoe high up in the lime trees. Mistletoe loves the fibrous quality of lime tree bark on which to root itself.

Cross the stile. If you wish to visit Loseley, turn left up the track to the house and grounds (to retrace your steps after your visit). Otherwise continue straight on until the footpath compels you to turn left. On reaching the track, turn right to Polsted Manor ('steading by the pool', the pond still being there), where you should turn right up the bridleway for 50m and turn left up the steps to continue. After 1km you will reach Coneycroft Farm, now devoted to horses.
Coneycroft is on record in 1841, but presumably is older. Judging by its name it is perhaps connected with the rabbits that may have been kept in the warrens. Perhaps this was the abode of the warrener. Until the nineteenth century an adult was a coney and a baby was a rabbit. Now we have rabbits and bunnies. Today Coneycroft looks modern and horsey.

Take either the left or right path around Coneycroft. In either case turn right on reaching the road, which takes you back to the Watts Gallery (almost immediately) or turn left to return to the Watts Chapel.

For the parish church of St Nicholas, another important building, continue past the Watts Chapel to the end of the lane, turn left down the main street for about 250m. St Nicholas stands on your right.

ST NICHOLAS CHURCH
St Nicholas is the real treat in Compton. It is one of the most remarkable churches in Surrey, and architecturally unique in England. Standing on a sandstone knoll, it is built with Bargate stone, chalk and flint.

THE EXTERIOR. As one approaches up the south side of the church, admire its long 'catslide' roof, the kind of Surrey roof which inspired the Arts & Crafts movement's enthusiasm for vernacular architecture. The Saxon tower with its shingled broach-spire is made of Bargate rubble, hardly the material one would expect to last so long, or to be the oldest part of the building. It is a real shame that a large window has pierced the west side of the tower, as it jars with the tower's Saxon period and style. The outer walls of the chancel are late eleventh century, while those of the aisled nave are probably about one hundred years later. The porch is nineteenth century.

THE INTERIOR.
(a) **The Chancel.** The building's great claim to fame is its Romanesque two-storey sanctuary, dating from the late twelfth century, the only surviving example in all England. Its purpose remains a tantalising

mystery. In order to build the upper storey a second inner skin was built inside the existing chancel walls (the plaster of the original walls was discovered during restoration a century ago).

The Norman guardrail of nine arches on the upper storey is cut from a single plank, reputedly the oldest carved woodwork in England.

The east window of the lower sanctuary contains a small glass panel of the Virgin and Child, either twelfth or thirteenth century.

The arches of the two sanctuaries, and also that of the chancel entrance are twelfth century, with their different Romanesque decorations. Over the chancel arch is a recently discovered (1966) twelfth century lozenge mural, unusual inasmuch as one might more reasonably expect a crucifixion, or a doom depiction here.

Before leaving the chancel look out for the 'squint' in the south wall, the angled window of a small oratory or cell, perhaps for an anchorite. On excavation six male skeletons were found beneath the floor, perhaps successive inhabitant anchorites.

Finally, on the same south side of the chancel is the graffito of a knight, scratched on the chancel arch wall. This, too, is twelfth century and it is easy to speculate, but with no evidence, that he may have been a Crusader.

(b) **The nave** seems to have been rebuilt about twenty years after the creation of the double sanctuary. The nave arcades are, like the outer walls, late twelfth century, with the local speciality of crimped plasterwork, and also scalloped capitals made of clunch. Others have Early Gothic foliage above solid drums.

THE FURNISHINGS. The font is made of carstone (p.236) probably sourced locally on the south side of the Hog's Back. There are holes in the rim for a locked cover, made mandatory from 1215 to prevent the theft of consecrated water for necromancy. Our obsession with the ghoulish, routinely trundled out at Halloween, has a long pedigree.

NEARBY PLACES

Opening times will be on the respective websites:
The Watts Gallery: www.wattsgallery.org.uk
   or telephone: 01483 810235
Loseley Park: www.loseleypark.co.uk or telephone: 01483 304440.

Puttenham Village and Common

Distance 7km/4 miles: 2 hours
OS Explorer Map No.145

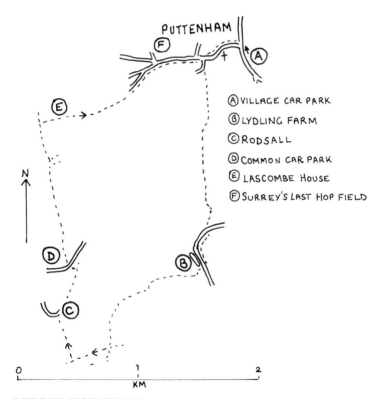

PUTTENHAM

Ⓐ VILLAGE CAR PARK
Ⓑ LYDLING FARM
Ⓒ RODSALL
Ⓓ COMMON CAR PARK
Ⓔ LASCOMBE HOUSE
Ⓕ SURREY'S LAST HOP FIELD

N

0   1   2
KM

BEFORE YOU WALK

This walk across Puttenham village lands shows the contrasting soils villages typically possessed: pasture at the outset of the walk, followed by mixed woodland, the sandy heath of the common land, and a glimpse of the most fertile arable in the lee of the Hog's Back, now the site of

Surrey's last hop field. An optional brief exploration of Wanborough, lying opposite Puttenham on the far side of the Hog's Back, is added as a postscript.

If car-less: Take bus No.65 to the Hog's Back Cafe, Puttenham from Guildford (10 mins). On alighting **walk back 300m** and take the marked footpath down into the village. On reaching the main street, turn left, pass the Good Intent pub and immediately right down Suffield Lane, following walk instructions at ➲ seven lines below.

Refreshment: The Good Intent (tel. 01483 810387), on Puttenham Street, at the end of the walk.

Start at the car park [GR 9350 4777] opposite The Harvester on the B3000.
The Harvester was once the Jolly Farmer when it was also the villagers' favourite and ancient pub.

Cross the road, turn right and after 200m turn left along The Street into Puttenham Village. Turn left opposite the Good Intent pub, ➲ down Suffield Lane (marked to Elstead and Cutmill) and almost immediately, where the road turns right, continue straight on, along the marked footpath [GR 9315 4774].
On the left lies the drive to Puttenham Priory. There is a glimpse of the house later in the walk. As one walks southward, the principal reward is visual, rather than informational.

Follow the path between hedgerows and fencing, then past conifers planted in the gully on the right, then straight across the fields, following the marked route, 'The Foxway'.
Crossing the open fields, note the slight bank just to the right of the route, evidence of a hedgerow which has been grubbed out.

Turn right along the road when you reach it for 250m (or, to avoid walking on the road, you can cross to the far side where there is a permitted path marked by occasional posts through the edge of the hazel coppice until brought down to the road opposite Lydling Farm, and its pond). Turn right up the track past the pond and along the left side of Lydling Farm [GR 9318 4611].
The noticeboard will tell you a little of the Aberdeen Angus breeding exploits of Lydling Farm. 'Lydling' may mean 'slope by a stream', which certainly fits the farm's location. Look out for the farmhouse, up the track

just beyond the farm outbuildings. It was built around 1700 in the style of Wren, very unusual for Surrey, but elegant in its plainness.

Follow the track which progressively turns into a sunken lane (see p.242), then a footpath. After 300m note a plantation of Scots Pine on your right.
Pass a few eucalyptus trees on the right, exotics from Australia, introduced to Britain in the 1830s. The change to nutrient-poor sandy soil is very noticeable, with consequent bracken growth.

After another 300m watch for a change to deciduous planting. After another 200m turn right at the first marked junction, following the path gently downhill.
Underfoot one will see lumps of Bargate stone in the sand, the poor natural building material of Surrey, too small and friable to be shaped, let alone dressed (for how it is quarried, see p.122). On either side of the path there is substantial sweet chestnut coppice (for its uses see p.81).

After 350m turn right again on a marked path [GR 9214 4532].
After 75m look out for the beeches growing out of the wood bank on the right of the path. Beech branches very happily grow into each other, 'inosculate', a process suggestive of intelligent recognition of the same species. It may be this that made beech a popular woodland boundary tree species.

After almost 400m the path forks at the very end. Take the right fork and follow the road past the front of Rodsall Manor.
Rodsall is old, even if the present farmhouse has been refurbished often. Indeed, while the first written mention of Puttenham was in 1199, Rodsall, 'the red miry place', features in Domesday in 1086, as one of a string of settlements with the assets of woodland and meadow. A sub-manor of Puttenham by 1200, it illustrates the way feudalism was beginning to weaken at this time: the lord of the manor allowed a farmer to lease Rodsall for life, at a yearly rent of fourteen shillings and a rose. He needed payment in money rather than in feudal service. (Seven hundred years later, a rose was still being paid annually by the occupants of Rodsall farm, but no longer.)

Rodsall was on the direct route from the south coast to Bagshot Heath, a notorious entrepôt for smuggled goods destined for London in the eighteenth century. Robert Keen, the tenant of Rodsall, would leave food and fodder in a nearby dell, Puckstool Bottom, to refresh the gentlemen and their horses. (The woodland you have just walked through was known 150 years ago as Puckstool Wood, and Puckstool Bottom is likely to be in the low ground behind your left.) Keen would find gifts of contraband left in appreciation. A 'puck', by the way, is a Wealden term for a goblin, immortalised in Kipling's *Puck of Pook's Hill.*

Pass the handsome Stable House on the left, and shortly after, Rose Cottage on the right. Fifty metres after Rose Cottage take the left fork and keep walking for 300m. Watch out for and take the steps up to the left [GR 9213 4607]. (If you pass a marked path on your right, you have just overshot).

John Aubrey, exploring Surrey in the years before and after 1700, 'was wont to admire how Lanes came to be worn of so great a depth, which is only in sandy Ground, where the Water washes them away.' It is not difficult to imagine the muffled hooves of ponies carrying contraband up these sunken lanes. Gertrude Jekyll heard a nice tale about a squire, recently arrived hereabouts:

> One morning before he was dressed, his valet brought him an urgent message from the bailiff to say that he wished to see him. The master said he must wait, as he was not dressed. The message came again, still more pressingly worded.
>
> 'Well, send the fellow up,' said the unfinished squire.
>
> The man came in with a mysterious air and watched the servant out of the room, and then said in a hoarse half-whisper: 'There was a run last night, Sir, and I've marked four.'
>
> The squire had not the least idea what the information meant, and on being enlightened he burst out indignantly: 'But I can't have anything to do with smuggled goods; why, I'm a magistrate. How dare you come to me with such a suggestion.'
>
> The bailiff stood his ground quite unabashed. 'If you'll take my word for it, sir, if you don't do as others do, you'll have trouble.'
>
> The squire continuing to protest vigorously, the bailiff said, 'Well, sir, will you ask the parson?'
>
> He did so, and the rector's answer was: 'If you wish to live in peace with your neighbours you had better fall in with the custom of the country.'

Gertrude Jekyll, *Old West Surrey* (1904)

Cross the road and follow the track up the right side of the Car Park. Stick to the east (right hand) edge of the Common, either walking on the vehicle track or keeping close enough to join it later. You are welcome to explore to the left but the myriad paths make it impossible to provide fool-proof directions.

The car park area offers a magnificent view across the landscape to the south-west.

Puttenham Common is medieval or possibly Saxon in origin. Because of its acidic, sandy, nutrient-poor soil, it can never have been under the plough. But it was apportioned to the feudal tenants as a location in which they could graze animals 'in common'. This right was for the use, but not ownership, of the land, which always remained with the lord of the manor. The lord's steward, or reeve, would ration the number of beasts each tenant might be allowed to graze, known as the 'stint', hence the phrase "don't stint yourself". The livestock, sheep and cattle would crop tree growth, thus creating a characteristic heath landscape.

Puttenham Common will have acquired much more tree cover since the collapse of common grazing in the late nineteenth century. Just over a century ago, George Sturt learnt about this grazing from his neighbours:

> … men who, if you lead them on, will talk of the cows they them-selves watched over on the heath – two from this cottage, three from that yonder, one more from Master Hack's, another couple from Trusker's, until they have numbered a score perhaps, and have named a dozen old village names.
>
> It all actually happened. The whole system was "in full swing" here, within living memory. But the very heart of it was the open common.

Another of his neighbours recalled as a girl in the 1830s she would

> see the cows come slowly down the valley, each to its own stall – for in those days half the cottagers kept cows, which only a boy herded on the common all day. And of evenings the air would grow fragrant with the smoke of turf fires lit for the evening meal.
>
> George Bourne [Sturt] *Change in the Village* (1912)

Manorial tenants were allowed to cut turfs and peat (which can be found in wetter, poorly drained areas) for fuel.

Turf and peat cutting was still going on here in 1800 and probably only ended in the late nineteenth century. Sturt, reminiscing about his child-hood in the 1860s, recalled:

> Turfs were the common fuel. They were cut on the Common (by the privileged) and the farmer carted them to the labourers' cottages not

*Cutting turf on the heath, c. 1890.
The man is holding the broad
crosspiece at the top of the haft in order
to give the cutter the whole weight of
his body.*

for money, but for the ashes when they were burnt, which made valuable manure…. Or was this rather peat? For that was spoken of. Peats or turfs – they were brought home and stacked in sheds, or in the open, then their owner thatched them over. And since the ashes were so valuable it was not uncommon to keep a fire burning night and day all through the winter.

Then as to lighting only people "rather aristocratic" burnt composite candles, and then perhaps only on festivals. The common candle of tallow was ordinary; labouring people had to be content with rush-dips…. The dip was a manufactured article, bought at a shop: the rush light was home made. About 18 inches long it burnt long enough to go to bed by.

George Sturt, *A Small Boy in the Sixties* (1927)

After 1km pass a modern red brick house on the right, then ignore two footpaths to the right, one very shortly after the other, but after another 350m take the next path to the right [GR 9180 4725]. It will lead you along the south edge of Lascombe House grounds, giving you a good view of the house.

Lascombe, begun in 1894, was an early commission for Edwin Lutyens, then only twenty-five. It was completed two years later. It is white roughcast on a brick plinth, with handsome gables and a massive chimney. This is classic Lutyens, nodding to the vernacular tradition of Surrey but on the large scale, a giant cottage one might say. It proclaims, like many other Arts & Crafts houses in the area, the arrival of the wealthy classes fleeing London in search of a rural arcadia. Yet it also speaks of something else, 'England's Summer', the two decades before the First World War when England's future seemed set fair, with barely a cloud in the sky. 1914 changed all that. (America's moment of untroubled imperial power was of no greater duration, from 1945 until the Cuban crisis, the death of Kennedy and the growing shadow of war in Vietnam.) The name Lascombe long predates the house but its origin seems to be lost.

Walk through the Lascombe building complex (an old pig farm), and follow the lane till it joins The Street.
The Hog's Back runs along the skyline on the left, the last remnant of the North Downs, its chalk structure both tilted and fractured, hence its dramatic narrowness. On the right, one of the older farmsteads of Puttenham, Suffield ('South Field'), nestles at the bottom of a sweep of fields, where the Lower Greensand gives way to Weald. In the distance ahead the Palladian frame of Puttenham Priory is visible among the trees. It was built in 1762, a pattern-book builder's work, and one of the few such examples in Surrey.

Before setting off down The Street, go 100m down the track to the left of the topmost cottage on the left side, to see the last hop field in Surrey.
This hop field supplies the local Hogsback Brewery with Fuggle hops, one of a handful of favoured varieties. By 1600 Puttenham had become a hop-growing village. By the end of the eighteenth century 'the passion for hop grounds [had] … then risen to a degree or rage,' around Farnham, when casual workers, often from the Traveller community, were required to help harvest. There would be a narrow interval – ten days – for harvesting. On completion of the picking there would be 'finishing frolics'. The agriculturalist William Marshall described these in the 1790s, evoking a world that Thomas Hardy would have instantly recognised a century later:

> the pole puller [the pickers' leader] wears a sash ornamented with ribbons, given him by the pickers, the women decorate themselves with such hankerchiefs, ribbons and finery, as they purchase at the shop, to

Eileen Stevens and Emily Marshall hop picking with a little help from Eileen's daughter, Sharon, c.1970.

carry home with them. Some of the companies parading in the streets of Farnham; – perhaps with a fiddler at their head, – singing, shouting, in tones of true licentiousness, the evening being usually closed by a dance, and always with copious libations, – doubtless to the goddess of the hops.

The itinerants, who live at a distance are (by agreement) sent home in waggons; forty or fifty perhaps in each; with a fiddler in the midst of them, and with their various colors flying. Altogether, a sort of glee and merriment which, in these decorous times, is rarely met with.

Once harvested, the hops would be dried in the kiln by means of a charcoal furnace.

Hop cultivation almost petered out after 1945, and in the 1970s a new dryer rendered the old kilns redundant. In the heyday of hops, there was a line of hop gardens running all the way along the foot of the Downs from Farnham into Kent. As recently as 1922, there is a note in the Puttenham school logbook: 'I am instructed to keep open the school for another week on account of the late hop-picking.'

The Street, Puttenham

BEFORE YOU WALK ALONG THE STREET: In the Middle Ages, Puttenham's dwellings were almost exclusively sited along The Street and the same is nearly true today. Village expansion has been neat and un-obtrusive. Villagers would have graduated from crude turfed hovels to cruck dwellings in the thirteenth century. By the fifteenth century they were beginning to afford timber-frame thatched dwellings. Each would have had a strip of cultivable land at the back, and beyond lay the common fields at the west end of The Street. William Cobbett gives us a glimpse of what we might imagine from his grandmother's dwelling, not that far away from Puttenham, in the late eighteenth century:

> It was a little thatched cottage with a garden before the door. It had but two windows; a damson tree shaded one, and a clump of filberts [hazel] the other....her fire was made of turf cut from the neighbouring heath and her evening light was a rush dipped in grease.

Until the twentieth century, a stream ran much of the way down the right side of the street, each front door having a paving slab to bridge it. There are plenty of houses worth noting, many of them with that Surrey speciality, galletting (p.236).

George Sturt reminds us what life was like just over a century ago along a street like this. Village life, he wrote,

> … subsisted in the main upon what their own industry could produce out of the soil and materials of their own countryside. A few things, certainly, they might get from other neighbourhoods, such as iron for making their tools, and salt for curing their bacon; and some small interchange of commodities there was, accordingly, say between the various districts that yielded cheese, and wool, and hops, and charcoal, but as a general thing the parish where the peasant people lived was the main source of the materials they used, and their well-being depended on their knowledge of its resources.

And he paid tribute to:

> the general handiness of the people, who with their own hands raised and harvested their crops, made their clothes, did much of the building of their homes, attended to their cattle, thatched their ricks, cut their firing, made their bread and wine or cider, pruned their fruit-trees and vines, looked after their bees, all for themselves.

George Bourne [Sturt], *Change in the Village*

John Heath in c.1920. He took over the forge (now the Old Forge) from his father. In 1900 there were four blacksmiths in the village, an indication of how much ironwork was required to satisfy the villagers' needs.

As you walk down The Street

ON THE LEFT at the top of The Street is a pair of eighteenth century cottages. The Heritage is a collection of cottages knocked into one. We forget that until the twentieth century, most people lived several to a room.

ON THE RIGHT, up the steps, No.139 was inhabited by a couple of sisters in the nineteenth century who apparently held a monopoly on the laying out of the deceased and were known as The Puttenham Sharks. One is left darkly speculating why. Possibly at the same time, but no one knows for sure, the house was home for three elderly pauper women.

ON THE LEFT, the houses in the row commencing at No.138 are mid-twentieth century award-winning council houses, blending well with the local vernacular.

ON THE RIGHT, the modern house Honey Wood admirably makes no attempt to pretend to be other than what it is, a brave thing in The Street. There is always a real dilemma building in an ancient and organic street like this: pastiche or modernity?

ON THE LEFT, No.106 is the Old Forge, certainly the blacksmith's shop in the nineteenth century as the chimney above attests, but its previous history is unknown.

Also on the left is Street Farm; the white building on the left of the drive was built, though it may not look it, before 1550. The old farmyard at the back has been built upon.

ON THE RIGHT Nos.87 and 89, recessed, are attractively faced in flint, a reminder of the way in which the lack of a single good building material in Surrey results in many buildings being a mixture of different materials, perfectly illustrated by the village church (see below). Next to it, Hillside House, built in 1872 by a successful local farmer is an architectural mistake, portentous where the other houses have warmth and intimacy.

ON THE LEFT, No.86 is eighteenth century, while No.78 beyond, from the late seventeenth century, was clearly inhabited by relatively prosperous tenants, with a dedicated washhouse on its right side.

ON THE RIGHT, Nos.77-81 were originally a terrace of six dwellings of the mid-eighteenth century. (In 1902 they were advertised for sale as freehold cottages which 'share a well, bake house, washing house, and closet' to be used as weekly hiring to labouring families.)

ON THE LEFT, PAUSE AT SCHOOL LANE to enjoy the seventeenth century cottages just before the lane. The village pond was in front, where the lawn is now. If you turn around you can see on the opposite side of The Street the bricked up culvert where the street's open stream ran out. On the opposite corner of School Lane is Old Cottage. It is truly old, for it was built in the fifteenth century with dressed clunch, the hard version of chalk, another of Surrey's many building materials.

CONTINUING ALONG THE STREET: on the right, on the corner of Suffield Lane, stands Winters Farm, like Old Cottage probably late fifteenth century and timber-framed.

ON THE LEFT, 'The Good Intent' is eighteenth century but more importantly it is where you will need to refresh yourself. The pub sign, of course, is a pun. Villagers of the 1640s, however, would hardly have seen the parliamentary soldier depicted today as 'good', even if they had sympathised with Parliament more than with the king, for its troops were billeted here in the period 1643-44. The villagers, by no means prosperous, found themselves having to provide food and lodging for young men with large appetites, for which it is unlikely they were properly compensated. Moreover the soldiers did not disappear at the end of the Civil War.

In May 1648 people in this part of Surrey had demanded the re-instatement of the captive King Charles and the disbandment of the army, and an uprising was planned. To nip it in the bud, Kentish Roundheads occupied much of west Surrey, and 'behaved themselves as in a conquered country, insulting and plundering the inhabitants.' By July 1650 they were still there, throwing their weight around. John Evelyn, a Royalist, travelling through Surrey, expressed his own disgust that, 'the country was now much molested by souldiers, who tooke away gentlemen's horses for the service of the State, as then call'd.'

ON THE LEFT, adjacent to The Good Intent are two old cottages, possibly late sixteenth or early seventeenth century. Just beyond is No.48, an elegant Regency house. Further along on the left, Priory Farmhouse stands in front of more hop kilns, skilfully and elegantly converted into dwellings. A few paces on is Home Farm, with probably an eighteenth century barn in its yard. (On barns see the note on Wanborough at the end of this walk.)

Until the mid-nineteenth century The Street ran to the south of the church, not to the north of it, but the then inhabitant of The Priory disliked the villagers being able to gaze upon so fine a mansion as they passed by and had the road re-routed.

ST JOHN THE BAPTIST CHURCH

In spite of heavy and destructive restoration in 1861, the church of St John the Baptist is still worth a visit.

THE EXTERIOR. As you enter the grounds the principal village well is on your left. The nave is probably early twelfth century, the northern aisle mid-twelfth century and the chancel and north chapel late twelfth century. The chapel on the south side is late fourteenth century. The tower, built c.1400, once carried a timber spire, which was lost to fire in 1735. The tower's stone parapet is modern, and there are plenty of repairs in brick and tile and buttressing to keep it upright. The fabric is a delightful mix of various Surrey materials available at different junctures.

THE INTERIOR. Despite renovation, the interior has a lovely village feel. Bath Stone replaced the original Bargate windows, and triangular dormers were inserted into the north pitch of the roof in 1861. The principal attraction must be the four-bay Norman nave arcade, built in c.1160, boasting a very local Surrey feature: the crimped plasterwork in the arcade surrounds. The remarkable thing about the arcade is that the bases rise from bay to bay as if the original floor had sloped up to the east. Admire the recent installation of a kitchen at the foot of the tower, so neatly done. There is a nice brass of Edward Cranford, rector 1400-31, reset in the chancel floor.

⊃ If you are car-less, to return to Guildford, continue to end of the Street, turn left, pass under the A31, climb up to east-bound carriageway, and the bus stop is a short way west (to your right).

POSTSCRIPTS

1. In case you are still unimpressed with Puttenham, consider the words of commendation of Puttenham's rector, Thomas Swift, shortly after he had taken over the living in 1694:

    > The Situation of this Place is so healthy... Such is the Salubrity of its Air, as did those wealthy Citizens know it, who want nothing so much as Health.... for in this little Spot you see.... such a Tribe of Patriarchs within Doors, as if this Place were exempted from the Feebleness and hasty Decays of this last Age of the World and hasty Death confin'd to keep his due Season for harvest, mowing down none, until Time has ripen'd them for his Scythe.

    The salubrity kept Swift going till 1752, when he was 86. So, if you think longevity would add to the meaning of your life, you know what to do.

2. On the far side of the Hog's Back stands **WANBOROUGH**, a hamlet of delight. Try as I might, I could not integrate it into a walk because of the traffic thundering along the A31. Thus one is denied a walk across the unique geology of the Hog's Back. A brief visit by car or on foot (walking the Wanborough road under the A31) would be worthwhile.

    Wanborough means 'the settlement of the Hump', the hump being either the rise in the Hog's Back above this hamlet, or perhaps a Bronze Age barrow once sited on the summit. Situated on the spring line, this settlement is probably prehistoric, dating back to the Bronze Age, possibly to the Neolithic period, five or six thousand years ago. Nairn & Pevsner describe it as 'unlike any other village in West Surrey – small, hard-bitten brick, huddled around a circular concrete silo. Really just one big farmyard.' Yet the barns surrounding the yard are magnificent.

THE TITHE BARN (95ft x 30ft) was used by the Cistercians (see below) to store wool from their downland flocks.

WANBOROUGH MANOR. Without infringing its privacy, an oblique view may be gained from outside. It was built around 1670.

ST BARTHOLOMEW. The flint chapel is worth visiting. The original church had been Saxon, but the present one was built by the monks of Waverley (see p.99) after the manor of Wanborough had been purchased by the abbey in 1148. If you are not up to speed on your saints, St Bartholomew was one of the twelve apostles, of whom we know nothing. Whereas not a single church in England had borne his name before the Conquest, a rash of churches in Norman England were dedicated to his memory in the twelfth century. So whatever this chapel lacked in size, it made up for in fashion.

The building has inevitably been tinkered with since it was built. The west front was rebuilt with brick, and the whole building restored in 1861, fortunately with a relatively light hand. Things to look out for:

- Surrey crimped plasterwork above six windows, including the east window.
- On the north wall is a memorial plaque dedicated to the memory of the women and men of the Special Operations Executive (SOE) who trained at Wanborough Manor during the Second World War.

Just to the right of the church is an ancient yew-lined lane, the old route up to the drove road running along the Hog's Back. Barely a century ago livestock would routinely have been driven up this track to market, in Farnham or Guildford or further afield.

The Wotton Estate

WALK

10

Distance 10km/6 miles: 3 hours
OS Explorer Map No.146

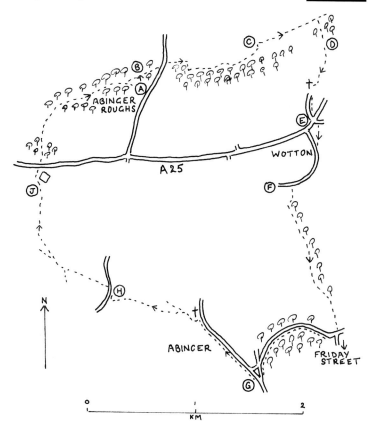

Ⓐ CAR PARK
Ⓑ WILBERFORCE MEMORIAL
Ⓒ PARK FARM
Ⓓ VALE HOUSE
Ⓔ WOTTON HATCH
Ⓕ WOTTON HOUSE
Ⓖ GODDARDS
Ⓗ RAIKES FARM
Ⓙ PADDINGTON FARM

BEFORE YOU WALK

Wotton simply means 'settlement, or farm, in the wood'. The Wotton estate is located on the lower greensand, and as you walk you will notice its composition varies. The estate was acquired in the late sixteenth century by the Evelyn family. Of this family, John Evelyn (1620-1706) was one of the most eminent men of Surrey and one of England's greatest diarists. His *Diary* gives a wonderful and entertaining glimpse of gentry life in England and on the Continent from the 1640s until the end of that century: as a courtier who knew Charles II and his brother, James II; as a country gentleman who grew up at Wotton and then spent his last decade here; as a leading intellectual of the day and, finally, but most relevantly for Wotton, as one of England's first landscape gardeners and tree experts. His book, *Sylva*, was primarily intended to encourage tree planting after the devastation of the Civil War (1642-45), but it remained an essential reference text until well into the nineteenth century.

It is difficult for us today to understand the centrality of timber (load-bearing stuff) and wood (smaller pieces) to the pre-1850s economy, but imagine a world without petro-chemical products, gas and oil, without mass-produced metal wares, and with all iron and steel expensive. This is what Evelyn himself wrote to impress his readers, whom he clearly feared would not take his polemic seriously:

> Since it is certain and demonstrable, that all arts and artisans whatsoever must fail and cease, if there were no timber and wood in a nation.... I say, when this is well considered, it will appear, that we had better be without gold than without timber.

His writings not only exhorted and instructed regarding trees, but laid the groundwork for the explosion of the English landscape movement in the following generation. As for his diary, it is a great pleasure and is not difficult to obtain second hand. You have his company on this walk.

If car-less: Take the No.32, 22 or 21 bus from Dorking (or alternatively from Guildford) to Wotton Hatch and pick up the walk at ➲ on page 155.

PRACTICAL POINTS BEFORE YOU WALK:

1   *Refreshment:* Food and drink are obtainable at Abinger Hatch (tel: 01306 730 737) on Abinger Common, just over halfway through the walk, or at the Stephan Langton (tel: 01306 730 775) at Friday Street.

2   If you wish to see John Evelyn's garden behind Wotton House, it is
    now private, and you have to walk through the house, a Principal
    Hayley hotel, to get into the garden. So please either telephone hotel
    reception beforehand (tel. 01306 737 000) where permission should
    be sought, or make yourself known at reception on arrival (and take
    light footwear or carry your boots to walk through the house if you
    fear your boots will be muddy).

**Start: The National Trust Car Park, Abinger Roughs [GR 1105 4800] up Critten
Lane opposite Crossways on the A25 (travelling east up the first turning to the
left after Abinger Hammer, travelling west up the second turning on the right
after the Wotton Hatch pub).**
'Abinger' probably means 'the farm of Abba's people'. However, the
Roughs (rough ground) were known until around 1900 as 'Terry's
Roughs'. Terry must have been a local farmer.

**Take the footpath leading north out of the car park (just on the left of the
information board) and walk downhill to the granite memorial.**
The granite memorial is to Samuel Wilberforce (1805-1873), the third
and favourite son of the emancipationist, William Wilberforce. As bishop of Winchester, Samuel became one of the most important Anglican
churchmen of the Victorian era. He was already a sick man when he fell
from his horse here. He had had a couple of heart attacks and his fall may
have been caused by another. He may, indeed, have been dead before he
hit the ground. A man of boundless energy, he was also a gifted word-
smith, both in speech and writing. People were lulled by his charm. It was,
perhaps, for this quality that he became known as 'Soapy Sam', so much
so that a critic characterised one of his arguments as 'a well-lubricated set
of words, ...so oily and saponaceous that no one can grasp it.'
    One of Wilberforce's weaknesses was to charge into the fray with-
out adequate reflection. He hastily joined the attack on Darwin's *On the
Origin of Species*, rashly relying on his friend Richard Owen, the distinguished palaeontologist, in dismissing the book as bad science. Darwin
thought Wilberforce's review was 'uncommonly clever.' Ironically,
Darwin also frequented the Roughs for recreation.

Opposite stands Leasers Barn. Leasers Barn is an old lambing barn, now
revived by the National Trust, and used for sheep rearing. 'Leasers' is a

corruption of the Old English word *laeswe*, meaning a pasture. The sheep kept here now are principally of two breeds: a recent introduction, the French Charollais breed, which first arrived in Britain in 1976, and the Jacobs, so named after the brindled brown and white livestock allocated to the Biblical Jacob by his father-in-law, Laban. Their arrival in Britain is not that long either, having been introduced from Spain in the mid-eighteenth century. The Charollais, recognizable by their white faces, produce excellent meat. They are also prolific. Compared with other species, the lambing is easier, the lambs are generally more robust, grow and mature sexually faster, all of which is good news for the shepherd. A century ago, however, you would probably have seen Southdown sheep here (see p.210).

Facing the barn, turn right, and after 100m cross the road and take the marked Bicycle Track No.22 (slightly left of directly opposite) eastwards [GR 1125 4820], with an open field on your left and woodland on your right.
Half left on the North Downs skyline is the spire of George Gilbert Scott's church at Ranmore Common (p.203) 5km/3 miles away. (If you cannot see it, you will get a better view once you have gone round the dogleg in the path.)

On your right is Deerleap Wood, a name which is probably 400 years old. Deer leaps were ramps by which deer could be driven over the fence, or pale, into an enclosed park. A deer park became the fashion accessory for any Elizabethan country gentleman who could afford one. This woodland, no good for agriculture, was a place for hunting game. We know there were plenty of red deer running wild around here, because in about 1724 Daniel Defoe looked down from the Downs nearby and wrote:

> The vale beneath this hill is for many miles, east and west, called.... Holmsdale.... in the woody parts of which are often found outlying red deer, and in the days of King James II or while he was Duke of York, they have hunted the largest stags here that have been seen in England; the Duke took great care to have them preserved for his own sport, and they were so preserved for many years, but have since that been most of them destroyed.

The woodland contains Scots pines, native to much of Scotland but hardly so further south, where they are virtually all planted, as they do well on poor sandy soil. In about 1650, Evelyn must have been among the first to plant pine this far south:

....there is a beautiful sort of fir, or rather pine, bearing small sharp cones, growing upon the mountains [of Scotland]; which, from the late Marquess of Argyle, I had sent me some seeds, which I have sown with tolerable success.

You will notice how sandy the path is, and will wonder how the farmer can stabilise the surface of the fields with sufficient humus and dressing to make it productive.

After 1km you will reach Park Farm, a name dating back to 1719 or earlier. Note the wonderful and typical Surrey barns, with their long roofs, now sadly dilapidated. If they collapse they are gone forever: a real dilemma for the owner. The second on the right, built on sandstone block plinth, with sandstone and brick duly 'galleted' on the east side, is late eighteenth century. The farmhouse looks as if it was already standing then, perhaps newly built, with a plain but elegant front.

By around 1800 Park Farm had acquired the prefix 'Limekiln'. From the eighteenth century there were numerous limekilns classically sited either side of the North Downs where the chalk met the adjacent geological beds. The lower chalk was superior for producing lime than upper chalk, and this made the foot of the escarpment, as here, more desirable than chalk obtained on the dip-slope. Most farms had their own limekilns. These usually stood on slopes, which made the manual filling or emptying of them easier. The lime was burnt from chalk and limestone, but since water is an essentially ingredient, for 'slaking' the lime to render it useable, it made sense to quarry and extract lime close to the spring line at the base of the chalk. The fuel used was principally furze (gorse), which

The entrance to a disused lime kiln. The interior is a circular stone construction in which the chalk was burnt.

could reach a high temperature very quickly.

Lime produced hereabouts enjoyed a national reputation. The principal commercial works were based in Dorking. The agriculturalist, William Malcolm, writing in 1805 declared: 'At Dorking are the best pits in the country, if not the kingdom. The stone that is here burnt into lime is sought after by every mason and bricklayer in London as well as in the country.' The Wey & Arun Junction Canal of 1814 (see p.22) stipulated the use of 'the best Dorking water lime'. The demand for Dorking lime faded away in the late nineteenth century.

Continue straight on Bicycle Track No.22, past the buildings, for 500 metres, and just 50m beyond a small dwelling on the right of the track, turn right up a narrow footpath [GR 1263 4853].

On the left you pass a plantation of larch. European larch was introduced to England in about 1620. Evelyn knew the value of this wood and planted them himself:

> the *larix* [is] among the trees which shed their leaves in Winter but not before there is an almost immediate supply of fresh…. The change of the colour of the old leaf, made an ignorant gardiner of mine erradicate what I had brought up with much care, as dead; let this therefore be a warning: The leaves are thin, pretty long and bristly; the cones small, grow irregular, as do the branches… Of the deep wounded bark, exsudes the purest of our shop-turpentine…That it flourishes with us, a tree of good stature sufficiently reproaches us our not cultivating so useful a material for many purposes, where lasting and substantial timber is required.

Evelyn had been in Venice and seen its use in the palaces surrounding the Piazza San Marco. In the words of a modern classic: 'No tree ever introduced to Britain has proved of so much value, or been so extensively planted. For many years its economic importance exceeded that of any other tree – even the oak.' In about 1850, however, it became vulnerable to a virulent fungoid parasite, with whole plantations destroyed. *Phytophthera ramorum* now threatens to banish larch from our shores.

Emerge after 200m in what was once the farmyard of Vale Farm.

The old rectory, now Vale Lodge and House, stands ahead on the left, a magnificent late Victorian pile indicative of the status once enjoyed by the parish parson.

Continuing in the same direction, over the stile to the right of Vale House, take the footpath up the narrow gully. The path itself narrows past the two tiny ponds on the left. When it widens again, look out for the church of St John's half hidden behind trees above on your right, and take the steep path up to it.

On entering the churchyard one can see the three original lancet windows (c.1200) in what is now the Evelyn Chapel. Even if you cannot get inside St John's, it is well worth a pause to enjoy the site, which goes back to Saxon times. The building is Bargate stone, with a Horsham slate roof. The early Norman tower was once the central feature of a structure, the west end of the nave, part of the pre-Conquest church, having at some stage been demolished. One can still see the blocked arch on the west side of the tower. Most of the church, except for the Evelyn mausoleum (c.1680), the vestry and the south porch, dates from 1190-1220, so this is one of the older extant churches of Surrey.

Born at the House in 1620, John Evelyn recalled in his diary receiving his first schooling: 'I was not initiated into any rudiments till I was four years of age, and then one Frier taught us at the church porch of Wotton...' It was presumably where the present 1857 porch, with its magnificent bargeboards, stands.

The tower has a two-staged pyramid roof, unusual for Surrey but similar to some churches in the Welsh border marches, and probably put onto the tower in the seventeenth or early eighteenth century.

If you get inside the thirteenth century church door, there are some nice seventeenth century monuments with kneeling figures in the Evelyn, chapel on the north side. Richard Evelyn's memorial of 1640 shows his son, John the diarist, as the second of the boys. John has his own plain but heavily inscribed slab under the chapel's south window. Also look out for the memorial to George Evelyn, 1829. Dr Arnold of Rugby School is at his most headmasterish in his inscribed eulogy: 'His early years gave a beautiful promise of vigour of understanding, kindness of heart and Christian nobleness of purpose.'

John Evelyn was buried in the family vault just north of the north chapel. In the churchyard is an eighteenth century Evelyn monument: a marble slab supported by two iron Doric columns and two iron Evelyn griffins.

Before leaving by the main entrance to the churchyard:
Note the brief avenue of limes. There was a fashion for lime trees in England when Evelyn was writing *Sylva*. Initially they had to be imported

from Flanders and Holland, where they were already all the rage for directing the eye across a landscape or for lining avenues. (Evelyn was the first to use the French term '*avenue*' for the approach road to great houses in England.) Evelyn himself must have seen some lime avenues during his self-imposed exile (see below). He certainly liked their qualities: casting good shade whilst keeping a reasonably compact shape, compared with the spreading habit of beech, oak, ash or chestnut:

> thus it will become (of all other [trees]) the most proper, and beautiful for walks, as producing an upright body, smooth and even bark, ample leaf, sweet blossom, the delight of bees and a goodly shade at distance of eighteen or twenty five foot. They are also very patient of pruning...

Charles II used them for the 'goosefoot' avenues radiating from Hampton Court Palace. Queen Anne used them for the 'ride' laid out across Windsor Great Park in 1708, by which time not only were there several nurseries in England producing lime saplings but also, on account of William of Orange's accession to the English throne in 1688, the humble lime tree had become closely associated with the Protestant ascendancy.

Evelyn was an enthusiast for the usefulness of lime wood:

> And because of its colour, and easy working, and that it is not subject to split, architects make with it models for their designed buildings; and the carvers in wood not only for small figures, but large statues and intire histories, in bass, and high relieve... The trophies; festoons, frutages, encarpa, and other sculptures in the frontoons, freezes, capitals, pedestals, and other ornaments and decorations to be seen about the choir of St Paul's and other churches; royal palaces, and noble houses in the city and countrey.

Indeed, he not only knew Grinling Gibbons but had advanced his career:

> This day I first acquainted his Majesty [Charles II] with that incomparable young man Gibbon, whom I had lately met with in an obscure place by meere accident as I was walking neere a poor solitary thatched house, in a field in our parish [Deptford], neere Sayes Court.
>
> *Diary*, 18 January 1671.

(Sayes Court was Evelyn's home. He returned to Wotton after the death of his nephew, when it was clear he would be his brother's heir, in 1694).

Continue along the drive to the A25 and cross.

⮑ **Alight from the bus on the A25.**

Walk through Wotton Hatch (a 'hatch' is a fenced plot) pub car park to find the footpath that veers to the right across an open field, and cross the stile onto the drive about 50m before the end of the field. Follow the road down towards Wotton House. If you do not wish to visit Evelyn's garden turn left across a stile at the marked footpath [GR 1236 4709] just before the pasture and grounds of the House (and shortly before the tile-hung house on the right of the drive), and pick up the walk overleaf at ⮑.

If you wish to see John Evelyn's garden, go to reception to ask if they are happy for you to look at it.

George Evelyn, a Surrey man, purchased Wotton in 1579. His family acquired the royal monopoly on gunpowder making, which took place on the Tillingbourne (see p.197). An Evelyn descendant still owns the Wotton estate. In John Evelyn's time the house was a complex of multi-gabled Tudor buildings with a U-shaped courtyard on the north side. Over time, the complex has been extensively altered, first in the second half of the seventeenth century, then in the eighteenth century the north front was given a Georgian centre, and yet later the west wing was rebuilt in a seventeenth century manner. Finally, in 1864 the east wing was rebuilt in mock-Tudor, the work commissioned by William John Evelyn who is more notable, perhaps, for creating a menagerie here. The animals duly escaped, and the kangaroos were last seen legging it towards Leith Hill. Clearly they knew a good place to hide.

Meanwhile the house became the Fire Service College for 30 years following the Second World War, and was then leased by British Telecom until 1986. It was taken over by Principal Hayley as a conference centre and hotel in 2000, after extensive refurbishment.

The principal attraction is the garden, which John Evelyn designed for his brother in 1643. His artificial terraced hill remains intact. It probably took about seven years to create. John Evelyn absented himself from England for a while, finding Cromwellian rule unbearable. In his absence his cousin, George, who had pretensions to architecture, built the temple into the artificial hillside. It seems John was not thrilled, commenting ruefully in his diary, 'he over-built everything.' Nevertheless, the whole effect is one of romantic enthusiasm. It holds an important place in the history of English gardening, for it is the first English attempt at an Italian Renaissance garden.

To the west of this central garden is another curious construction, the Tortoise House, consisting of an Ionic portico in front of a pool. It is probably dated around 1820. The idea apparently was that one took tea on the upper floor and watched terrapins brushing up their breaststroke in the pool below.

Retrace your steps from the house 200m, going back 200m up the drive to resume the walk by turning right over the stile at the marked footpath [GR 1236 4709], just after the tile-hung houses on the left of the drive.

➲ Follow the path southwards and uphill through the trees. Almost immediately turn right at the T-junction with another track.

Look out for traces of hazel coppice (see also, p.172). Evelyn was an enthusiast for coppiced hazel, for its multiplicity of uses for rods, wattles, hoops, forks, angling rods and charcoal. 'Furthermore, there is no wood which purifies wine sooner, than chips of hasel.' He had a tip, too, for thickening coppice, by plashing a 6 metre long stem:

> …. giving it a chop near the foot, to make it succumb; this fastned to the earth with a hook or two, and cover'd with some fresh mould at a competent depth will produce a world of suckers, thicken and furnish a copp'ce speedily.

On your right you will soon notice the string of ponds on this, the principal tributary of the Tillingbourne. The first of these was a bathing pond. John Evelyn left an exhortation to his grandson, also John, 'Endeavour to store your streams with Coarse fish', and would have been glad to learn that his grandson eventually did so, channelling the stream and creating the fishponds in the 1730s. It is one of the earliest 'serpenting' schemes in England. But grandson John may have got the idea from Castle Howard in Yorkshire, which he had just visited.

Do not ignore the magnificent beeches. Beeches were usually planted for decorative purposes, as here. Evelyn noted, 'that which I would observe to you from the wood at Wotton is, that where goodly Oaks grew, and were cut down by my grandfather almost a hundred years since, is now altogether Beech.' He did not state whether these had grown

The approach past the millpond to Friday Street as it looked a century ago.

naturally or been planted by his grandfather. Beech was never valued for its qualities as timber. Yet Evelyn quotes from a ditty about its domestic value for Surrey villagers:

> Hence in the world's best years the humble shed,
> Was happily, and fully furnished:
> Beech made their chests, their beds and the joyn'd stools,
> Beech made the board, the platters and the bowls.

But there was a warning he failed to attach. Woodworm adores beech. Fortunately it loves alder more. Inside beech chests and cupboards, therefore, villagers would put branches of alder, which would attract the pest away from the furniture.

After about 1 km pass a gate and bridge on your right but continue straight ahead for another ½ km until you reach Friday Street millpond.

The millpond was created late in the sixteenth century, probably by George Evelyn, after his purchase of Wotton manor in 1579. It was apparently for a corn mill, although a gunpowder mill may also have stood here briefly. This is not wheat country, and the mill or mills here were closed in the 1730s, when the pond became purely ornamental. The channel seems to have been steepened, to facilitate the 'serpenting' mentioned above. The scene has been decorative rather than useful ever since.

The common room at Goddards. Gertrude Jekyll had a hand in the common room, with its 'old West Surrey' feel: oak flooring with hand-made rush mats, and rush-seated ladder-back chairs. Even the door catches were hand-made by local craftsmen.

(If you wish to visit the hamlet of Friday Street, including the Stephan Langton pub, it lies 200m further up the valley.)

Otherwise turn right and walk along the road through woodland for almost 1km, until you reach a triangular green at the south end of Abinger Common.

The chief attraction at this end of Abinger Common is a Lutyens gem, Goddards, which lies mainly hidden, like almost all Lutyens houses, at the south-west extremity of the green. (But you can enter one of its two gates in the high hedge to get a glimpse of its entrance, and there is a side view on the north side by the cattle grid.) Lutyens built the house in 1899 for a rich shipping magnate and his wife, not as their home but for the use of 'ladies of small means', by which they meant governesses, nurses and the like who worked long hours in London and who could not afford to go away on holiday. They could come and stay here for a week, living communally, using the common room and skittles alley indoors, with walks in the countryside beyond.

Both internally and externally Lutyens lavished much attention on detail. The tall chimneys and other brickwork, the roof of tiles and Horsham slate speak of Surrey, but the off-white roughcast deliberately invokes the harled walls of Scotland, the land of his clients. Since Goddards is now a Landmark Trust property, you can yourself savour the house by taking it for a week provided, that is, you are not of small means.

Take the lane (Abinger Lane) on the west side of green, till you come to Abinger Hatch pub, where refreshment awaits.

The Evelyn Hall, side on to the pub, was built at the end of the nineteenth century in the Arts & Crafts Movement style, and works well within the ensemble of buildings here.

ST JAMES'S CHURCH is worth a brief visit. Until the twentieth century the church boasted a Norman nave, a thirteenth century chancel and a fifteenth century belfry. In 1944 a flying bomb destroyed most of the building except the north chapel (on the right as one approaches from the pub). Following rebuilding the bell turret was struck by lightning in 1964, and the ensuing fire caused widespread damage. It was skilfully restored a second time.

THE EXTERIOR. This is classic Surrey vernacular, with a shingled bell turret. The walls are made of Wealden sandstone, and the nave has high lancet windows on either side.

THE INTERIOR. The timber tie beams for the restored nave come, appropriately, from woodland on Leith Hill. The chancel is Victorian in Early English style. The two large tie beams in the chancel are made of thirteenth century timber. The modern stained glass of the east window is described by Nairn & Pevsner: 'Much the best modern glass in the county, portraying the Living Cross in vivid abstract colouring.' It was created by Lawrence Lee in 1967. Look out for three fine fifteenth century alabaster reliefs respectively by the altar, the font and the porch.

THE CHURCHYARD. The war memorial in the churchyard was designed by Edwin Lutyens. From 1919 when Lutyens designed the Cenotaph, he became increasingly identified with the power and success of the British Empire, notably with New Delhi in 1931, a far cry from his earlier, intimate Surrey houses.

Walk through the churchyard, and at the back take a footpath [GR 1135 4600], passing the remains of a Norman motte (fortified mound) in the garden of Abinger Manor on your left.

The motte is probably eleventh century and once had a wooden palisade and tower on stilts. By the twelfth century fortifications were almost invariably built in stone.

Follow the footpath as straight ahead as possible, ignoring any path to left or right. After 700m or so, disregard the track forking to the right towards the farm buildings, but stick to the footpath between high hedgerows until you can turn right through the yard of Raikes Farm, dogleg through the farm yard taking the marked footpath to the road. Turn right onto the road and after 20 paces turn left along the marked footpath across open fields [GR 1068 4624].

'Raikes' may well be a corruption of the Saxon word *hraca*, meaning throat. The farm lies at the head of a narrow valley, making sense of Raikes Lane which runs down it.

Resist any footpaths to the left and follow the track diagonally across the large field. Having crossed it, veer half right along the track (it swings northwards, directly toward the North Downs) for ¾ km, downhill to Paddington Farm.

Paddington Farm is a real treat. It is one of the oldest of Surrey's farm buildings. It was built in fifteenth century with timber and roughcast plaster, and enlarged in the early sixteenth century with an 'oversailing' gable at each end. It is still miraculously unspoilt by rebuilding or modernisation. The outbuildings, barn and stables, are pretty good too. The manor dates back to before Domesday. Paddington (along with Towerhill in Gomshall) was in the ownership of William de Braose, to whom King John richly demonstrated that he was a cad (see p.167).

Pass the millpond on your right.

There was a mill here by the time of Domesday, 1086, and successive mills over the centuries, used for fulling cloth in the early fourteenth century, and for an iron hammer (see p.25) in the mid-sixteenth century. The last of these mills is still standing, marked 'W. J. Evelyn, 1867'. It fell into disuse probably a century ago, now happily restored as a dwelling. To the left there are extensive watercress beds, as there were in the nineteenth century.

Cross the A25, and continue up the footpath first enclosed by hedgerow, then across an open field and into the woodland for 1½ km. Follow the main path veering round to the right through Abinger Roughs, and follow the track back to the Wilberforce memorial and the car park.

Shere and its hinterland

Distance 7km/4 miles: 2 hours
OS Explorer Map No.145

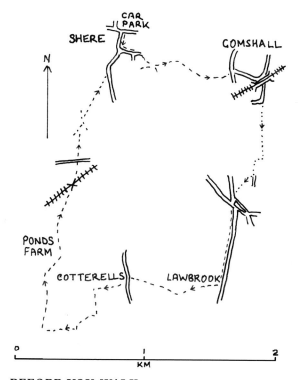

BEFORE YOU WALK

This walk explores the buildings and some of the landscape of a lower greensand parish, and demonstrates some of the changes over the centuries. Much of the soil is astonishingly poor, and one is left wondering how farmers have ever made a living here. But they have. They even established moderately prosperous villages like Shere and Gomshall in the valley. Today Shere is composed to a considerable extent of retirees and commuters, as are most other pretty villages in England. In one important respect, however, Shere is quite unlike other Surrey villages. Its inspired squire in the first half of the twentieth century, Reginald Bray, ensured that by retaining ownership of many village dwellings he could protect the indigenous community from dispossession by moneyed incomers. (To read about him, see the introduction to Walk No.12, p.171.) That said, the old country ways, with the squirarchy and villagers living close to the soil, have in many places given way to a richer, less rooted society, and the social and economic climate has changed. In some ways it is for the better, with the banishment of acute rural poverty, but as one walks this landscape one can see that it has also, in some ways, been for the worse.

Shere has some lovely examples of Surrey's vernacular architecture, and the walk starts through the village. The name Shere derives from *scir*, Old English for 'bright', and is probably the Saxon name for the Tillingbourne.

If car-less: Take the No.32 bus to Shere from Dorking or Guildford.
Refreshment: The William Bray (tel. 01483 202 044), as you walk back into Shere Lane at the end of the walk or the White Horse (tel. 01483 202 518), opposite the village square.
Other attractions: Shere Museum, Gomshall Lane, is delightful and the perfect coda to the walk's exertions. It is open January to December weekends, bank holidays (except Christmas/New Year) 1-5pm, and from April to October on Tuesdays and Thursdays (10am-3pm), www.sheremuseum.co.uk.

Start at the car park just north of Shere's principal T-junction [GR 0735 4800]. Walk to the road, turn left and along Middle Street (the village shopping street), enjoying some of the older houses.

A East Lodge does not pretend to be other than it is, a simple but elegant Arts & Crafts gatehouse for the manor house. It shows such self-confidence that it is no surprise to learn that it was designed by Edwin Lutyens in 1894.

B Manor Cottage, to the left on the opposite side of the road, is late fifteenth century, perhaps a weaver's house. In the 1920s it was a sweet shop run by the Misses Batcock.

SHERE VILLAGE

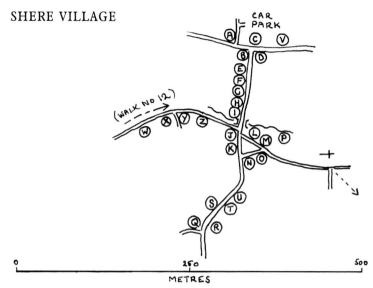

C At the head of the junction stand Vine Cottages, once a very small farm of seven acres. They date from c.1500, but with part dating to the fourteenth century. The front of the west wing was rebuilt in c.1610.

D A merchant's house. The south cross-wing is all that survives of the original late fifteenth century building. The central part was rebuilt in c.1600 and the north cross-wing rebuilt shortly thereafter. By then the ground floor is thought to have been used for weaving fustian, a cotton and flax twill. (Fustian was first made in Egypt, and means 'of Fustat', Cairo's name until 973 AD.)

E Forge Cottage and Bodryn are essentially one building, a few fragments dating from the fourteenth century. Bodryn was a sixteenth century reconstruction in a grander manner undertaken to incorporate a parlour. The forge seems to have been here only from about the mid-nineteenth century.

F The Forge, a timber built blacksmith's forge, was re-fronted in 1914 with old barn timbers. Lutyens had a hand in the design, and his two salamanders may be made out on the gable front. These lizard-like mythical creatures live in fire. By allusion, fire purifies good metal but consumes rubbish.

G The Restaurant next door was designed by Edwin Lutyens in 1892, intentionally in harmony with the older buildings.

H The wooden public toilets started life as the Shere & Albury Volunteer Fire Brigade Station in 1885, as indicated on the proud escutcheon.

I The Pound by the Tillingbourne was sited here in the mid-nineteenth century, and the much-lowered walls are all that remain. It was used for impounding stray animals found in the village street. Claimants had to pay a fee to recover their beasts.

J The bridge over the Tillingbourne is eighteenth century.

K The White Horse was originally built in about 1425 but was fronted with brick and re-roofed in the late seventeenth century. It suffered the indignity of faux-timbers applied to the exterior a century ago. During a restoration in 1955, kegs of brandy were found in a bricked up cellar, confirming tales of smuggled liquor from the early eighteenth century.

Turn left into The Square

L A pair of cottages, once a single white-plastered timber-framed house, which was probably built in the early seventeenth century.

M Pantrys and Minns Cottage (5, The Square). The east end is early seventeenth century with an eighteenth century brick front.

N This cottage was built about 1550, with some rebuilding about 125 years later. It became known as Vaughans, after the bakers here for much of the nineteenth century.

O The shop and part of Haven Cottage were built in the second half of the fifteenth century, probably as a single-storey hall.

P Sayers is L-shaped, built handsomely in brick in 1797. The eighteenth century introduced to country gentry and yeomen high ceilings, tall light-giving windows, with sash openings rather than casements, which were previously the preserve of the aristocracy.

ST JAMES'S CHURCH

St James's is Norman, dating from the late twelfth century, and occupying a perfect village site. Nothing illustrates the shortage of decent stone in Surrey better than this church. The makeshift fabric looks like the work of scavengers. It is composed of two lower greensand kinds of sandstones (Bargate and Carstone), clunch and flint from the North Downs, Horsham slates for the roof, imported Caen stone, recycled Roman tiles and Tudor brick, not to mention a quantity of nondescript rubble.

THE EXTERIOR. Enter by the lychgate, designed by Lutyens in 1901. The central tower is Norman but it was heightened in the mid thirteenth century, while the shingle spire is late fourteenth century. The west doorway (c.1220), by which one enters, has Petworth marble shafts, while the door, dated 1626, boasts a magnificent lock.

THE INTERIOR. The Norman style is heavy. The chancel contains a squint and 'quatrefoil' in the (left) north wall, the remains of an anchoress's cell built against the outside wall, giving the hermit a view through to the altar. On the south side of the interior, there is a fine connecting arch of Petworth marble with leaf capitals between the Bray chancel and the south aisle. The south doorway boasts a zig-zag chevron pattern around the arch.

THE FURNISHINGS. The font is c.1200, one of the oldest in the county. The large chest is thirteenth century, possibly a 'Crusader chest' one of the many installed in churches by Pope Innocent III to raise money for the First Crusade. There are two small medieval memorial brasses in the floor, of Robert Scarcliff the rector, dated 1412, and John Lord Audley, who died in 1491. Look out for the tiny thirteenth century Madonna and Child, mounted on the wall of the south aisle, near the Bray chancel. It was lost by its owner in a nearby field and only discovered in 1880.

On leaving the church, turn left to exit onto the street as it runs along the south side of the church. Take the footpath running south-east, on the left of Church Hill and on the right of the sign Church Lane [GR 0745 4775]. Walk for approximately 200m and at the junction turn left [GR 0755 4765], to follow the track to Gomshall, barely 1km away.

If you are interested in the complexity of the lower greensand layers beneath your feet, see the cross section on p.233.

As you approach Gomshall, look north across the valley. Netley House stands on the slopes of the North Downs, just below the tree line. Originally dating from 1786, it was rebuilt in 1860 after an extensive fire.

The Old Malthouse, Gomshall.

After ½ km, as you pass behind housing on your left, follow the track round to the left (marked in red: No.22 cycle route). Cross the Dorking-Peaslake road and continue straight ahead, along High View (also signposted No.22).

Immediately on your left, on the corner, stands Gomshall Lodge, built around 1820 but now with Arts & Crafts colours: white and green. Next door, the empty plot boasts the exotic trees: a mature Monkey Puzzle, an Atlantic cedar and another very tall conifer, suggesting it was once part of a large handsome garden, perhaps that of Gomshall Lodge itself. Yet even 150 years ago, it was already an open field hosting these mysterious exotics.

The name Gomshall is Saxon and probably means 'Goma's terrace' or shelf of land.

Walk along High View for 250m to the corner.

On the very corner, opposite the railway bridge, stand Malthouse Cottages, once a single medieval house. The south wing (on the corner) is early seventeenth century, and much of it was re-fronted in about 1700 with Bargate stone. Part of it was either a malthouse or the house of a maltster.

Turn right under the railway bridge [GR 0841 4751] (again marked No.22).

Once the railway was laid, Gomshall got terrible stick from an agricultural expert in the 1850s:

> An hour and a half's [train] ride from London.... A state of rural management as completely neglected as ... in the remotest parts of the island... undrained marshes, ill-kept roads, untrimmed hedges, rickety farm buildings, shabby looking cows of various breeds, dirty cottages – nothing indeed exhibiting care or attention, except covered drains from the farmyards, which ostentatiously discharge the richest part of the manure into the open ditches by the wayside.

Thus, while the rest of England was busy improving the soil with manure, bone fertiliser, guano and superphosphates, Surrey – even here in its principal valley – was an embarrassment.

Just beyond the railway bridge on your left stands the Towerhill Farm, one of Surrey's larger domestic houses. Towerhill was once a separate manor connected with Paddington (in Abinger, see p.160). Both estates had been conferred on William de Braose by King John. De Braose, like King John, was a bully. When the two fell out, de Braose, took 'his revenge on those below him, by harassing and oppressing his vassals, and murdering his miserable neighbours in Wales.' Once he knew that his own life was in danger de Braose legged it into exile in 1210. He thought he knew the character of his king. However, thwarted of his quarry, 'that merciless tyrant' King John chased de Braose's wife and son to Corfe Castle where he starved them both to death, amply confirming our Robin Hood view of John as a Baddy. William died in exile in 1212, but must have learnt the fate of his wife and son.

The back of the present house dates from the sixteenth century when it was described as 'a house within a mote'. Moats, it should be noted, were essentially fashion accessories, not a means of defence, except occasionally used to safeguard livestock from theft at night. The main house you now see was built in c.1605 by the family Bray which expanded from Shere to take over this manor also. Its handsome south façade was rebuilt in chalkland red and grey brick in c.1740.

Follow the road but after 200m, where it turns right, continue straight up the footpath for about ½ km.

As you walk up this sunken lane, you will see that it is sufficiently worn away that sandstone rocks occasionally protrude. Sandstone and sand is close to the surface across much of Shere parish, and looking at the ground one is constantly reminded of the poverty of the soil.

Gilbert White, just over the Hampshire border at Selborne, was used to such hollow lanes in the lower greensand, worn away by hooves, feet and rain. Writing to his friend, the hardy Welsh traveller, Thomas Pennant, in 1787, he said of these lanes:

> In many places they are reduced sixteen or eighteen feet beneath the level of the fields; and after the floods, and in the frosts, exhibit very grotesque and wild appearances, from the tangled roots that are twisted among the strata, and from the torrents rushing down their broken sides; and especially when those cascades are frozen with icicles, hanging in all the fanciful shapes of frostwork. These rugged gloomy scenes affright the ladies when they peep down into them from the paths above, and make timid horsemen shudder while they ride along them; but delight the naturalist with their various botany.

On the right, the trees along the side of the lane widen into a 'shaw', a narrow parcel of woodland, with lapsed hazel coppice, which probably served as a windbreak.

At the T-junction [GR 0843 4698] turn right to continue. Immediately on emerging onto a track with houses on the left, fork right along a narrow path with a garden lawn on your left [GR 0835 4681].
The path is hardly welcoming for the walker, hemmed in on either side by relatively modern dwellings with their gardens. The path is old, perhaps even medieval, and must have been used by country people long before the invention of the internal combustion engine and these houses that followed the advent of the car in the 1920s.

Think of Gomshall's labourers, walking out at dawn to the fields or the livestock that needed tending, and returning homeward at dusk, through the seasons of the circling years. The pattern finally petered out only about a century ago. One cannot be sorry that the grinding poverty of such workers has now ceased, but it is not clear that as a society we are happier, and we can certainly regret that the sense of connectedness with the land has now gone. The inhospitable narrowness of this path hints at that. George Sturt spoke with affection of the typical labourer who was his neighbour, who wrested his living from the soil by a familiar knowledge of its properties:

> From long experience – experience older than his own, and traditional amongst his people – he knew the soil of the fields and its variations

almost foot by foot; he understood the springs and streams; hedgerow and ditch explained themselves to him; the coppices and woods, the water-meadows and the winding heaths, the local chalk and clay and stone, all had a place in his regard.

No one, driving across the landscape but not working it by hand, can have that kind of intimacy with what is underfoot.

On reaching the road, turn left but immediately after the road junction, turn right along Lawbrook Lane [GR 0820 4656], passing Lawbrook House after 600m.

'Lawbrook' is probably a corruption of *læge* (fallow, unploughed) and *broc* (low-lying land).

The great house looks eighteenth century, but may be older, while its modern electronic gates signal a greater degree of privacy than country folk traditionally sought. In the mid-nineteenth century a Scottish artist, Edwin Douglas, lived here with his wife, Christiana Feake-Martin. They were early Victorian settlers in Surrey. Belonging to gentry families, both were keen riders. Edwin belonged to the Surrey Union Hunt.

Edwin Douglas' portrait of himself and Christiana Feake-Martin.

Turn right immediately after Lawbrook [GR 0815 4604], following the footpath for 1 km along field boundaries.

Look to your left. On the skyline to the south stand the conifers of Winterfold, once Shere's large expanse of heathland but first planted with Scots pines probably by William Bray (see p.179) about 1800. On the right, there is a good view of Burrows Lea, a large Victorian mansion built on a promontory at Burrows Cross in about 1880 by a successful London lawyer. It typifies the radical transformation of Surrey that took place in the second half of the nineteenth century, as City professionals took possession of the Surrey countryside.

On reaching the next road turn left and admire, if you can, the frontage of Cotterells.

The name refers to the one-time landholder, Stephen de Cothulle, in the 1270s, and his name is probably based on local place name ('hill with a small dwelling on it'). The extra syllable is likely to be a corruption in parlance.

Cottrells was probably built c.1750. It may be a 'copybook' house but it is attractive in its simplicity, its plain brickwork telling you that what you see is what you get, and what you get is pretty nice though, until it tones down, the bright white mortar gives the façade a doll's house effect. Building standards had undergone considerable improvement from the mid-sixteenth century onwards. Roofing with tiles and the introduction of brick as the standard building material for infilling a timber frame had transformed the quality of housing in the sixteenth and seventeenth centuries. By 1700 indoor rooms were larger and a good deal more gracious, and the upper storey rooms no longer cramped under the eaves but elegant in their own right. Sash windows, allowing larger areas of glass without stone mullions and transoms, let in far more light and so replaced casement windows except for labourer's cottages. The vertical sash was probably a Dutch invention. It was introduced to Britain in the 1680s and rapidly swept the board.

Once again electronic gates remind us that those who now inhabit these large houses seek exclusion. It seems that the richer we are, the more apprehensive we become of others. And judging by the yew trees now growing along the front, those outside are perhaps not meant to see inside either, a trait characteristic of many larger Surrey mansions today.

A century ago there was more openness in Surrey, even when houses were grand. Landowners traditionally knew their workforce and the conditions in which they lived. The good ones recognised their community duties. And the irony here in the parish of Shere is particularly acute. Since the end of the fifteenth century the manor belonged to the family Bray. They still own 1,700 acres of common land mainly on the high ground of Hurtwood and Winterfold to the south.

The Brays have long maintained an exceptional interest in their environment and the wellbeing of the community in their charge, none more so than Reginald Bray (1869-1950). He was well aware of the rapidly changing social

Reginald Arthur Bray, Shere's remarkable, far-sighted and enlightened squire.

order in a period of urbanisation and deep agricultural recession, and he devoted his energy to managing the difficult transition. His priority was to safeguard the viability of the estate on which a community of 2,500 people depended. He took his responsibility for decent housing in the community as an absolute duty. He also welcomed opening up the Surrey countryside for people to enjoy, particularly Londoners of low income. Cyclists from London had 'discovered' Shere as early as the 1880s. When Bray began to administer the estate on behalf of his father, he welcomed this new class of visitor. He thought that those of modest means living in cities should benefit from enjoyment of the countryside. So he was among the first in Britain to provide hostels for the YHA, at Holmbury St Mary and at Ewhurst. Alongside this, he set up a network of voluntary agreements with other landowners to protect the hills from speculative builders. Thus Leith Hill, the Hurtwood and Winterfold, and the crest and southern slopes of the North Downs are as they are today, open countryside without despoiling developments. Reginald Bray strove to preserve the community and the landscape from the worst excesses of private wealth and open the latter for all to enjoy.

Living as we do at a time of astonishingly rampant capitalism, we owe such visionary people and the movements they helped establish, like the YHA and the National Trust, an enormous amount.

Turn right along the footpath immediately on the left of Cotterells [GR 0739 4604].

The soil here is not quite pure sand but nearly so, with a thin friable top-soil. It seems almost a miracle than anything beyond bracken will grow. The farmer here is committed to organic farming and this, perforce, is pasture. Plough it up, and without massive dressing with humus it would probably turn to a dustbowl. Unlike the Weald with its heavy clay just 4km away, this is a fragile landscape demanding gentle treatment.

Follow the path, which doglegs around the field. On the dogleg, go through a wicket gate and turn right through a second, walking down into a dip. Resist the temptation to turn right in the dip (down the track beside the metal fencing enclosing young oaks) but continue straight ahead, over the knoll and down through the next field.

You will pass an old oak fence on your left just before reaching Pond's Lane. It marks the edge of Dilton Farm, which has been here since the Middle Ages, if not earlier. Now very old and frail, its rails look crude and crooked but they are infinitely superior to modern sawn rails. These have been cleft, a method which does not break the cellular structure of the grain. Cleft oak rails survive far longer than sawn ones, since a saw will cut through the cells, leaving them exposed to rain and fungal attack, both of which more than halve the life of the rail. The whole fence was assembled without the use of a single nail, the shaven ends inserted into mortised posts, and dowelled. The makers of this fence, who probably died almost a century ago, knew what they were doing.

On reaching a vehicle-width track (Ponds Lane), turn right [GR 0670 4570].

Note the hazel coppice lining the road. Hazel used to be a lot more common than it is today, with large areas devoted to coppice. It is to be found in hedgerows and on the peripheries of woodland, since it cannot endure much shade. Its principal use as coppiced wood was to make hurdles for livestock enclosures and wattle (as the framework for applying daub) for the walls of buildings, most of which have since been replaced with brick. Hazel was also used as thatching spars, and for making the hoops of barrels. The two great virtues of hazel rods are that, while green, they can be split down the middle, and also that they can also be twisted back on themselves without snapping, and are thus brilliant for weaving hurdles (see p.34). The decline of hazel coppice occurred with agrarian enclosures, first in the Tudor period and then more intensively in the eighteenth century, when so many hedgerows were planted, thus greatly reducing the need for portable hurdles. Likewise, (hazel) wattle-and-daub gave way to brickwork in the seventeenth century. Finally, wire fencing reduced the surviving hazel in hedgerows.

Until the catastrophic advent of the American grey squirrel a century ago, hazel trees provided villagers with a good crop of hazel nuts. There were red squirrels around in 1910, when the American species was introduced. By 1950 the red squirrel had virtually vanished. Today, grey squirrels will strip any hazel trees bare.

Such a valuable tree is commemorated in many place names, in Surrey most notably in Haslemere. John Evelyn reckoned his surname was derived from the Latin name for hazel, *avellana.*

After ¾ km, pass Ponds Farm.

The house is set back behind a wall and half-hidden behind the breeze-block barn. You will start to note the dramatic change of soil to sand underfoot.

After another 400m you will reach a row of houses on the right of the track.

Until 1920 there was an orchard here and a single dwelling. A commercial laundry was built in about 1925. Most of the houses look as if they are conversions from the original laundry.

Turn left to cross the railway.

It is an apparent contradiction to think of the railway line as a contribution to nature. Yet, unlike roads where the traffic is frequent, flycatching bird species, like the red-backed shrike, have learnt to wait patiently for a passing train, ready to strike when it disturbs the insect life in the foliage.

Once across, turn right immediately across wooded heathland (Shere Heath). Follow the main path (resisting forking right at the cross path after 150m).

Shere Heath comes as a sharp reminder of the drifts of almost pure sand to be found in virtually every parish, land that could be used for livestock grazing by landless or almost landless rural labourers, and for harvesting timber, underwood and turf for fuel. They called it the 'waste', but this land had its own valuable qualities and the word meant something quite different from the meaning we give it in our truly wasteful society.

Cross a tarmac road and follow the path in the same direction till it descends. Where it runs into another path, turn right but almost immediately, on joining another sunken lane, turn left downhill and then almost immediately up a track to the right [GR 0703 4728]. Once over the rise, the main path descends, and fields open up on either side. On your right is a house anxiously growing a cypress screen to hide the housing estate opposite. Walk straight through the housing estate, joining Shere Lane at the top of the village. Turn left.

Houses of note walking back into Shere:

Q Dial Cottage is probably mid-seventeenth century.

R Knaveshurst, opposite, is late seventeenth century, and made of brick and Bargate stone.

S The long industrial building is an old malthouse, built around 1830.

T Yew Trees and Trenchmore are seventeenth century.

U Gallandes was built in c.1742.

Retrace your steps to the far end of Middle Street, but at the T-junction instead of turning left back to the car park, turn right and walk for 50m.

The roughcast Village Hall (**V**) on the left was built in 1920 as a memorial following the First World War, a nice example of its epoch. It stands on the right of its predecessor, the brick hall built in 1897 to mark Queen Victoria's Diamond Jubilee, now the hugely enjoyable Shere Museum.

Shere, the Downs, Newlands Corner and Albury

Distance 10km/6 miles: 3 hours
OS Explorer Map No.145

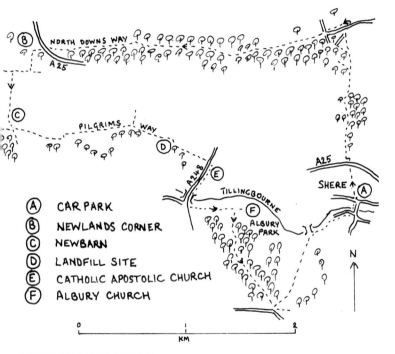

Ⓐ CAR PARK
Ⓑ NEWLANDS CORNER
Ⓒ NEWBARN
Ⓓ LANDFILL SITE
Ⓔ CATHOLIC APOSTOLIC CHURCH
Ⓕ ALBURY CHURCH

BEFORE YOU WALK

This walk takes you across the geological divides between the lower greensand, the gault, the chalk and the clay-with flint. Its principal points of interest are Newlands Corner on the chalk, where there is refreshment and a magnificent view, and Albury Park where there is a remarkable and very old church, and the pretty village of Shere, where refreshment is plentiful.

The first part of the walk does not command lovely views, but from

Newlands Corner onwards, it is one pleasant prospect after another. I hope that you will be struck not merely by its beauty but how different generations have seen the landscape.

As you walk, you may wonder how it has all been so well preserved. Your democratic instincts will be challenged, for we owe the loveliness of Shere and much of the land surrounding it to the passion of the family Bray, the Shere squirarchy. In the early twentieth century Reginald Bray (1869-1950) used his powers to ensure that Shere remained lovely for future generations. (For his portrait, and more about this man, see p.171.) His family held land up to the crest of the North Downs and as far south as Farley Green. He lived frugally and devoted his energies to steering Shere through the cataclysmic changes that so transformed (and spoilt) much of Surrey. And when he was not saving Shere for posterity, he was active as a social reformer in low-income Camberwell. Bray's plan for protecting the countryside, in the words of one historian, 'was out of all proportion to the area of land involved on account of the high landscape value of the districts concerned and the example they set to others….[and] it was his ability to expound their principles as never before in English planning which finally won the day.' In brief, by his personal commitment and local influence, Bray laid down the foundations for the concept that became the Green Belt, with the notion that the landscape should be protected for all of us to enjoy. Just occasionally, the principle of enlightened paternalism achieves things which democracy, committees and local government seem less able to do. We can all be deeply thankful for Squire Bray.

Bray's descendants are still here. They still own about forty village properties, not as a family milch-cow but in order to foster the community of Shere and its rootedness in the village, through secure tenancies. Shere is not simply beautiful. It stands in wonderfully defiant contrast with most Surrey villages where the old community is long since gone, edged out by moneyed professionals.

If car-less: take the No.32 bus to Shere from either Dorking or
    Guildford, and go to the car park, tucked behind the T-junction.
Refreshment: The White Horse, Shere Lane, opposite the village square.
Other attractions: Shere Museum, Gomshall Lane, a gentle reward
    after the day's exertions. Open weekends and bank holidays,
    1300-1700, and April-Oct also Tues and Thurs 1000-1700,
    www.sheremuseum.co.uk.

Start: At the car park near the T-junction in Shere [GR 0735 4800]. Turn right out of the car park entrance, up the unmetalled track running straight uphill.
As soon as you have walked under the A25, find the very first opportunity (within 40 paces of the bridge) to dogleg up onto the parallel path to the left. Continue walking straight uphill.
You will immediately be aware of crossing onto chalk, since the flora will change, most notably with an abundance of yew trees.

After ¾ km you will reach the top of the hill at Hollister Farm.
The name 'Hollister' may be based upon the one-time prevalence of holly trees hereabouts. Today, however, you will notice lots of young sycamores on either side of the path, a sign that you have left the chalk and reached the clay-with-flints. Sycamores love clay. Originally they were planted here, perhaps without awareness of how easily they propagate themselves. Sycamores were probably introduced to Britain in the early Middle Ages, but no one knows exactly when. In north Britain they do well, as hardy and valued hedgerow trees. In the south they often seem more like a weed. John Evelyn was the first to express his disgust in writing, the sycamore being:

> ... much more in reputation for its shade than it deserves; for the honey-dew leaves, which fall early (like those of the ash) turn to mucilage and noxious insects, and putrifie with the first moisture of the season, so as they contaminate and mar our walks.

In south Britain the sycamore remains unloved, except among ornithologists who know that it harbours more aphids and other invertebrates for birds than most other trees.

Near the farm entrance, the North Downs Way sign points to left and right (westwards and eastwards). Turn left past the entrance to Hollister Farm and then follow the track for ½ km, ignoring a couple of tracks branching left, the first seductively downhill, the second more or less on the flat.
These two tracks lead down into a wonderful gully called Combe Bottom, an ancient track only accessible, sadly, if you run the gauntlet of impossible traffic in the adjoining lane. This was a favoured smuggler's route. An old shepherd who worked on the chalk downs and who was eighty-two years of age in 1889, told how smugglers used to bring their pack-loads of brandy by Combe Bottom and hide them among the thickets of juniper, thorn, and bramble. It only remains for me to quote what I learnt

at school (in case you didn't), about the 'run' from the Sussex coast to London:

> Five and twenty ponies,
> Trotting through the dark –
> Brandy for the Parson, 'Baccy for the Clerk.
> Them that asks no questions isn't told a lie –
> Watch the wall my darling while the Gentlemen go by!
>
> Rudyard Kipling, *Puck of Pook's Hill* (1906)

After almost ½ km you will reach a T-junction [GR 0720 4940]. Cross the road, turn right for 15 paces, then turn sharp left along the footpath marked North Downs Way (i.e. in a westerly direction).

There is a mysterious concave concrete pit by the turning, probably of Second World War vintage. Its purpose is unclear.

After 250m cross a road, and walk through the car park.

It is well worth taking a look at the car park noticeboard, where the Surrey Wildlife ranger will have posted a seasonal newsletter about the landscape.

Continue walking along the North Downs Way through the woodland for 2½ km, until you emerge at Newlands Corner [GR 0440 4920].

This terrain, of course, is clay-with-flints, hence it is wooded, not tilled. Flint is notorious for breaking ploughshares. Were the flints to be cleared, itself a backbreaking job, the clay would still make only indifferent arable. Traditionally the woodland would have been used principally for coppice.

With our preference for the importation of cheap softwoods, we have largely lost the economic value of native hardwood species on which our forefathers depended for construction materials, vehicles, tools and fuel. Here one can see stands of exotic trees planted, it seems, by the county council about 35 years ago. They comprise hemlock, Lawson's cypress and western red cedar. The plan is progressively to thin them over a number of years and to allow for natural regeneration, the likely colonisers being birch, ash (which loves chalk, if it is not eliminated by ash dieback) and the prolific sycamore.

On the right are the remains of an old wood bank, with one or two venerable yews. Where there are deciduous trees there is also magnificent liana-like wild clematis, or old man's beard (another chalk lover), hanging from the branches.

It is frustrating that the tree cover on the left (south) side obscures the fine view from the North Downs, although the reward comes at Newlands Corner. If you suffer boredom walking along this track, here is a little more about two other Shere Brays.

The man who brought the family to Shere, and also to eminence, was also named Reginald. He had been involved in a plot to overthrow Richard III in 1483, supporting Henry Tudor's aim to wrest the crown from the House of York. He may have been at the battle of Bosworth in 1485 and is credited with finding Richard's crown under a thorn bush on the battlefield and placing it on Henry Tudor's head, but of this we cannot be sure. He was appointed chancellor of the duchy of Lancaster later that year and remained one of Henry VII's closest advisers. He was rewarded with the gift of several estates but he purchased Shere outright in 1495. At their greatest extent Reginald Bray's estates, obtained by gift or by purchase, were to be found in eighteen counties.

The other eminent family member was William Bray, a distinguished antiquary, who lived from 1736 to 1832. He grew up at Shere and became a lawyer. He wrote the earliest account of baseball after a game on Easter Monday in 1755, in which he had participated, along with the sublimely named Miss Molly Flutter. As steward to many Surrey manors, he became immensely knowledgeable about their history. Consequently, as co-author, he ensured the completion and publication of the most important printed work on the county, *The History and Antiquities of the County of Surrey*, published in three volumes, 1804-1814, having rescued what was going to be the work of one individual, Owen Manning, whose eyesight suddenly failed in 1796. Bray and Manning became very close friends while working on the project with Bray, literally, seeing it through.

We owe William Bray another major debt, for it was he who, in 1818, transcribed John Evelyn's manuscript journal into the delightful *Diary* (see p.148) we have today, over a century after Evelyn's death. It is a work of great scholarship on Bray's part (and recommended reading). He also introduced Scots pine to the Hurtwood heathlands in about 1800.

Newlands Corner: cross the road and walk to the car park before turning left onto the greensward to enjoy one of the most spectacular south-facing views of Surrey.

To enjoy Newlands Corner one needs no more than the magnificent view southwards. Yet here is a ridiculous fact worthy of Monty Python, and one which tells you about those who see the landscape in purely utilitarian terms. Following the rise of the Volunteer movement, the precursor of the Territorial Army, in 1859 (see p.125), Newlands Corner became a popular location for manoeuvres. Forty years later a new fangled contraption made it possible to report that,

> Newlands Corner, the centre of the rifle clubs of Surrey, has been made the scene of assaults and counter-attacks made by Volunteer cyclists against defending bands of riflemen. The riflemen have held their own under the severest fire; Ministers and distinguished soldiers have watched them.

It is hard to imagine the fittest of cyclists, on his wretchedly heavy machine, being remotely capable of engaging 'the enemy' if he had just pedalled up from the valley. Bicycles remained part and parcel of army equipment well into the 1960s, when the author himself mastered the intricacies of army bicycle drill. And who, having been thus drilled, has not thrilled at the cry: Prepare to Mount?

Walk a little way down the slope, looking out for the black barn and buildings of Newbarn in the valley below, slightly right of centre. That is what you are making for. Descend straight downhill and turn right along the path (running just in front of the belt of trees), walking for about 150m to a small, green, walkers' sign pointing you ahead; but ignore it and turn left, through the tree belt to find the wicket gate and path leading you to Newbarn.

The chalk hillside has a very attractive sweep to it. Newbarn stands in the narrow belt of arable land, just off the chalk, but where chalk has washed down to render the narrow band of gault and the adjacent lower greensand more fertile. This narrow belt of arable runs virtually the whole way along the foot of the escarpment, from Farnham to Folkestone. It was probably the first land in Surrey to be settled by humans in prehistoric times, before they ventured onto the Downs, and then into the Weald. Walking through Newbarn farmyard, note the dark carstone (presumably extracted from St Martha's Hill on your right, p.193) used for one of the outbuildings to your left.

Pass Newbarn, and after 120m turn left along the marked bridleway, part of the so-called Pilgrim's Way [GR 0417 4850].

The fantasy of Chaucerian pilgrims making their gentle way along here is almost irresistibly seductive. However, resist it you must. The term 'the Pilgrim's Way' was first coined in the appendix to a book about Canterbury Cathedral by Arthur Way, a local antiquarian, in 1855. It might have died a natural death had not an amateur archaeologist and captain in the Royal Engineers, who had read the appendix, been assigned to survey the first large-scale map of south-west Surrey for the Ordnance Survey. It is, therefore, Captain Edward James RE whom we must thank for inventing the Pilgrim's Way, which has run across OS maps ever since. In fulfilment of his fantasy, a series of books, of which Hilaire Belloc's, *The Old Road* (1904) is the most famous, have dribbled their way into print ever since. The argument runs thus: 'if pilgrims had made their way from Winchester to Canterbury to pray at the shrine of St Thomas Becket, the most obvious trackway to use was the one that ran partly along the foot of the North Downs and partly along their escarpment.' Conveniently, there were indeed very old tracks along stretches of the alleged route. Yet those tracks that did exist, both at the foot of the escarpment and on top of it, might as easily have been for the benefit of local droving. As a whole they were disjointed and for significant parts of the supposed route, most notably the stretch from Winchester to Farnham, no such track existed at all. Nor was there any documentary evidence to suggest that the Pilgrim's Way had ever existed. This proved no discouragement to Captain James. He eagerly invented.

James and his successors ignored the argument that such pilgrims might well have travelled further north, perhaps making use of river transport to London or to Dartford, and then following that nice Roman road to Canterbury. Or they might just as well have travelled along the valley tracks from one settlement to another, from Farnham to Guildford to Dorking to Reigate and so on, benefitting from the hostelries in these settlements along the way. Indeed, the townsfolk would have been anxious not to lose passing trade. Such practical considerations were swept aside in pursuit of romance.

By the early decades of the twentieth century a new argument had been thrown into the ring: that the route the pilgrims took was much older, possibly dating back to the Bronze Age or before, the track along the chalk ridge taking travellers, for example, from Stonehenge to the Kent coast where they could cross to the Continent. There are two problems about this theory. One would expect to find substantial evidence of pre-historic settlements and activity along this supposedly arterial route. There is such evidence along the Thames valley, yet precious little to suggest a route along the Downs. The second problem is that the population was so small and the number of folk actually trading between the Continent and Wessex so few, that no arterial route as such is likely to have existed. That parts of the track are old is not in question. We simply have no evidence to date them, nor to say who might have used them apart from people on local business.

After ½ km dogleg left and right around Water Lane Cottages to maintain the same direction. After another 400m look back before entering the belt of trees on your right.

The views here, both east and west are redolent of that attractive 1930s art which typified travel posters of the time. Yet imagine what a Victorian water colourist would have made of this, something more detailed, more intimate and very much sweeter. Go back further to Turner and we risk being swept away with emotion, the hillside bathed in the setting sun. In the early eighteenth century the landscape might only have been a parkland backdrop, to a great house or to a portrait. In the seventeenth century few but the Dutch would have deemed the landscape worthy of attention and before then, in the late Middle Ages it would have served simply as a backdrop to the Holy Family. The truth is that across the centuries, artists have persuaded us to see the landscape differently. Long may they continue to do so.

Follow the path for another 400m.

If you are intrigued by the use of holly on the woodbank on the left, see p.65.

Resisting the path branching left, continue straight past Timbercroft, and shortly thereafter (150m) take care to veer right up the footpath [GR 0540 4850], away from the made up track as you approach Sand Pit landfill site. Cross the access road to the landfill site.

It is worth pausing to see the horrific rubbish mountain on your right and to absorb the enormity of what we throw away. It really is no joke. Every schoolchild should, among other things, be brought to see a landfill site to learn about the wilful wastefulness of the adult world.

Continue through the trees and across the field, and turn right along the A248, but cross to the east (church) side, where there is a footpath.

On your left stands the so-called Catholic Apostolic Church, now closed, a piece of pseudo-Perpendicular. The Catholic Apostolic Church was the brainchild of a Scots Presbyterian, Edward Irving (1792-1834), the son of an Annan tanner. It was as a preacher in London in the 1820s that Irving became famous, and people flocked to hear his bizarre blend of Presbyterianism and ritual, and his belief in the imminence of the Second Coming. The joint founder of the so-called Irvingite Church was Irving's close friend, Henry Drummond (see below), who happened to own Albury Park, hence the church, built in 1840. (The architect was a minor Gothic Revivalist, William McIntosh Brooks.) The church closed in 1901, but remains ready, at a moment's notice, for the Second Coming.

Just after the road crosses the Tillingbourne, turn left and left again for an ecclesiastical treat [GR 0575 4787]. Walk through Albury Park to the church of St Peter and St Paul.

WHY ALBURY CHURCH IS NOW BEREFT OF ITS VILLAGE

The grounds of the Park were once the site of Albury village. The green abutted the village church. This idyllic scene was sharply disrupted when Captain the Hon. William Clement Finch RN purchased the Albury estate from his brother, the 4th Earl of Aylesford, in 1782. He had the money, having recently captured a valuable Spanish ship. Finch may have lived cheek-by-jowl with his crew at sea but he was most certainly not prepared to do so with the *hoi polloi* ashore. Like many landowners, he decided to remove people who lived near his house. It was the beginning of the golden age of social hierarchy, public schools and class deference from which, since the 1960s, we are mercifully emerging, albeit too slowly.

Finch's first act was to obtain magistrate's orders to re-route village roads, and to enclose the village green. (The traces of ground disturbance remain visible.) Then he commandeered part of the churchyard. He also started to harass the villagers until, one by one, most moved to Weston Street, where the present village now stands. Finch died in 1794, with the giddy rank of rear-admiral. For a few years the villagers enjoyed a respite, but in 1811 a new landlord took up where Finch had left off, demolishing virtually all the remaining cottages and re-housing their inhabitants in Weston.

In 1819 the estate was purchased by Henry Drummond (1786-1860). Drummond's wealth derived from his senior partnership in Drummond's Bank but he had wide interests, endowing a chair in political economy at Oxford (Adam Smith already having established this vital field with his *Inquiry into the Nature and Causes of the Wealth of Nations* in 1776), entering Parliament (to which he returned in later life as member for West Surrey), and embracing the Catholic Apostolic faith. After twenty years' residence, Drummond obtained a licence to build a new Romanesque-style church (also by Brooks) for the villagers in Weston. He closed the church here in 1842 and removed its internal fittings to the new church. He decided to make the old church into a mortuary chapel for his family. Drummond may have been a patrician but he did not share his predecessors' desire to marginalize the ordinary villagers. It is to his credit that he strenuously organised relief for the villagers during 'the Hungry Forties' when the potato crop failed causing widespread hunger, and that he was a pioneer of the allotment system.

Before entering the church it is worth glancing down to the valley bottom, the Tillingbourne and the garden beyond.

In 1667 John Evelyn designed a new garden here for his friend, Henry Howard. It was of a geometric design, influenced by the French gardens he had seen during his years of exile during the Civil War, its centrepiece being a rectangular canal where the Tillingbourne ran, no less than 400m long and 80m wide, a very considerable expanse of water. Sadly, it had no chance of survival against the later English landscape movement. The canal was filled in and the geometric features erased. We know they must have vanished by the time William Cobbett rode this way in November 1822, for he pronounced of the gardens, 'without any exception, [they] are, to my fancy, the prettiest in England; that is to say, that I ever saw in England.' Cobbett, with his hatred of all things foreign (which, within his generous ambit, also embraced Scots, Jews and Quakers) would never have given the time of day to a geometric garden that smacked of foreign-ness.

THE CHURCH OF ST PETER AND ST PAUL

THE EXTERIOR

- The tower seems to be Norman (c.1140), but is built on Saxon foundations, and its small windows are thought to be Saxon.
- The unusual shingled cupola is probably seventeenth century, replacing the typically squat shingled spire characteristic of many churches in the area. The chancel was a ruin until repaired and re-roofed in 1988.
- The porch is one of the best preserved in Surrey, late fifteenth century woodwork, while the door hinges have been recycled from the previous early fourteenth century door.

THE INTERIOR

- The nave is built on the Saxon foundations, with a small area of Saxon herring-bone rubble low on the north wall.
- The south aisle was rebuilt c.1300. The faded wall-painting, c.1480, depicts St Christopher carrying the Christ Child, although what can now be seen is only the head and shoulders of the saint, to his left a hermit's cell and to his right a ship. The mural was originally much more extensive, and seems to have been done at the same time that the north porch was built and (presumably) the south door filled in, thus allowing the painting to extend across most of the south wall. It seems it was plastered over to protect it from the Puritans. At some point the old south door was re-opened, thereby destroying a substantial part of the image. The remains of the painting were discovered when a chunk of plaster fell away in 1884. A description in 1919 indicates the saint, wearing turban, shirt and mantle, fording a river with a staff in his hand, bearing on his left shoulder the Christ Child. To the right was a castle, and over this an estuary in which two ships seem to be in combat. Whether as a result of exposure, or the repeated attempts at conservation, most of what was visible in 1919 has now been lost.
- The monumental brass on the floor is of Sir John Weston, 1440, whose family had held the manor of Albury from c.1200.
- The south transept has been converted into a 'mortuary chapel' for the Drummond family. Drummond commissioned the prime Gothic

Revival designer of the day, Augustus Welby Pugin, and this chapel is, according to Pugin's biographer, one of his most successful works. In 1847 Pugin's design, which used elements of various Drummond armorial bearings, was executed by a little known painter, Thomas Earley. The eagle is the Drummond crest, while the entry screen bears the Drummonds' motto in Scots, 'Gang Warily', a reminder of the dangers of life in the Borders but which, translated into today's mild Surrey, means 'Mind How You Go.'

On leaving the church gate strike off to the left at roughly 45 degrees.
If you are thirsting to know about the house, it was damaged in a severe fire in 1697, and today is private accommodation, partitioned into individual flats.

As you cross the open parkland, take a sign-posted path through a wicket gate on the edge of the woodland [GR 0620 4775], and up to the summit of the hill and beyond. Keep following the path without deviation.
Part of this walk is through oppressive conifer plantation. Before emerging from the estate, note the avenue of old chestnut trees on your left, an old approach to the house.

Albury Park as it looked before it was rebuilt after the fire of 1697.

Albury Park after its exterior was extensively remodelled by Henry Drummond.

When you reach the exit to Albury Park, just before reaching the tarmac turn sharpest left (marked Shere Parish Millennium Trail) [GR 0660 4700].
You will find yourself walking through venerable parkland, down another magnificent but unusual avenue of sweet chestnut pollards. They must be at least 500 years old.

When you reach the valley bottom, turn left and right immediately through 'Vicky's Gate', just before the footbridge (Chantry Bridge) over the Tillingbourne [GR 0690 4765].
Tillingbourne is not the original name of this stream. Its previous Saxon name was Sherbourne, 'bright stream', hence the village of Shere.

Follow the Lime Walk through to Shere, where refreshment awaits.
Dwellings of interest (on map, p.163) along Lower Street, from the fourth on the right, are

W Wickhams and Weyside is a timber-framed two-storey house, mid-seventeenth century. It once had a smoke bay, later converted into a loft for smoking salted bacon. For this, Gertrude Jekyll tells us, the

Village tradesmen standing on the Tillingbourne bridge in Shere, c.1910.

favoured material was the outer oak bark, which the tanner did not want:

> This rough bark, the 'sole', as country people called it, is put aside for bacon-curing, and sells readily for sixpence a sack. When once alight it keeps on smouldering a long time. No kind of resinous wood, such as fir or pine can be used for smoking bacon.

The smell of smoke, however, was easier to endure than that of salted bacon, as in one case Jekyll knew:

> It was proposed to turn the space to account as a cupboard; but, in spite of thorough cleansing and lime-whiting, its walls were so deeply impregnated with the briny infiltration that they have received from the tons of salted pig-meat that have hung against them for centuries, that the place cannot be used for any other purpose than the keeping of crockery.

John Wickham owned the house from 1727-1771, passing it to his daughter, Elizabeth. So it comes by its name honestly.

X The Old Prison is probably early seventeenth century and was formerly part of a larger holding demolished in 1786. That the front wing was once the lock-up is hearsay. The barred window means nothing, for all windows were thus barred before glass became cheaply available.

Y The Old Forge, on the corner of Orchard Road, was probably built in the first half of the seventeenth century. It contained a butcher's shop when it was sold in 1795, and in the nineteenth century it was a wheelwright's shop, with the forge in the outshot, the tall chimney clearly for the forge furnace.

Z Willow and Ash Cottages were once part of a row of dwellings known as Stiles, built in 1475 as a single bay hall recessed in the Wealden style. The chimney and floor were installed in the mid-sixteenth century. One must bear in mind that the floors of most dwellings prior to this time were usually a hardened mixture of clay, dung and ox blood, the surface of which could be burnished but would, of course, have remained damp. Look out for the hollow mouldings on the fascia boards. In the nineteenth century it was owned by the same wheelwright who used the forge next door.

(For other Shere dwellings see pp. 162-64.)

Turn left for the car park, turn right for the White Horse and the William Bray beyond.

WALK

13

The Romancy Vale: St Martha's Hill and Chilworth Powder Mills

Distance 8¾km/5 miles: 2½ hours
OS Explorer Map No.145

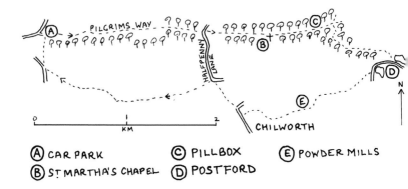

ⒶCAR PARK ⒸPILLBOX ⒺPOWDER MILLS
ⒷST MARTHA'S CHAPEL ⒹPOSTFORD

BEFORE YOU WALK

This walk takes you eastwards up onto the geologically extraordinary ridge of St Martha's Hill, from where there are stunning views southwards, then down into the Tillingbourne valley to return through the heartland of the Tillingbourne's industrial past, notably the ruins of its famous gunpowder mills. The return is by one of the old routes along the lower slopes of St Martha's Hill.

If car-less: From Guildford Station, either follow the road sign for the A281 to Shalford for 1km, and turn right up Pilgrims Way to the car park (on the unmetalled extension, where the road name changes to Echo Rd) or take a quieter route: in Guildford High Street turn right through Tunsgate, continue in the same direction across Castle Square, South Hill, Warwicks Bench Rd, taking the footpath in same direction where road turns sharp left. Continue along the footpath across Chantry View Road, emerging where the Pilgrim's Way turns into Echo Road, opposite the unmetalled extension to the car park.

Refreshment: halfway through the walk, from the Powder Mills one can walk to the A248 for the Percy Arms, Chilworth (tel. 01483 561765, www.thepercyarms.net).

Make a day of it: visit Guildford: Museum, and Castle Arch, open Mon-Sat, 1100-1700 (tel. 01483 444751, www.guildford.gov.uk/museum), the Cathedral, and also Dapdune Wharf, Wharf Road, Guildford (tel. 01483 561389, www.riverwey@nationaltrust.org.uk).

Start at the Pilgrim's Way car park on the south-east side of Guildford. The car park [GR 0035 4835] is on the unmetalled extension of the Pilgrim's Way, itself a turning off the Shalford Road, the A281, which runs south from Guildford town centre.

Follow the track of the Pilgrim's Way (aka North Downs Way) from the end of the car park straight on through Chantry Wood (Chantry Cottage, the old Keeper's cottage, stands on the right of the Way) for 1.5km without deviation. The wood was an endowment for a chantry in Holy Trinity Church, Guildford, where prayers were said for the soul of Henry Norbrigge, Mayor of Guildford, who had died in 1512. With the Reformation occurring only 22 years later, the woodland must have passed into secular hands, although the name survived. Enjoy the beautiful woodland, either side of the track. As you walk you will notice pieces of carstone (see p.236) in the track, a very dark, high-ferric content variant of Bargate stone. After 1km or so, there is a field on either side of the track, which becomes as sandy as the seashore, yet up to the left rises the chalk escarpment of the North Downs. After the field, the woodland on the left was once known as 'Farthing Copse', a long time ago presumably coppice rented for a farthing. On the right lay Halfpenny Copse.

On reaching the tarmac lane (Halfpenny Lane) turn left and immediately right to continue along the Pilgrim's Way. After about 400m, with the ground rising, ignore the lower right fork of the track (marked 'bridleway') and take the higher track (marked 'footpath') straight up the hill to reach St Martha's Church [GR 0280 4830]. Walk into the churchyard and take a well-deserved seat.

ST MARTHA'S CHURCH

This is the church of the parish of Chilworth, in the valley below, the only one in England to be dedicated to St. Martha. It may be a misnomer. The church is possibly referred to in the Domesday Book, and

St Martha's Church in its ruinous state in the 1820s.

surviving fragments of stonework indicate that it was certainly standing before 1150. There has been plenty of speculation that its name was once 'Martyr', on account of the fact that St Martha's was granted to Newark Priory (see p.217), originally founded in 1199 and then dedicated to the memory of St Thomas Becket (martyred in 1173) as 'Sancti Martyris'. So one can see how the name might have morphed into Martha. Critically, we seem not to know what it was called before 1173. In the sixteenth century the hill was still 'Martyr's Hill'.

By the mid-nineteenth century the building was largely a ruin. The present chapel was built in 1848-50 by a well-known local restorer, Henry Woodyer, using the materials of the Norman ruin and locally available carstone, which you will see underfoot as you walk. No attempt was made to replicate what had already gone, but it was rebuilt faithfully in the strictly plain Norman style. The original building had a tower over the west door. That tower has now disappeared, and the west doorway is set into the original early twelfth century archway. Inside (if it is open) the four-pointed crossing arches of the transept, beneath the present central tower, are largely made from reused material from the original, c.1170. The twelfth century font is a fugitive from Hambledon, decoratively carved in 1850, copying an authentic pattern of the period.

The reconstruction unleashed huffing and puffing on the part of some pundits. To the authors of *The Victoria County History*, it is 'An object

Rippled paving stones.

lesson in the mischievous results of fanciful restoration', while it receives praise from others. Nairn & Pevsner reckoned, 'The result is an impressive job in the Norman style, making no attempt to be a copy, but at the same time expressing the spirit of the lonely exposed site perfectly.'

As for the view, enjoy, as John Aubrey described it in 1718, 'this little Romancy Vale.' Beneath the chapel on the southern slope are the remains of five circular banks, each about 30m in diameter, indicative apparently of Bronze Age henge monuments, some of the very few Bronze Age sites that actually abut the Pilgrim's Way (on this fraudulent name, see p.181) along the crest of the ridge. At the bottom of the valley lies Chilworth, and on the far side, first the Blackheath Forest and then Winterfold Wood running up to the lower greensand escarpment, with the Weald hidden beyond.

The relative hardness of the pieces of carstone you will see, either in the church fabric or underfoot, explains the existence of St Martha's Hill. Some of these pieces have the ripple marks we are all familiar with on sand at the seaside at low water. The ripple marks survived as the sea first receded, then returned millions of years later, depositing sand on top, and eventually chalk. One might think that ripple-stone is a curiosity of little practical use, but the larger slabs were laid 'to meet the chafings of the steel-shod horses' hoofs as they clatter into the stables.'

It is extraordinary to think that the whole of St Martha's Hill, and the view southwards across the lower greensand hills, and across the whole of the Weald was once covered in a carapace of chalk, of which only the North and South Downs remain.

Resume walking in the same direction, keeping to the broad sandy downhill path along the southern (right hand) edge of the ridge, with the view southwards, and resisting any temptation (signposts to left or right) to leave the ridge. There is the occasional sign confirming the North Downs Way. After about 400m, you will come to a Second World War pillbox just to the left of the path.
The structure has a brick skin, presumably to absorb the shock of ordnance fired at it, with hard concrete behind. It was part of the line of defence ('the GHQ Line') which ran along from Somerset, across high ground in Hampshire and in Surrey along the Hog's Back and North Downs to the Medway, a desperate attempt to render London defensible after Dunkirk. We can be grateful it was never put to the test, though pundits are agreed that a German invasion would have been unlikely to succeed.

One must assume here that a better field of fire was achieved by clearing much of the nearby undergrowth. Nevertheless, during the dark days when invasion was expected, you may imagine the Home Guard manning these defences nightly, in case of an enemy parachute drop to seize the high ground. Anyone familiar both with Dad's Army and with how deceptive the first hint of dawn can be, with odd-shaped bushes morphing into malignant enemy infiltrators, can easily imagine any number of false alarms raised by nervous and unseasoned guards.

After the pillbox, continue straight for 200m exactly, keeping to the right side of the path where there are forks. You should then find yourself close to a wooden signpost on your right [GR 0347 4842]. Since this is not as easy as it may seem, read the following first. There is a method for those numerically challenged. Most of us take about 110 paces for every 100m. So if you get muddled counting, pick a couple of fern fronds and discard the first frond after 100 paces, and likewise when you discard the second you know you have twenty paces left to walk. If, like me, you forget where you are well before 100, take 11 fronds, each frond for 20 paces. When you run out of fronds, mercifully you will be exactly on target. (The method works. In a happily distant army career, I navigated several miles through very dense secondary jungle in Malaysia simply using this method and a compass. If it had not worked, I would not be here to tell the tale.)
    You should find yourself standing close to, or in sight of, a wooden signpost on your right, with a four-directional sign. Three signs are marked as bridleway

but follow the fourth, marked footpath, to the right, down the steep slope into the valley. Keep descending, turning left after 200m when you reach a gully with a beautifully sculpted open field opposite. The path will take you to Postford in the Tillingbourne valley.

The woodland down this slope is now known as Colyer's Hanger. One's first instinct is to think that this woodland here came by its name because of charcoal burners operating here, but apparently not. It is named after a Richard Collier (whose forebear clearly was a collier) who must have lived here. Its previous name was Lythie, meaning 'hill-slope' (like Leith Hill). Nevertheless, the valley bottom was indeed devoted to alder coppice to provide charcoal for the Chilworth gunpowder works. As you approach the bottom, the alder trees – no longer coppiced – are apparent.

Turn right at the bottom, [GR 0410 4807], (past Millpond Cottage), crossing the bridge over the small mill race that powered one of the five powder mills of Upper Chilworth, and follow the tarmac road to the right.

On your left is the channel leading to the larger of the two millponds with alder carr (swampy wood) beyond.

Cross a small millrace whose water runs through the modern housing estate.

Upper Chilworth Powder Mills here at Postford were part of a much larger complex of mills sited on a two-mile stretch of the Tillingbourne through Chilworth. The Evelyn family (p.155) established England's first powder mills at Wotton, Godstone and Tolworth in the sixteenth century, but by the early seventeenth century they had sold the rights, and manufacture under Crown monopoly became centred on Chilworth. In 1626 a contract required the proprietors to provide Charles I with roughly 28 tons of powder annually. With a royal grant in 1636, the works were expanded, whereby annual yield was increased tenfold. During the Civil War, Chilworth sided (like almost all the south-east) with Parliament, which consequently enjoyed a far better powder supply for its army than did the Royalists.

Postford's five mills (the other four sited off this larger millpond) produced gunpowder from about 1650 to 1700. The water was channelled along a race from Albury to the two ponds here in order to obtain a sufficient head of water. Both the Upper (by the nineteenth century known as Postford Mill) and Lower Chilworth mills produced paper in the nineteenth century, leaving only the Middle Chilworth mills (see below) as the site of powder manufacture through to the twentieth century. None of Postford's mill buildings survive. The last mill was still producing animal feed until the 1990s when it was demolished and the site redeveloped for residential use.

After the last house on the right, cross another bridge, and go half right along the marked but narrow footpath, between trees and a wire fence. Follow the path as it continues across an open field. Just before a stile one must cross a stream.

This stream fed a network of channels, one of which lies to the left of the path. It was probably dug some time between 1650 and 1700, part of a meadow irrigation system. The 'floating' of meadows became a widespread practice across southern England in the seventeenth century. Water meadows such as this would be flooded through the winter, and then drained off at the end of February. Meantime, sheep would be folded on chalk or lower greensand arable lands, and fed on roots while they manured the land, ready for spring sowing. Winter flooding kept the soil warmer and accelerated grass growth once drained, ready for lambing. One acre of water meadow would support up to 400 ewes and their lambs for a day, which would be rotated from field to field. By late April the sheep would be banished and the meadow flooded again, this time to produce two or three hay crops by the end of September, when cattle would be put out to manure and crop the stubble, before the cycle re-started with November. The practice died out with the collapse of grain prices in the nineteenth century.

These fields subsequently became the site of gunpowder production, as this expanded in the 1860s, and of cordite production from the 1890s. The ruins of the cordite factories can still be seen, standing in the field off to the right. The invention of cordite provided the army with the best smokeless propellant, of crucial value in the concealment of guns on the battlefield.

Continue straight, with the remnant of one of these irrigation channels on your left, eventually reaching a metalled track. Turn right over a bridge on the millstream.

The lump of concrete on the left of the bridge is the remnant of a Second World War roadblock.

HOW GUNPOWDER IS MADE

a Gunpowder is made from 15 per cent charcoal, 10 per cent sulphur and 75 per cent saltpetre (potassium nitrate). At first saltpetre was obtained from bird droppings in dovecotes, but by 1700 it was being imported from India. Sulphur came from Sicily and the nearby Aeolian Islands, and alder charcoal, of course, came from local colliers harvesting the alder carr.

b These ingredients were milled separately before being mixed to produce the 'charge' for processing in 'incorporation' mills. Initially these incorporation mills used mortar and pestle to pound the mixture, but in the eighteenth century this method was replaced by 'edge runner' millstones. Unlike corn grindstones which revolve on a horizontal plane, these millstones, like a vehicle wheel, turned on a vertical axis, the edge grinding the charge which was placed on a horizontal bed (there are plenty of these to see later), to produce 'mill cake'. (In the nineteenth century stone was replaced with iron-edged runners.)

c The mill cake was pressed to make dense slabs, 'press cake'.

d These slabs were then granulated to powder, or 'corned', in a corning house.

e The powder was dusted and glazed to render it moisture resistant, dried and packed in barrels and stored in the magazine until despatch.

Turn left immediately to enter the site of the Middle Chilworth Powder Mills [GR 0330 4767].
It is time to pause to read the signage, which explains the Chilworth site. (You will find a commentary and rudimentary sketch map overleaf, to help as you walk.) You are standing at the entrance marked on the right of the map, and will make your way along the main path through to the west end. The first crucial thing as you walk is to imagine the site to be tree-less and open. The tree growth is less than a century old. Once you realise that the saltpetre and sulphur were obtained abroad, you will also be wondering why powder mills were sited here. The answer lies in waterpower and the immediate availability of alder charcoal, the best charcoal for making gunpowder.

At its apogee, in the last quarter of the seventeenth century there were 17 or 18 powder mills on the Tillingbourne around Chilworth. John Aubrey visited the mills perhaps around 1700:

> In this little pleasant Valley, the springs serve not only to water the Grounds, but for the driving of 18 Powder Mills, 5 whereof were blown up in little more than half a Year's Time. 'Tis a little Commonwealth of Powder-makers, who are as black as Negroes.
>
> Here is a Nursery of Earth for the making of *Salt-Petre*. There is also here a Boyling-House where the *Salt-Petre* is made, and shoots; a Corneing House, and separating and finishing Houses, all very well worth the seeing of the Ingenious. I had almost forgot the Brimstone Mill and the Engine to search it.

From which we know that manufacture was complicated, dangerous and dirty: the danger arising from the potentially unstable nature of gunpowder (in 1901 a corning house exploded, killing six men) and the dirt from the ground alder charcoal.

Follow the main path.

The interpretation board at the entrance indicates where many of the installations were. Unfortunately most of the structures have disappeared, or are so ruinous as to be difficult to interpret as you walk. Perhaps the most striking feature is the number of millraces that run under the path, each producing power for some part of the process. Much of the path follows the line of the narrow gauge tramway, used to carry materials around the site. The sketch map below indicates the more visible features.

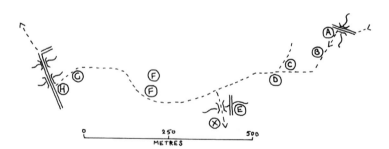

A The remains of a charcoal mill, mixing house and charge house lie in the dip on the right of the path.

B A row of six incorporating mills was built here in 1885, equipped with iron edge-runners. This is the most impressive building on the whole site. A lever arrangement, still visible at roof level, ensured that an explosion in one mill triggered a drenching mechanism in all six mills. These mills produced brown prismatic powder with brown charcoal made from straw. Its advantage was that it was almost smokeless.

C Just before a path comes in from the right, note the remains of a protective earth and corrugated iron embankment (known as a Chilworth mound).

D Opposite, on the left, lie the foundations of an 1860s corning house, with steam engine bed.

E After 200m a path to the left leads to a wooden footbridge. To its left the remains of a tramway swing bridge crosses the stream.

⊗ To the Percy Arms.
   (If you wish to take refreshment, cross the footbridge and follow the path across the fields to the main road. Turn left and walk for 150m to the Percy Arms. When sated, return to resume walk.)

F Continuing alongside the main path, you pass a row of edge-runner millstones, and 30m behind them, the ruins of the older steam-powered incorporating mills which had used these stone edge-runners.

G A barrel vaulted brick storage shed stands on the left of the path.

H On the left of the exit is West Lodge, where the workforce clocked in, and past which the finished gunpowder left the factory to be stored before despatch in a large magazine about 250m south west of the gate.

(This description is an abbreviated version of Glenys Crocker's *Guide to the Chilworth Gunpowder Mills*, Surrey Industrial History Group, 2005)

Walking through the old factory grounds one can only be astonished at the ingenuity devoted to the destruction of other humans. For me these grounds are the prime example of Blake's Dark Satanic Mills.

Turn right on exit [GR 0246 4746], crossing the first of two channels of the Tillingbourne.

On your left is the site of a paper and print mill, which replaced the gunpowder mill here in 1704, a reminder that, after all, the Pen is mightier than the Sword. One leaves the dark brooding remains of the powder mills for open country with some relief.

Continue over the second channel, to the sharp corner. Leave the road and follow the footpath on the left, leading uphill, on the outside angle of the corner of the road.

Had you been walking here in the early evening of Wednesday, 25th September, 1822, you might have met a genial but highly opinionated rider coming the other way from Merrow Down on the north side of St Martha's Hill, none other than William Cobbett himself:

> We *steered* for St Martha's Chapel, and went round at the foot of the lofty hill on which it stands. This brought us down the side of a steep hill, and along a bridle-way, into the narrow and exquisitely beautiful valley of Chilworth, where we stopped for the night.

It was in contemplating this delectable valley that Cobbett gave vent to one of his many trenchant views:

> This valley, which seems to have been created by a bountiful providence, as one of the choicest retreats of man; which seems formed for a scene of innocence and happiness, has been, by ungrateful man, so perverted as to make it instrumental in effecting two of the most damnable inventions that ever sprang from the minds of man under the influence of the devil! namely, the making of *gunpowder* and of *bank-notes*!

It was the banknotes that particularly got Cobbett down, 'spreading misery over a whole nation', an opinion worth contemplating when our capitalist credit system has got the nation into such a mess.

Emerging after 250m on Halfpenny Lane, turn left immediately [GR 0214 4785] onto another footpath along the left side of the field.

Cobbett loved this valley, 'skirted partly by woodlands and partly by sides of hills tilled as corn fields'. Looking at the extremely sandy soil here one might dispute his verdict that, 'the land is excellent particularly towards the bottom,' but one can agree, looking up to the right, that 'the arable fields are in some places, towards their tops, nearly as steep as the roof of a tiled house.'

After 300m, pass old ivy-clad barn buildings on your right and continue.
A spring is marked on the map, so you will not be surprised to see willows growing on your left.

On reaching the attractive farmstead (Manor Farm), dogleg right and left to continue along the path.
Manor Farm takes its name from the manor of East Shalford, which dates back to the times of King Edward the Confessor, before the Conquest, if not earlier.

Continue straight at choices.
Ahead, the skyline with a radio mast on it is the Guildford end of the Hog's Back (Walk No.8)

Continue until you reach the tarmac road and turn right [GR 0034 4802]. After about 30m, where the road bends to the left, follow the footpath straight up the hill, alongside back garden fences. Continue straight for 350m to return to the car park.

14

Ranmore and Polesden Lacey

Distance 6km/4 miles: 2½ hours
OS Explorer Map No.146

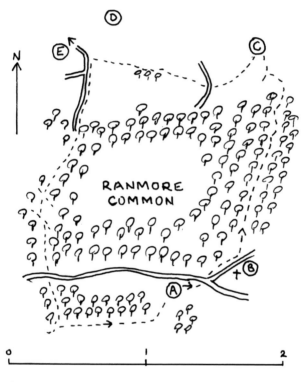

Ⓐ NT CAR PARK   Ⓓ POLESDEN LACEY
Ⓑ St BARNABAS   Ⓔ TO VISIT THE HOUSE
Ⓒ BAGDEN FARM

BEFORE YOU WALK

This walk takes you off the clay-with-flints cap on the North Downs escarpment, onto the 'dip-slope' of the chalk, past the National Trust property of Polesden Lacey, an opportune moment to visit (but if it is muddy underfoot, take light shoes for indoor wear) and for refreshment. The walk returns up to and just over the edge of the escarpment with the remarkable panorama over the Tillingbourne valley and Dorking.

Clay-with-flints, the principal geological terrain of this walk, is a tease. The name was first given in 1861 to clay containing whole and shattered flints. The spread of clay-with-flints is considerable, sheets of it occurring from Hertfordshire to Sussex, and from Kent to Devon. Geologists once thought it was a residue from the slow dissolution of chalk. It is now more widely believed that it is a series of more recent (Eocene and Pleistocene) deposits. It may be significant that it only occurs south of ice sheets of the glacial epoch.

Ranmore, now a long green running along the escarpment, is an old name. It probably means 'boundary strip', as the old parish and manorial boundary ran along this escarpment. Manorial boundaries in Saxon times and in the Middle Ages tended where possible to follow natural features: a ridge, watershed, valley bottom or stream. There was a practical purpose to this. It made for fewer disputes.

If car-less: There is no public transport to Ranmore Common. Your best bet is to arrive at Dorking West station and walk up Ranmore Road, 1½ km, or take a taxi from Dorking station to St Barnabas, Ranmore. (On your return you are walking downhill.)

Refreshment: en route at the National Trust restaurant, Polesden Lacey.

Make a day of it and visit: Polesden Lacey, house and gardens, half way around your walk, or drive there afterwards. (www.polesdenlacey@nationaltrust.org.uk).

Start at the Ranmore NT Carpark [GR 1415 5035].
Facing the road, turn right and walk for 200m. Fork left at the sign marked to Bookham and West Humble, along the minor road, and pause at St Barnabas.
St Barnabas was built in 1859 for George, the wealthy son of Thomas Cubitt, London's greatest nineteenth century developer. It was after

Thomas' death in 1855 that George, having been forbidden by his father from taking holy orders, built the church here. George Gilbert Scott designed it. It is unashamed gothic revival, with a solid, not to say knobbly appearance, with its walls of un-knapped flints, and the dormers above the belfry. It is an improbable building in rustic Surrey. As for St Barnabas, he was a Cypriot Jew who teamed up with Paul in his missionary travels. Together they defeated the pro-circumcision faction in the early Church, but later fell out over the choice of travelling companions.

Thomas Cubitt himself had lived at Denbies, a bombastic Italianate building he had built nearby on the escarpment in 1849, and which was demolished in 1953. Cubitt's mansion was not the first to be here. Jonathan Tyers, an impressario and the proprietor of the fashionable Spring Gardens in Vauxhall, lived in a previous house on the site from 1734 till his death in 1767. His garden revealed a morbidly sepulchral side to his theatrical nature: one could enter 'The Valley of the Shadow of Death', the centrepiece being two up-ended stone coffins surmounted by human skulls. He thus anticipated the birth of the Gothic novel by a whisker. (Horace Walpole's *The Castle of Otranto* appeared in 1764.)

Just beyond St Barnabas stands the old school, while over the road is the rectory, just out of sight, but to which you will come shortly. Both are also by Scott and, true to the ethos of the era, exude authority rather than intimacy. In retrospect one cannot help thinking of this as a psychological mistake, whether in matters pedagogical or spiritual.

Turn left along the marked path opposite the school, down the side of the old rectory house [GR 1460 5050].
The old rectory house may speak of authority – as a miscreant member of the Sunday School one can imagine the terror, indeed fear of damnation, of being summoned to the Rector's Study within – but it is also unusually fine and elegant.

Keep walking, deviating neither to right nor to left.
As you walk through the woodland you will notice that the soil is clearly clay-with-flint, muddy with flint cobbles, fit really only for woodland, notably oak, ash, and beech. In his *Rural Rides*, Cobbett took the view that this soil was worth working:

In coming up the chalk hill from Westerham [just inside the Kent border], I prepared myself for the stiff red clay-like loam, the big yellow flints and the meadows, and I found them all.... Everywhere upon the top of it [between Newbury and Folkestone] I have found a flat, and the soil of all these flats I have found to be a red-stiff loam mingled with big yellow flints. A soil difficult to work; but by no means bad, whether for wood, hops, grass, orchards or corn.

Well, Cobbett may have said that, but ploughing clay-with-flints was heavy going and hard on the ploughshare and for that reason it was not worked when other arable land was available. It was an irony that, as Cobbett observed, labourers were better off on the clay-with-flints than in the richer valleys. However, the reason for this lay in land ownership, as he admitted: 'All is not appropriated where there are coppices and wood, where the cultivation is not so easy, and the produce so very large.' Another problem with clay-with-flints is that it also contains drifts of infertile sand.

As you walk note the lapsed coppice-trees to right and left. Coppicing was a major activity all along the North Downs. Occasionally one may see an uprooted tree, displaying the soil quality on its roots: sandy clay with lumps of flint in it.

After just over 1km the path emerges into an open field, almost exactly where the soil underfoot changes to chalk, good for pasture. Continue down for about 300m to Bagden Farm on the left of the track.

The name is on record in the thirteenth century but must be older, for it probably refers to the Saxon owner and means 'Bacda's Valley'. On the right is Old Dene, a handsome Victorian mansion, with what looks like an Edwardian loft-conversion.

Turn left just before the farmhouse, through the farmyard, to admire the old flint walls, sheds and wooden barn buildings [GR 1476 5195]. Follow the path along the valley bottom.

Crossing this field, there is a curious bank on the right, the remains of an old wood bank or hedgerow, with one surviving oak tree, with the characteristic lean for one growing out of a bank. There was a proper track here in the nineteenth century, though the hedgerow had already disappeared, except for a few trees. Up to the left the trees along the edge of the field have the characteristic 'browse line' of trees nibbled by livestock.

Go through the gate, turn left and after a few paces turn right [GR 1440 5175] through another gate, to continue up the valley bottom.

A Youth Hostel lies half hidden in the tree line at Tanner's Hatch, in the far left of the field. It is unclear whether this was the cottage of someone called Tanner, or was actually the site of a tannery. If the latter, it is isolated for a good reason. Tanning is an extremely smelly process, so tanners usually lived well away from other habitation. A 'hatch' is a fenced-off plot.

At the end of the field take the wicket gate down into the wooded valley bottom.

The woodland is largely hazel coppice, a vital asset on any estate before 1850 or so (for its uses see p.172). It is clear that the great quantity of flints washed down the hillside has made the land unattractive as arable or pasture, but still of value as coppice. After the woodland a vista of parkland opens up on the left, so you know the field can be seen from the house, Polesden Lacey.

On emerging, follow the right side of the field.

Polesden means Poll's valley, the Saxon name as it first appeared in a written record in 1198, but 'Lacey' remains an unidentified manorial suffix. The house stands on the hilltop on the right, to be seen from a vantage point later on.

Follow to the right of the farm and its outbuildings. When you emerge onto a track, turn left and walk past Polesden Farm and straight up the hill [GR 1350 5180], unless you wish to visit the house in which case turn right and keep turning right at choices to enter the grounds of the house from the north side, just over 1km.

Underfoot, the clay-with-flints with its high sand content has washed down the hillside onto the chalk.

After 400m, just before the cottage (Prospect Lodge) and the woodland there are seats on the right enjoy the view back to the house.

Polesden Lacey is wonderfully sited. It is unclear how many buildings may have been on this site previously. In the Middle Ages, the manor belonged to Merton Abbey, so there was probably a grange (a monastery

Polesden Lacey in 1850. In the foreground the farmer supervises bringing in the harvest, grown on the chalk slope. The stooks have been assembled, the labourers enjoy a rest and refreshment.

farm). After Henry VIII's dissolution of the monasteries, the manor was given to the Sackville family, which probably built a house here in the Tudor period and certainly had one during the seventeenth century.

Thomas Cubitt rebuilt Polesden Lacey in 1823 in the neo-Grecian Regency style, as one can still see on the south face, which has since been skilfully extended. The interior was expertly re-modelled on Edwardian lines in 1906, and contains a family collection of fine paintings, furniture and porcelain. The gardens are lovely. Definitely, as Michelin would say, worth the detour if you have not already visited it.

Continue up the track, past Prospect Lodge.

On the right is a wood bank, on the left through the trees one can see a patch of hazel coppice.

Keep following the track for about ½ km passing through a gate, and after another 250m of more open ground walk through a woodland clearing. You will reach another gate and then a major cross track. Turn left along the track, but after 50m fork right along the marked path and continue without deviation.
This woodland has probably never been totally cleared but, over the centuries, has been harvested for useful timber and wood, and in some areas coppiced. Out of sight, 500m to your right, lie Hogden and Pigden cottages on Hogden Lane. The lane runs down a gully. Den means valley, but it is also a Wealden term for designated woodland swine pasture, or 'pannage', as the Normans called it. It is unclear whether these names indicate the gully or the pannage, but they are likely to date back to the early Middle Ages, or even to Saxon times.

Cross the tarmac road [GR 1320 5042] and continue (down the track with the signage for the Dorking Scout Council). After about 300m the track starts to descend steeply to reach the North Downs Way [GR 1330 5010]. Turn left but dogleg through the gate into the field on your right, and take a seat.
The view is a stunning contrast with what has gone before. The valley below, from Folkestone in the east to Farnham on the edge of Hampshire, was the scene of early human colonisation of this part of England. Slowly the settler communities pushed into the hills north and south to make use of the grazing areas on offer, while the valley became the principal zone for settlement and agriculture. As a consequence, most of the community settlements which eventually became manors, later called parishes, stretched north, usually to the escarpment, but a long way southwards beyond the hills (Leith Hill, Holmsbury and the Hurtwood hills) far into the Weald, into which swine- and cowherds drove their livestock for the summer months, and where colliers lived in the deepest woodland producing charcoal (see p.242).

Follow the path eastwards, just below the treeline, in order to enjoy the magnificent view. It will eventually bring you up to Ranmore car park.
Classic chalkland flora will be found on these slopes: box, wild clematis, dogwood, privet, the wayfarer's tree, the spindle tree and common buckthorn. Until about 1900, sheep would have been grazed here through the summer months, coming up from the valley, perhaps from a water meadow (see p.196), once lambing was successfully completed. The tradition of sheep grazing must date back more than two millennia, broken

so recently by the internal combustion engine. We do not know precisely what breed of sheep was here in the Middle Ages, but the animals would have been the size of small dogs. We do know that the meat was delicious. John Evelyn complained that the mutton of new 'improved' larger breeds did not compare with the 'small and sweet mutton' with which he had grown up but which was increasingly hard to obtain.

We get a lovely glimpse of the shepherding life on the North Downs from Evelyn's friend, Samuel Pepys, near Epsom in July 1667:

> I walked upon the Downes, where a flock of sheep was; and the most pleasant and innocent sight that ever I saw in my life — we find a shepherd and his little boy reading, far from any houses or sight of people, the Bible to him; so I made the boy read to me, which he did, with the forced tone that children do usually read, that was mighty pretty, and then I did give him something, and went to the father, and talked with him.... He did content himself mightily in my liking his boy's reading, and did bless God for him, the most like one of the old patriarchs that ever I saw in my life.... We took notice of his woolen knit stockings of two colours mixed, and of his shoes shod with iron shoes, both at the toe and heels, and with great nails in the soles of his feet, which was mighty pretty: and,

A nineteenth century shepherd's crook, designed to catch a sheep's hind leg.

taking notice of them, "Why," says the poor man, "the downes, you see, are full of stones, and we are faine to shoe ourselves thus; and these," says he, "will make the stones fly till they sing before me." I did give the poor man something, for which he was mighty thankful, and I tried to cast stones with his horne crooke. He values his dog mightily, that would turn a sheep any way which he would have him, when he goes to fold them: told me there was about eighteen scoare [360] sheep in his flock, and that he hath four shillings a week the year round for keeping of them...'

A variety of different breeds were probably here in the early eighteenth century, but by the 1790s the most common breeds hereabouts were

A rare sight now, a pair of Southdown rams.

North Wiltshire Horned and Dorsetshire sheep. They were not destined to last, since in the second half of the century breeders started to improve stock dramatically. Foremost was John Ellman, who lived near Lewes. He transformed the Southdown in the 1780s from a light and long-legged animal into one that was solid and compact, excellent for mutton and still good for wool. The Southdown remained a favoured downland sheep well into the twentieth century. Today most of the sheep kept on the Downs are Texels.

The path will take you back to the car park on the escarpment, at the end of the woodland on your left.

The River Wey Navigation and Newark Priory

Distance 6km/4 miles: 2½ hours
OS Explorer Map No.146

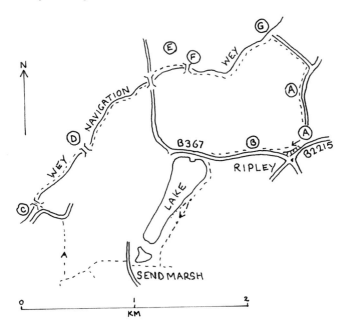

(A) CAR PARK

(B) DUNSBOROUGH PARK

(C) TANYARD FOOTBRIDGE

(D) PAPERCOURT LOCK

(E) NEWARK PRIORY

(F) NEWARK LOCK

(G) WALSHAM LOCK

BEFORE YOU WALK

The prevailing theme of this walk is water, and the contrast between how water, be it in river, canal or lagoon was once integral to the economy and how today it has become integral to leisure. The walk takes you past an enormous flooded gravel pit, and later along the Wey Navigation, one of the earliest of Britain's canals.

If car-less access: Take the No.462 or 463 bus from Guildford (25 mins) or from Woking (35 mins) to Ripley, and pick up the walk at ➲ on Newark Lane (B367) outside Dunsborough Park (see below).

Refreshment: Ripley has plenty of hostelries, but the principal one is the Talbot Inn, on the High Street (tel. 01483 225188).

Make a day of it: if you wish to pursue themes of the River Wey: in Guildford the River Wey and Godalming Navigation & Dapdune, Wharf Rd, Guildford (www.riverwey@nationaltrust.org.uk), and the large timber-framed Shalford Mill (www.shalfordmill@nationaltrust.org.uk).

Nearby: Clandon Park (www.clandonpark@nationaltrust.org.uk), West Clandon or Hatchlands Park (www.hatchlands@nationaltrust.org.uk), East Clandon. RHS Wisley (tel. 01483 224234, www.rhs.wisley.org.uk), just off the A3 north of Ripley.

Start at Ripley Green on the west side of the main road (B2215). There are a number of small car parks [GR 0534 5690]. With your back to the main road, turn left and start walking (south-westwards) past the houses with the green to your right. On reaching it, veer right along the road (B367).

➲ Immediately on your right stands the imposing gatehouse to Dunsborough Park. It would have you believe it is Tudor. It looks Edwardian but was only built in 1939. Behind lies the house, a seventeenth century pile with subsequent additions, and gardens which underwent the opening phase of restoration by that eminent gardener, Penelope Hobhouse, in 1994, and demand a visit (with your diary, check www.antique-garden.com).

After 250m cross a small bridge over a brook, and after another 120m, having almost passed the boundary wall of Homewood Farm, take the footpath on the opposite side of the road [GR 0447 5672]. You should see a sign through the shrubs: 'Angling – Papercourt'. Follow the footpath with the lake to your right.

This lake (14 hectares) is the result of massive river gravel extraction undertaken in the mid-twentieth century. The extent of the gravel is an indicator of the one time immense width of the Wey. Before the extraction, the area was still open fields.

It is the wide flatness and huge skies which remind you throughout this walk of the once mighty river. During interglacial periods in the past 600,000 years, the gravel was borne down the Wey and Thames valleys as ice-melt flood waters swept across southern England, putting down pebbles smoothed by their journey from the West Country. Gravel was extracted in the twentieth century from sites along the Thames Valley from Ham westwards, for the construction of road networks and the spread of suburbia (apart from anything else, just think of all that fashionable pebbledash of the 1920s). With the exhaustion of the deposits here, the hole has been filled with water to become an anglers' resort.

After 350m the paths fork. Take the left fork, which veers slightly away from the lake edge. After almost 500m, you will reach the corner of the field, with a wooden footbridge on your left [GR 0405 5582]. But turn right, following the path which shadows the perimeter fence on your left. After 250m the path reaches a tiny car park. Turn out of the car park onto the road. Cross the stile (and gate) opposite (just to the right of 'Danesfield' but to the left of the Rio industrial estate) [GR 0375 5588]. Pause at the allotments.

Before proceeding, look at the allotment noticeboard, for here you will see a map of the current allotment holders. Read the names. What you are witnessing is a profound expression of the English with their fingers in the soil. There have always been smallholders. The present ones are spiritual descendants of the tenant peasantry of Saxon and Medieval periods. The first phase of enclosure of common fields from the time of Queen Elizabeth I caused major distress and impoverishment. In some cases small allotments of land were provided for tenant cottages. By the middle of the nineteenth century landlord enclosures led to legislation to protect the rural poor with the provision by the local authority of 'field gardens', a quarter acre per household. This concession was motivated by fear of revolution and the growing power of the Chartist movement.

The two world wars and the imperative to maximise food production led to the hey-day of the allotment movement. By 1943 there were 1.4 million allotment plots. Today there are in the order of 300,000 plots. They survive thanks to the passion of their cultivators, people who on the whole believe in organic and fresh food. If you are tempted to think meanly of allotments, think again. They may be less efficient in terms of labour than conventional agriculture, but they remain much more efficient in terms of land use. They are restorative particularly for those condemned to commute to work during the week and, as importantly, they are an admirable act of defiance against the grip of supermarkets and capitalism. Ask any allotment holder: small is not only beautiful but incontestably best. Think about getting a plot.

Continue walking along the boundary (and back gardens) on your left. Follow it along the field edge for 300m. Ignore the small footbridge to the left which offers a path towards attractive buildings across the field, on the road. Keep following the edge of the field for just over 200m. On reaching a T-junction on the far side of the field [GR 0320 5573], turn right, with a stream on you left. After about 150m turn left over a wooden bridge through the hedgerow line to continue following the stream but by the narrow path on its left side. Shortly thereafter there is a pond on your left. On reaching the road turn left, and after 200m turn right down the side of No.1 Tannery House.

On reaching the River Wey, look at the wharves to your left, which used to be a hive of industry. There was once a mill here, and also a tannery established in 1717 and still operating in the late nineteenth century. Tanning was an industry that would have polluted the waters here and caused the most almighty stench. One can immediately understand why it was both a good distance from and usually downwind of Send.

Cross the first (Tanyard) footbridge [GR 0295 5636]. (Beyond one can see a second footbridge. This crosses Broadmead Cut, a flood defence mechanism dug in 1930, which shadows the Navigation.) Turn right along the River Wey Navigation, which by-passes the meandering Wey which is 250m to the west along this section.

The Wey Navigation, one of England's oldest canals, was the brainchild of a local landowner, Sir Richard Weston. He was obsessed with the idea that if the Wey were navigable, an enormous amount of freight could be conveyed between Guildford and London. He also had a bee in his bonnet about the newly invented pound lock, the one we are familiar with, consisting of two pairs of gates with a 'pound' between them to accommodate a vessel as it adjusts to the different level of the water. All previous gates were 'flash' locks, that is a single gate which let the water down in a whoosh. This was fine when travelling downstream, but time-consuming and very laborious when hauling a vessel upstream, as the flash lock had to be closed to allow the upper side to fill and become navigable again, which might take some hours. Weston's pound lock obviated this inconvenience.

Weston started work on the 25km/14 miles from Guildford to Weybridge in 1635. He was a man of conviction, and proved it by selling off his Clandon estate to the Onslow family to raise sufficient capital. Then, disaster struck with the outbreak of the Civil War. A Catholic and Royalist, Weston was in strongly Parliamentarian country and was forced to flee to Flanders. In 1650, with the Civil War over, Parliament allowed him back on condition that he completed the canal, and guaranteed half the capital cost. He set to with enormous energy but died in 1652 with 10 out of the 14 miles of the Wey canalised. The work was completed the following year and opened in November 1653, equipped with 10 locks, 4 weirs and 12 bridges.

From upstream and downstream along the Wey came timber, wood in finished form, and fuel faggots (bavins, to use the local term). By 1664 the Wey Navigation was carrying 4,000 barge loads of timber annually, let alone other goods. These other goods included corn, flour, and even gunpowder from the Chilworth Mills up the Tillingbourne (see Walk No.13). Coal was the principal commodity brought back from London.

So useful was the Navigation that it was lengthened by another 7 km to reach Godalming in 1760-64. This was the real hey-day of canal construction in Britain, Eventually the Navigation became part of a far wider system. In 1794 the Basingstoke Canal connected with the Wey Navigation at Byfleet, and in 1816 the Wey-Arun Junction Canal was completed (see Walk No.1), connecting London by inland waterways to the south coast. By then the economic value of canals was drawing to a close. Yet the Wey Navigation did not finally cease carrying freight until 1983, almost 20 years after it had been taken over by the National Trust.

As you walk, drag your mind back two hundred years. The Wey here would have been full of barges, and the air thick with the coarse oaths of the bargees, a complete contrast to today's quiet anglers and the view of the opposite bank with its well-mannered lawns.

The vessels would have been small swimhead barges, shaped like punts with vertical sides and a flat bottom, a sharp right-angle at the joint (the 'chine'), with a length of about 22 metres/72 feet and a beam of 4.2 metres/13 feet 9 inches. These barges could carry up to 80 tons freight. They would have plied their trade as far as Basingstoke and Portsmouth. What you see today, moored along the riverbank, is one or two converted narrowboats. These are of the same length as the old barges but with a beam of only 2 metres. Furthermore, they have a more rounded chine between side and bottom, and also at the bow and stern. There are reasons for the changed shape. The riverine Wey Navigation consisted of both rivers and canals, but the later waterways to the Midlands, most significantly the Oxford Canal (opened in 1790), consisted almost entirely of canals, with no running rivers. This meant that every time a lock was opened, water would be lost from the higher level. Replenishing the canal level from a distant water source was time consuming, so locks were halved in width to 7 feet to reduce water loss, and narrow boats designed for them.

There was another reason for reducing the width of these canals. Unlike the Wey Navigation, much of which is a river in its own right, canals had to be 'puddled' with a clay lining to prevent water loss. Narrower canals reduced the amount of puddling necessary. Clay puddling is fragile and easily ripped and to protect it, the new narrow boats were designed with much more rounded edges than the older craft with their sharp chine. Anyone wishing to share the lucrative freight route offered by the Oxford canal and beyond it, to the Midlands, had to conform to the rounded shape of the new narrowboats. Within a very few years the old swimhead barges had disappeared from the Wey.

Follow the Wey Navigation to Papercourt Lock, where the path moves to the right canal bank.
After about 200m the river Wey (including Broadmead Cut) comes in from the left.

On reaching Newark New Bridge (carrying the B367), turn left over the bridge and immediately right to follow the Navigation left bank.
Until about 50 years ago Newark Mill stood on the right bank, and a few outlying brick buildings with new additions still remain. In 1086 the Domesday Book recorded a mill on the Wey between Ripley and Pyrford. It was probably here. The mill was granted to Newark Priory by the local magnates, Thomas and Alice of Send in the early thirteenth century.

Newark Mill, c.1905, standing by the old bridge that would have been quite unable to stand up to modern traffic.

By 1900 Newark was the largest and finest watermill in Surrey, equipped with three waterwheels and eight pairs of grindstones. It burnt down in 1966, having finally fallen into disuse in 1942. A description in 1951 ran,

> Surveying the vast interior, every inch of timber, dusty and dry, it is not difficult to understand why so very few buildings of its period and its construction have been preserved – sooner or later they must inevitably be destroyed by fire.

It is easy to be suspicious, and perhaps the insurers were at the time.

After 100 metres look out for the ruins of Newark Priory to your left.

Newark Priory stands on private and inaccessible land. Like most of the larger monastic houses, Newark was built close to the riverbank, so as to facilitate the transport of the necessary building materials. The Austin Canons established Newark Priory in the early eleventh century but only moved here in about 1207 from an unidentified location. Once established, the power of the priory upon the neighbourhood would have been pervasive. No one could have escaped its economic, religious, political and social influence.

The Austin Canons had been established as a result of theological anxiety, the thought that man's failure to live a fully Christian life was what delayed the Second Coming of Christ. Marriage and property owner-ship were seen as impeding that heavenly journey. The Austin Canons were founded as part of the drive in the early eleventh century to reform the priesthood, in particular to end the taking of wives and ownership of property and to live a life in common as a Christian ideal. It is a meas-ure of their failure that by the end of the thirteenth century there were still married priests to be found, and many another who 'kept a girl in his house, who lit his fire but extinguished his virtue.' Nature will have its wicked way.

The Priory was built of flint rubble with Reigate stone dressings. Most of it must have been dismantled following the Dissolution for its valuable salvage material, particularly its dressed stone. A nearby farmhouse was recorded in 1806 as having ornamented floor tiles, some of them depict-ing men on horseback, which had been found at Newark.

Continue along the left riverbank, until compelled to cross to the right bank again at Newark Lock, where there is another view of the Priory. Continue walking for another ¾ km to Walsham Lock.

The original sluice gearing that was used on the Wey Navigation is still in place here.

A board fixed to the top of the paddle has a series of holes in which pegs were fixed to hold the paddle as it was slowly raised with a crow-bar, one hole at a time. The bridge is designed with shallow steps to allow barge draught horses to cross easily.

At Walsham Lock [GR 0500 5775] turn right along the footpath away from the Wey, until you reach the T-junction and tarmac road. Turn right to Ripley Green.

End of the walk: Despite the through traffic, Ripley main street has con-siderable charm with its old cottages and timber frame buildings. Look out for St Mary Magdalen's Church (south, just beyond the village cross-roads). With its prim bell tower, the nave is an unremarkable nineteenth century building, but the church also has a lovely Norman chancel. This is unusually made of 'pudding stone', a cheap alternative to Bargate stone or proper flint, and thus a commentary on the poverty of Ripley manor in the mid-twelfth century when it was built. In fact the chancel predates Ripley as a population centre, which only really grew after foundation of Newark Priory.

Pudding stone, as can be seen, is a conglomerate, made of fragments of sandstone and flint naturally cemented together by a silicon or zinc oxide substance. It is a geological feature of Surrey. It is not strong – hence the buttressing which has held it together for the past 800 years. Inside, the chancel is again the attraction, with the string course of Caen stone with diamond ornament, with mid-wall piers and single shafts in the corners that seem to have been intended to carry a rib-vault. There are nice scallop-like capitals set in the wall, unique in Surrey. On the north (left) side of the chancel are two surviving Norman windows.

WALK

16

Chobham Common

Distance 3½km/2 miles: 1-1½ hours
OS Explorer Map No.160

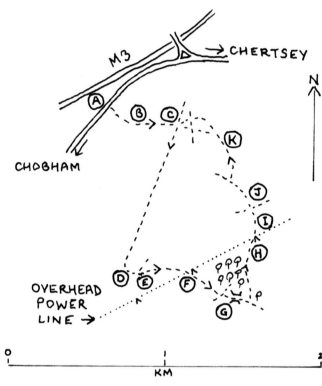

A STAPLE HILL CAR PARK
B GATE INTO GRAZING AREA
C MARKER POST L115
D LONE PINE
E MARKER POST H10
F MARKER POST H11

G LANGSHOT STUD
H MARKER POST 112
I MARKER POST 112E
J MARKER POST J12
K TWO BENCHES
   ON SUMMIT

BEFORE YOU WALK

Chobham Common is one of the best examples of lowland heathland anywhere. It is virtually the only heathland on Bagshot sands which is also permanently accessible to the public. Bagshot sands are geologically much younger than the drifts of sand in the lower greensand to the south. Those had preceded the chalk deposits of 150 million years ago. But the Bagshot sands flowed across the Thames basin only 40 million years ago, which is 20 million years *after* the London clay had also been deposited on the chalk. So, geologically speaking, it is just the other day. The Bagshot sands are composed of coarse infertile material carried eastwards by a huge freshwater river quite as large as the Ganges. Because of the comparative sterility of these sands, they have mostly been set aside for military training.

At the beginning of the eighteenth century John Aubrey came to Chobham and noted, '….in the Heath…. are found Pebbles of Hardness next to a Diamond, but of Lustre and Clearness inferior,' presumably a reference to the high level of silicon in many pebbles here.

Heathland is a man-made environment on sites where arable or pasture is not feasible. It was created originally for hunting and stock herding. It is maintained by constantly reducing tree growth, traditionally by grazing. It is impossible to say how old the heathland landscape is, but late Neolithic and Bronze Age tools have been found here, so one may be fairly sure that this landscape was cleared of much tree cover by 3,500 BC, and quite possibly two or three thousand years earlier. There are three barrows on the west side of the Common, indicating its antiquity.

Heathland has been maintained by livestock grazing for over 200 generations, but with the progressive reduction in livestock grazing from the late nineteenth century, human intervention has been necessary to cut trees down. Left to itself, the Common would become covered principally in birch in the short term. After about 30 or 40 years oak and holly would start to appear, which would eventually displace the birch. The birch would move on to colonise new open spaces. Gorse and broom, too, would grow where they were not within the shadow of the tree canopy. Although the Scots pines are now self-generating, they are an import and would not have been growing here, say, 800 years ago. They were probably introduced after 1750, in order that this highly infertile landscape might produce something useful, and to stabilise the sand.

If car-less: Chobham Common is very difficult to get to and would
require walking from the village. There are very infrequent trains
serving Long Cross station just on the north side of the M3.

Refreshment:
1 The Red Lion (tel. 0871 951 1000), Red Lion Rd, Burrow Hill,
    Chobham.
2 Four Horseshoes (tel. 01276 857581), Burrow Hill Green. To
    reach both drive west from Staple Hill Car Park and turn left onto
    the B383, Red Lion Road is the second turning on left, opposite
    the Four Horseshoes, across the Green on your right.

Local attractions: The Savill and Valley gardens at Windsor Great Park
(see David McDowall, *Windsor Great Park: the Walker's Guide* which
describes these gardens, Virginia Water and plenty else besides).

**Start at Staple Hill car park between Longcross and Chobham [GR 9720 6470].
This walk offers you an anticlockwise circuit of part of the Common. There is no
need to follow the prescribed walk, since one can easily identify the location of
the car park by the skyline of Scots pines just west (left) of it, and the isolated
tree clump marking it. Keeping track of this part of the skyline as you walk is
the surest means of not getting lost. The sketch map and marker post numbers
are intended to ensure you do not lose your way among the myriad paths on
the Common.**

Look out for small pools, boggy areas and wet-loving flora: reeds, deer
grass, and sedges. How, one might ask, are pools formed in sand? Bagshot
sands contain a very high ferric content. Millions of years of rainfall has
caused a reaction, iron oxide helping the sand to coalesce into a hard
water-tight crust of rock ('iron pan'), lying about one metre below the
surface and creating boggy areas and pools. Chobham had such a reputation for so much bogginess that locals were supposed to have webbed
feet.

**Cross the road at the car park entry and follow the path leading straight ahead
(past post K9N), without deviation.**

The most noticeable flora is the gorse, or furze, to give it its proper
Surrey name. It was also used to thicken hedgerows on indifferent soil. It
was once highly prized as fuel and used for bread ovens on account of the
high temperatures that could be rapidly achieved. In lean years, villagers
would have pounded the furze as fodder for livestock. This useful plant

was sufficiently valued that strict rules were applied regarding annual cutting to ensure fair distribution, and adequate regeneration. Furze was also used for drying clothes. Its prickles act as grips and when in flower, its coconut-vanilla scent is imparted to fresh linen.

After about 150m pass through a gate into a newly designated cattle grazing zone.

Cattle are selective grazers, where sheep are not. They have been found to enhance the biodiversity of a habitat by avoiding eating flower heads.

Follow across the boggy ground on the short wooden walkway. After another 200m reach a bridleway marked with post LIIS, and turn right [GR 9775 6473] and walk without deviation for almost 1km.

Daniel Defoe crossed this kind of heathland early in the eighteenth century, when exploring the landscape for *A Tour through the Whole Island of Great Britain*, published in 1724-6. Coming up from Farnham, this is what he had to say:

> I took the coach-road, over Bagshot-Heath.... here is a vast tract of land, some of it within seventeen or eighteen miles of the capital city; which is not only poor, but even quite sterile, given up to barrenness, horrid and frightful to look upon, not only good for little, but good for nothing. Much of it is sandy desert.... for passing this heath, in a windy day, I was so far in danger of smothering with the clouds of sand, which were raised by the storm, that I could neither keep it out of my mouth, nose or eyes, the sand appeared spread over the adjacent fields.... so as that it ruins the very soil. This sand indeed is checked by the heath, or heather, which grows in it, and which is the common product of barren land, even in the very Highlands of Scotland; but the ground is otherwise so poor and barren, that the product of it feeds no creatures, but some very small sheep who feed chiefly on the said heather.

Why was Defoe so negative about heathland? The answer must be because of its wild and unproductive nature. Appreciation of the 'wilderness' only arose with the romantic movement from the mid-eighteenth century, when agricultural improvements seemed to put humans in real control of the landscape, allowing leisured gentry to look at the landscape for the first time as a thing of poetic beauty.

Cross straight over at the crossing marked JIOE and ignore JIO.

Look out for clumps of broom growing beside the track, its whippy spineless branches once used for sweeping. Broom was the badge of Geoffrey of Anjou, and its Latin name, *Planta genista*, gave his son (Henry II) and his successors their nickname, Plantagenet.

Had you been married near heathland you might well have leapt a branch of broom, an invocation of fertility. And had you overeaten, you might well have taken an infusion using boiled branch tips.

After about 900m along this track, and a few paces before reaching the Lone Pine (as illustrated, it is about 50m before the wall of deciduous and conifer plantation trees and just to the left of two posts), turn left [GR 9747 6395], and take the path to the right of post HIO, leading under the overhead power lines.

In the absence of better soil, it is remarkable how some use can be found for almost any terrain. Here, the principal product was honey. Chobham, including its heathlands, had been granted to Chertsey Abbey as long ago as 675, or possibly even earlier. Until 1215, the dead of the village could only be buried at Chertsey, not in Chobham, and to obtain that concession the community paid the Abbey with 10lbs of beeswax yearly. When the Abbey leased Chobham to Geoffrey de Bagshot (a name somehow lacking in gravitas) in 1254, it required yearly dues, including an annual rent of 12 gallons of honey, which at the end of the seventeenth century Aubrey elegantly described as 'Mead Silver'. It is for this reason that 'Bee Garden' is still to be found on the OS map.

In the fourteenth century one of Chertsey's greatest abbots, John Rutherwick, had an enormous carp pond dug in the south-east part of the Common. Its name, Gracious Pond, is still on the map, although the pond was drained in 1810 and subsequently filled in. About a mile in circumference, it was still producing fine carp in the eighteenth century. Fish was important for the Friday diet of the abbey.

Another use for the common would have been for peat and turf cutting. In the words of George Sturt, writing of heathland near Farnham,

Turfs were the common fuel. They were cut on the Common (by the privileged) and the farmer carted them to the labourers' cottages not for money, but for the ashes when they were burnt, which made valuable manure.

Pass under the power lines to the right of a pylon and post HII. Follow the track until you are close to the fenced edge of the Common.

This is the north edge of Langshot Stud. Langshot is first on record in 1312. It is Saxon for a long angle or strip of land.

Follow the track until it is joined by another track coming in from the right, very close to the perimeter of Langshot Stud (the fields and buildings ahead), and continue with Langshot Stud now on your right. Cross the iron bridge [GR 9815 6378].

Look at the ferric content of the water. Bagshot sand carries a lot of iron (hence iron-pan). Travelling hereabouts 300 years ago, Aubrey came across a well, 'the Water whereof has a rough Taste, and with Powder of Galls, turns to a Purple Colour, which comes from Iron.'

50m after the bridge, fork left up the edge of the birch coppice.

Birch grows enthusiastically on this soil. Growing wood on heathland had to be balanced against the other benefits heath offered. Birch coppice would have been grown principally for fuel. But its brushwood (precisely that) would also have been harvested to make besoms, which most people now mistakenly think of as witches' brooms. Besom manufacture was one of the sandy heath trades from which a very modest living could be made. The most notable area for the trade was in the extreme south-west of the county, at Hindhead (see p.69).

(True 'witches' broomsticks', in case you are wondering, were potions of mind-altering drugs, including such things as fly-agaric toadstools, toad skins (which contain a powerful hallucinogen) and certain herbs, made into an ointment with hempseed oil, and administered vaginally with a dildo to give, apparently, a most astonishing trip. There is no accounting for human ingenuity. Substances for such a broomstick may have been collected on this particular blasted heath. No wonder Puritan men, anatomically denied this pleasure, were keen to condemn female herbalists as witches.)

A Cottager's bee-hives. Gertrude Jekyll in 1904, 'The old straw hive is still in use among the poorer folk… and the cottager's device for sheltering it… with a bonnet made of pieces of sacking, and broken halves of a red-ware washing pan, adds to the prettiness of the little bee-establishment.'

Cross the bridleway (past post II2), and continue.

Note the pebble drifts. These pebbles occur frequently in Bagshot sand. They have travelled a long way, as can be seen from their beautifully rounded shapes. In fact, as mentioned in the introduction, they were washed eastwards by a vast fresh water river 40 million years ago from Devon and Cornwall, as confirmed by granite particles here. The sands were first identified at Bagshot, hence the name, but another drift also extends from Hampstead to Highgate in north-west London, the geological basis for Hampstead Heath.

This landscape is hardly useful even for livestock, but a few beasts would have been grazed here. A village lad would have taken out the cows of the poorer tenants onto the heath and kept an eye on them. Remember the bees kept here. They would have been kept in skeps, made from straw plaited into 'ropes'. By 1900 skeps had virtually died out. Just a few Travellers continued to weave them, using long briar, or bramble, shoots to stitch the skeps together. By then skeps had largely been displaced by the beehives with which we are familiar today. As one writer a century ago observed, 'Bees nowadays would scorn to occupy one of those picturesque little domed huts – a straw skep – as a permanent residence; this is regarded in the bee-world as the equivalent of a caravan.' Yet china honey pots are still shaped romantically after the skep.

Pass a pylon and then pass post II2E. Cross the track past post JI2. After 200m the path forks (there's a post indicating horse riders to go left). Take the right fork to climb the hill.

As you reach the apparent summit of the hill, note the small pond on the right of the path, further evidence that even here, iron-pan provides an impermeable membrane.

Look out for exposed raw sand on banks on the climb up to the top of Tank Hill. These show just how richly yellow, almost orange, Bagshot Sand can be beneath the surface which is normally bleached by the sun and discoloured by humus.

The name 'Tank Hill', albeit a modern name, is a reminder that another use was found for the Surrey sands in the nineteenth century: the grand manoeuvres of the army. In 1853 Queen Victoria reviewed 8,000 troops on Chobham Common, well, 8,129 of them to be exact, according to an accounting mentality which ensured that this mind-numbing fact was placed on the memorial. This was erected in 1901, which gave him (it has to be a male of the species) plenty of time to do his sums, and sited where Victoria's podium had been, now separated from this side of the Common by the M3.

The review was the brainchild of Prince Albert, who was aghast that the army was obsolete in training and equipment, still using muzzle-loading guns cast to defeat Napoleon, almost forty years earlier. In the meantime, every continental army was equipped with more rapid firing breech-loaded guns. He had mentioned to Wellington some years earlier that Chobham be designated a permanent training area, but his suggestion fell on deaf ears.

In 1853, however, the nation was driven by one of its periodic fits of francophobia, and Albert at last got his way for 'a camp of instruction'. Two miles of tents were strung out, and the troops encamped in mid-June. A week later the Queen herself was here to watch. 'Upwards of a hundred thousand people shared in Her Majesty's enjoyment of what was in truth a singularly beautiful spectacle – a well contested, though bloodless battle, over ground broken by hollows, streams, marshes and woods.' Among these, inevitably, were quite a few Chobham locals who, in those days, did not enjoy a reputation for intelligence. It was maliciously put about that some of them put their pigs on the wall to enjoy the military bands as they went by.

Albert's elder brother, Duke Ernst, was in attendance, smirking with his German chums at the poor quality of what they saw, 'a few tactical evolutions, which appeared to be rather childish.' After the Queen's departure the camp was washed out with driving rain and a sea of mud. Albert

Eton College Volunteer cadets on exercise on Chobham Common, October 1905.

gallantly camped with the army, one morning writing early to Victoria, 'It has been raining since five, and it looks very doubtful it will cease... about nine we shall have to turn out; I will join my brigade.... The tents are convenient but both damp and hot during the night.' Albert was rapidly learning the discomforts of soldiering.

The review led to the establishment of Aldershot as a permanent military camp and the designation of hundreds of acres of north-west Surrey's Bagshot sands for army training. In short, the army suddenly became permanently local.

Pass the model aeroplane noticeboard (K12) on your left on the false summit, and continue to the actual summit beyond [GR 9800 6470].

From our twenty-first century perspective, heathland seems rather useless, fit only for military manoeuvres or for walking the dog. George Sturt knew from his neighbours how it had been in the years before 1850:

> .... when I had heard of the village cows, which used to be turned out to graze on the heaths, and had been told how fir-timber for cottage roof joists could be cut on the common, as well as heath good enough for thatching and turf excellent for firing; and when to this was added

Gertrude Jekyll writing in 1904: 'the old carter's smock-frock or round frock, still lingering, but on its way to becoming extinct, is centuries old. No better thing has ever been devised for any kind of outdoor wear that admits of the use of an outer garment. It turns an astonishing amount of wet, especially when of the ordinary local pattern... The frock is cut quite square, of two whole widths of the stuff, with side seams only. The shaping is made by the close gathering, either over the whole back and front, or in two panels on the breast and back near the buttons. It can be worn either way about; back and front are alike... The material is a strong, tough, closely-woven linen.'

the talk of bread-ovens at half the old cottages, and of little corn-crops in the gardens, and of brewing and wine-making and bee-keeping, I understood at last that my elderly neighbours had seen with their own eyes what I should never see – namely, the old rustic economy of the English peasantry.

One of those who had seen was William Cobbett. Chobham Common survived, but elsewhere landlords were busy enclosing so-called 'waste' and driving its inhabitants away, and he recalled:

I [used to go] around a little common [just inside Hampshire]... I found the husbands at home. The Common contained about 150 acres; and I found round the skirts of it, and near to the skirts, about thirty cottages and gardens, the latter chiefly encroachments on the

A 'Sunday best' embroidered smock, worn throughout a lifetime, Sunday by Sunday.

common, which was waste (as it was called)... I took down the names of all the cottagers, the number and ages of their children, and number of their cows, heifers, calves, ewes, pigs, geese, ducks, fowls, and stalls of bees; the extent of their little bits of ground, the worth of what was growing, the number of apple trees, of black-cherry trees, called by them 'merries'... I remember one hundred and twenty-five, or thirty-five stalls of bees, worth at that time ten shillings a stall, at least. Cows there were about fifteen, besides heifers and calves; about sixty pigs great and small; and not less than five hundred head of poultry! The cattle and sheep of the neighbouring farmers grazed the common all the while besides. The bees along were worth more annually than the common, if it had been enclosed, would have let for, deducting the expense of fences.... The cottagers consisted, fathers, mothers, and children, grandfathers, grandmothers, and grandchildren, of more than two hundred persons! I learnt to hate a system that could lead English gentlemen to disregard matters like these! That could induce them to tear up 'wastes' and sweep away occupiers like those I have described!

.... When I was a boy, country labourers' wives used to spin the wool, and knit the stockings and gloves that were wanted in the family.

My grandmother knit stockings for me after she was blind. Farmers' wives and daughters, and servant maids, were spinning, reeling, carding, knitting, or at something or others of that sort, whenever the work of the farm-house did not demand them.... I remember a little sort of fair that used to be held at a village [in fact, Chertsey] in Surrey. I remember the [men's] white smock-frocks and red handkerchiefs, and nice clean clothes of the girls that used to ornament the fair. By accident, I stumbled upon it in a rural ride [in 1822]. Not a tenth part of the people, and these, in general ragged and dirty, with some few girls drawn off in tawdry cottons, looking more like town prostitutes than country girls; and this was a pretty fair sample of the whole country.

Thus, change was already in the air as a result of the Industrial Revolution, well before the advent of rail and macadamised roads in the mid-nineteenth century. This led to a tidal wave of building, with suburbanisation along most of Surrey's Thames riverbank.

Go left and pass two benches from where one can see the path leading back to Staple Hill car park, on the last stretch passing post LIIS, retracing the path initially taken at the outset.

Background on the character of West Surrey

The Geology

Walking any terrain is infinitely more rewarding when one knows something about its geology, the consequent ecology and the way humans have used it. The purpose of the sections that follow is to help visualize the geology that has determined West Surrey's landscape, and human use of it.

Surrey contains two principal landscape features, both of which run west-east: the Weald formation; and the London basin of the Thames which, since it is so heavily urbanised, is of little concern to walkers.

ORIGINS OF THE WEALD FORMATION

The Weald Formation dominates Surrey, Sussex and Kent, creating a structural symmetry which one can see on a clear day, standing at Newlands Corner on the North Downs escarpment looking southwards. It is composed of an extensive centre, the Weald, which is 70 miles long west-east and 25 miles wide, surrounded by two rims, one of sandstone (lower greensand) and, allowing for a thin margin of clay, an outer rim of chalk (the North and South Downs).

In geological terms, these visible formations are recent. They were originally layers of deposits, one laid upon another under water:

(a) The so-called *Wealden Beds*, composed of both sands and clay, are the oldest. They were formed after the land had risen above sea level. They result from fresh water lake and river deposits, mainly sandstone, laid about 160 million years ago, probably over a period of about 20 million years as the water slowly drained eastwards.

(b) After a 20 million year interval the land sank and sea re-entered the area and laid down the *Greensand Beds*. The greensand was deposited in two phases, the more substantial one, lower greensand, was laid down about 120 million years ago, and a later much less substantial phase, upper greensand, was laid down about 110 million years ago. Between the two phases a thin layer of gault clay was laid (running through what became Surrey's 'central valley', running west-east

– the Tillingbourne-Holmesdale valley in which Guildford, Dorking, Reigate and Sevenoaks are located). The lower greensand is 200 metres thick, but the upper greensand, laid on the thin layer of gault clay, is so narrow in West Surrey as to be negligible for walkers. Walking the landscape, the lower greensand is obviously yellow, sometimes almost orange, but never green. However, it is so named because of the presence of a green mineral, glauconite, which only occurs in marine deposits. One never sees the green because on exposure oxidation rapidly turns glauconite yellow or brown.

The greensands vary from very hard rock with high silicon content, known as 'chert', which explains the unusual height and steep escarpments in the Leith Hill district, through a variety of more workable rocks with different local names, to friable sand. These have been laid down in layers over a period of time. A section from the hillside just south of Shere church illustrates the kind of variety to be found in lower greensand:

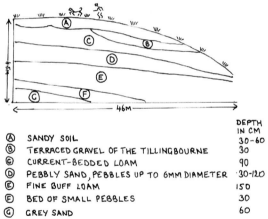

		DEPTH IN CM
Ⓐ	SANDY SOIL	30-60
Ⓑ	TERRACED GRAVEL OF THE TILLINGBOURNE	30
Ⓒ	CURRENT-BEDDED LOAM	90
Ⓓ	PEBBLY SAND, PEBBLES UP TO 6MM DIAMETER	30-120
Ⓔ	FINE BUFF LOAM	150
Ⓕ	BED OF SMALL PEBBLES	30
Ⓖ	GREY SAND	60

(c) Chalk was laid about 80 million years ago, as the portion of the tectonic plate of which England and Wales form a part was drifting northwards through the tropics. This deposit was principally the result of algal blooms. As they died, these minute crustaceans turned to pure limestone chalk. This deposit was laid at a rate of one centimetre per 500 to 1,000 years. In places the deposit is as much as 500 metres thick, suggesting that the time span of the deposit lasted tens of millions of years. This feature is particularly significant because, unlike other rock formations, there is no other example of such chalk beds currently being formed anywhere in the world. Furthermore, along with Normandy, England has the thickest and most extensive chalk anywhere in the world. Within the chalk, itself almost pure fossil, are flints, very hard pure silica lumps, consolidated remains of what were once sponges, sea urchins or similar sea creatures.

(d) Finally, on top of the North Downs there is a layer of clay-with-flints, a layer laid down over different phases, some possibly straight after the chalk, some probably more recently, which geologists are still trying to puzzle out. It is significant that clay-with-flints occurs only south of the last great glaciation.

THE FORMATION OF TODAY'S WEALDEN GEOLOGICAL LANDSCAPE

Between 20 and five million years ago a series of major 'earthstorms' caused massive folding of the landscape, most dramatically seen in Europe in the formation of the Alps. The Weald in Surrey, Sussex and Kent was pushed up into a whaleback-shaped dome, running west-east, and surrounded by water. One piece of evidence for this formation lies with the contrary behaviour of the rivers which, had they been formed *after* the earthstorms, would have logically run eastwards through the low-lying Weald. Yet the principal rivers run north, the Wey, the Mole, the Darent, the Stour and the Medway, off the side of the 'whaleback', cutting through the harder chalk of the North Downs, something they could only have done *before* the chalk top of the dome was eroded and the softer gault, greensand and Wealden beds were washed out. Meanwhile the Arun, rising close to the Surrey-Sussex border runs south.

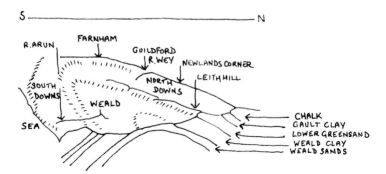

The River Wey has three principal tributaries, one from the south-west, which was once the headwaters of the Blackwater river from Alton in Hampshire. This river once crossed the Hog's Back three kilometres east of Farnham but was 'captured' during the long process of landscape erosion, and now flows on a more southerly route through Tilford (p.98); another tributary runs from the south, drains the Weald clay from close to the Sussex border and flows via Frensham to Tilford; and the third, the Tillingbourne, flows from the east, along the 'central valley' to join the southern Wey at Shalford.

THE FORMATION OF THE THAMES VALLEY

The London Basin, shared with Kent and the north bank counties, is of less importance to the walker as virtually none of the Thames' Surrey bank west of the River Mole is much of a pleasure to walk along. The story of the Thames started 80 million years ago, when the deposit of chalk was drawing to a close. Uplift of the west side of the country led to an immense river flowing eastwards. Sixty million years ago when the land was yet again submerged by sea, another major deposit, this time a layer of clay (London clay) about 80 metres deep, was laid across the sea-bed. When the land was uplifted, about 40 million years ago, a vast river drained eastwards leaving major sandbanks, of which the most notable for Surrey are the Bagshot beds, laid across parts of north west Surrey, and even along the ridge between Hampstead and Highgate on the north side of the basin. Astonishingly, the sand and pebbles had travelled from as far as Devon and Cornwall.

The folding of the chalk between 20 and five million years ago created the London Basin, edged by the North Downs to the south and the Chilterns to the north. The present path of the river Thames was only created two million years ago when the water cut through the Goring Gap at Maidenhead to flow eastwards across the Vale of St Albans. Half a million years ago the advancing ice cap forced the outflow along a more southerly route, cutting the present Thames Valley and Basin. Since then repeated glaciation and thaw has led to mineral debris: pebbles and finer gravels along the path of the Thames, hence the enormous gravel pits close to the river in north-west Surrey. The same process also led to the creation of river terraces, each succeeding phase of melt water cutting a new, deeper, trench through the clay, depositing a fresh layer of gravel and, as it slowed down, silt.

WEST SURREY ROCKS USEFUL TO HUMANS:

Cretaceous Sandstones (between 65 and 146 million years old)

1   *Horsham slates.* Horsham slates belong to a group of sandstone beds found in the Weald clay, with a high mica and quartz content. They are made from fissile Cretaceous sandstone laid down in phases under water, and which splits along the layers of deposit. Despite their heaviness, they were widely used for roofing in the southern part of the county.

2   *Bargate stone* is west Surrey's equivalent of Reigate stone and Kentish rag found further east, but it is less durable and more friable. It is found in considerable quantities in the lower greensand around Godalming. For its extraction see p.122. It is difficult to dress and is used roughly hewn. This makes the quality of mortaring particularly important. A Surrey speciality, 'galleting' or 'garneting', the insertion of small stones (usually *ironstone*, see below) within the mortar seems originally to have acted as wedges between Bargate blocks, to prevent them from rocking. But the elegant seventeenth century galleting at Dunsfold Church(p.40) and in many other places shows that it became decorative, though when Dunsfold church was built, around 1270, the original galleting may have been for stability.

3   *Ironstone*, but known as *carstone* in Surrey, is a fine-grained sandstone strongly cemented by its iron content, which renders it resistant to erosion. It is found in the lower greensand, most notably in St Martha's Hill where its hardness explains the existence of the hill. John Aubrey described carstone as 'Ragges, which look like cast iron.'

4   *Chalk.* Lower chalk (the oldest), being more compacted than Upper Chalk, can produce a soft stone, 'clunch', used occasionally in medieval buildings. Like pudding stone, its use indicates the paucity of more durable alternatives. The quarries have all fallen into disuse.

5   *Flint.* Flint, the compressed siliceous remains of sponge-like sea creatures, is formed into nodules and found on the surface of the North Downs, in the clay-with-flints deposits on top of the chalk. It is extremely hard and difficult to work except by splitting, or 'knapping'. No country uses flint so extensively as England for building, and most of Surrey's churches use flint. Examples in Surrey may be found of both whole flints and knapped flints, exposing the dissected nodule. It is slow to use, as each layer of a wall must be allowed to set

before adding another layer, to ensure its stability for the weight of the next layer.

6   *Chert* is a siliceous crystalline material in narrow beds of sedimentary rock, similar to but larger than flints, sharing the same brittle quality. It occurs principally in the Lower Greensand escarpment on the north fringes of the Weald.

Tertiary Sandstones (between 20 and 65 million years old)

7   *Sarsen stones* are fragments of sand and gravel deposits laid down after the chalk, the remains of a cap of tertiary sandstone. Among the sand and gravel, these stones have survived because of their extreme hardness resulting from their high silicon content. The name 'sarsen' alludes to their apparent strangeness, supposedly like a 'Saracen' or foreigner, which suggests that the term is medieval. They are grey and are found beneath the Bagshot Sands of north-west Surrey. The best examples constitute the waterfall at Virginia Water in Windsor Great Park (see *Windsor Great Park: The Walker's Guide*).

8   *Pudding stone* is another rock of the same period as sarsens. It is only in so stone-poor a county as Surrey that pudding stone came to be used for building. It consists of fragments of conglomerate rock, not very well held together by natural cement. The brown sandstone 'cement' is very friable, but contains fragments of flint. It is, inevitably, difficult to work. Galleting helps to stabilize pudding stone when it is used for building.

Extracted minerals

9   *Lime mortar*. By the eighteenth century there were numerous limekilns on either side of the North Downs, where the chalk met its adjacent beds, or on limestone. The lower chalk was superior to the upper chalk for producing lime, and this made quarrying at the foot of the escarpment more desirable than chalk obtained on the dip-slope (see p.151).

10   *Glass sand* is quartz sand which fuses under heat. Its presence was the basis of the Chiddingfold glass industry in the Middle Ages (see p.42).

11   *Fuller's earth*, *hearthstone* and *firestone* are found in the upper greensand in East Surrey but not in any meaningful quantity west of Dorking.

Humans in Surrey

PREHISTORY

The Ice Ages ended around 17,000 years ago, after which the warmer climate led to massive tree growth. Almost all Surrey was covered with trees, even allowing for the theory that large mammals, like mammoths, may have created clearings by breaking trees down. It was probably Mesolithic Man who started clearing the woodland, an extremely arduous process, achieved with fire as well as with flint implements.

Early humans settled where the soil was most dry, on hilltops or valley slopes. Mesolithic people established woodland clearings, but it was not until about 4000 BC that the North Downs began to be deforested by Neolithic people. They seem to have settled principally along the rivers Mole and Wey, and along the spring lines on the north and south sides of the Downs. They lived in clusters of beehive shaped circular huts, dug into the ground to ensure warmth.

There is little evidence of a Neolithic farming economy. There may have been the beginnings of herding, or perhaps hunting in the Wealden forest was so easy that there was little incentive to keep herds. It may have been population expansion that created the pressure for agriculture. With the slow growth of agriculture from the late Neolithic period (c.2000 BC) there must also have been greater emphasis on using soils that were fertile and manageable as meadow and pasture for livestock, and as arable, a process which determined the central valley (Farnham-Guildford-Dorking-Reigate valley) as the axis for future human settlement.

As settlement progressed and villages or hamlets were established, use was increasingly made of the unexploited landscape to north and south of the valley. By the Early Bronze Age (c.1600 BC) people were beginning to settle in the Greensand Hills also. (Yet even in the Middle Bronze Age, 1400-1000 BC, it was only the Thames Valley which was systematically settled.) Given the speed of technological development today, it is immensely hard to imagine the apparent slowness of human development over 3,000 years ago.

To the north of the central valley, the Downs provided immediate access to well-drained slopes on which to graze livestock, and on top, the heavier clay-with-flints was a good source for wood but remained deeply intractable for the plough. On the upper chalk slopes, however, both on the 'dip-slope' tilting into the Thames valley and the escarpment facing the south, sheep were grazed. Yet even in the Iron Age it was shunned as a place for settlement. The clay-with-flints must have put them off. Lower down, where chalk leached down onto the clay (London clay to the north, gault clay to the south of the Downs), the soil was not only good for arable crops. It also marked the spring-line, attractive for settlement.

To the south, Late Bronze Age folk had established camps on the high ground of the lower greensand escarpment, at Anstiebury, Holmbury Hill and Hascombe Hill. In the Iron Age these became part of a line, flanked in the west by Hillbury on Puttenham Common and in the east by a camp above Squerrys, just inside what became Kent. Were these a defensive line of strongpoints to protect the central valley to the north? It is not clear. They may have been trading points, or assembly points for herds taken into the Weald. Apart from these camps there seems to have been very little settlement on the Lower Greensand hills.

IRON AGE AND ROMAN SURREY

At the outset of the Iron Age the greater part of the population seem to have lived on the gravel and sand of north-west Surrey and to have exhausted it and moved away, leaving behind irredeemable heathland. People apparently led semi-nomadic lives. Some pastoralists ventured into the Weald for seasonal grazing. Others began iron working, for example at Hascombe.

One might think of the central valley across Surrey as rather remote from England's population centres, and perhaps it was. Yet plenty of gold and silver Iron Age coins have been found at Albury and on Farley Heath. Several that have been found bear devices imitative of those of a far wider world, one, for example, clearly derivative from the coinage of Philip II of Macedon.

There is no indication of any resistance to the Roman conquest of Britain. The people of Surrey seem to have welcomed and benefitted from Pax Romana. A main road, the A29 or Stane Street (p.50), ran from London to Chichester via Dorking. The A25 between Dorking and Guildford was probably an Iron Age track, metalled by the Romans. A few villas were established. Two temples have been found, near Wanborough and on Farley Heath, in both cases sited near a road. Some Romano-British temples seem to have been prominent in the landscape.

THE SAXONS AND SURREY'S SETTLEMENT PATTERN

It is in the Saxon period (from the early sixth century) that there is clear evidence of systematic colonisation of the North Downs, with plenty of burial sites on the Downs as well as in the central valley. Use of the Weald for summer grazing was a feature of Saxon agriculture, as it had been in the Late Iron Age. One should be surprised if that were not the case, since the people, albeit their language and culture had changed with the arrival of the Saxons, were still fundamentally the same. Surrey place names are overwhelmingly Saxon, an indication that those carrying Saxon culture were technically advanced and powerful, possibly in the same way that American culture has powerfully influenced the English language and, let's admit it, the culture of Britain over the past two generations.

There is no evidence of the wholesale killing or driving out of the British already living in south-east England. Rather, the indigenous people seem to have accepted the new dominant Saxon culture in the way they accepted Roman culture 500 years earlier and, more astonishingly, embraced the language of this new culture. Place names often indicate specialism: Gatton (goat farm), Merstham (horse enclosure), Banstead (bean cultivation) and Chipstead (marketplace). In the early Middle Ages more names crept in with suffixes like *–feld* (pasture), *-fold* (animal enclosure), *-leah* (woodland clearing); *-ersc* (stubble or ploughed land); *-wic* (a specialised settlement). Other suffixes often describe later settlement in the Weald, for example *-hurst*, another word for woodland clearing.

Anglo-Saxon coin hoards indicate that Surrey used the currencies of outsiders, principally the rulers of Mercia and the Kentish Jutes. Kufic coinage among these hoards indicates the long reach and economic influence of the Islamic Empire by the time of the Caliph Harun al-Rashid at the end of the eighth century. It must be about this time that Surrey, 'the southern district', became a distinct entity, probably detached from the Saxon territory on the northern bank of the Thames which itself must have shrunk into the county of Middlesex.

Surrey's most populated area continued to be along the Thames riverbank. Chertsey Abbey was founded in the mid-660s, and remained immensely important for 900 years, until the Dissolution in 1535. To the south, in the central valley, large single estates were rare. Instead there seems to have been a continuation of Celtic landholding patterns of several farmsteads making up a single parcel of land. One of the most important centres was Shalford ('the shallow ford'), a critical crossing point at the junction of the Wey, the Bramley Wey and the Tillingbourne. To the south, Surrey can at this stage have had no boundary, as the Weald had yet to be colonised.

The Weald was by far the biggest concentration of woodland in England during the Norman period, an area some 70 by 25 miles appearing almost as a blank in the Domesday Book. Settlements grew up as offshoots or dependencies of parent manors outside. It may have been autumnal encampments for pasturing pigs on mast, known as 'pannage', which turned into permanent settlements. Most of the tree clearance of the Weald took place between 1100 and the Black Death of 1349, when population collapse halted it.

Surrey is even better known for its heathland. Mesolithic people were the first to fell tree cover and Neolithic people the first to graze livestock on this sandy soil and thus develop and maintain the heathland ecology. Heathland survived in Surrey as a major man-made habitat, one that was too infertile to act as either pasture or arable, but which was still maintained with minimal tree cover by the practice of stock grazing. Stock grazing ended in the nineteenth century when Surrey was transformed by the intense building development and, coincidentally, by changes in agricultural practice across England which rendered it no longer worthwhile to graze animals on heathland. With the loss of stock grazing, Surrey heathland progressively reverted to natural tree cover, principally birch. Landowners also changed the character of the heathland by deliberately planting larch and Scots pine for their commercial value. As a consequence, we have lost almost all Surrey's real heathland, though there are two or three survivors, all now maintained heathland landscapes, for example Chobham and Frensham commons.

Unlike many counties, Surrey did not become wealthy until it was converted into a rural dormitory for London professionals in the nineteenth century. From the Middle Ages Surrey mostly had scattered hamlets and farmsteads rather than villages. Surrey's parish churches tend to be very small, or were enlarged only recently. They catered to small congregations. Their size was also inhibited by the paucity of decent building stone.

PARISH BOUNDARIES. The picture of settlement in the late Saxon and early Norman period is evident in parish maps of the area up to the 1870s: many parishes (the administrative boundaries of which had taken over from medieval manorial estates) were relatively elongated north to south, and narrowed west to east. This reflected the social and economic organisation for an increasingly crowded central valley, allowing equitable expansion north and south onto the less productive but still valuable lands. Droving from the central valley deep into the Weald led to the establishment of manorial 'outposts', plots of grazing land, miles away from the central manorial holding. Parish maps are one piece of evidence as to the longevity of these old land holdings. This is evident from the sketch map.

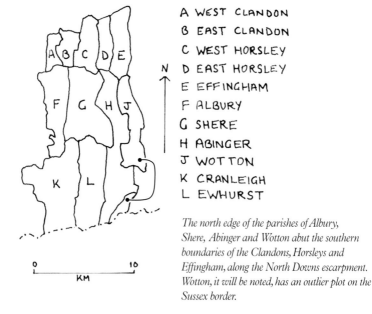

A WEST CLANDON
B EAST CLANDON
C WEST HORSLEY
D EAST HORSLEY
E EFFINGHAM
F ALBURY
G SHERE
H ABINGER
J WOTTON
K CRANLEIGH
L EWHURST

The north edge of the parishes of Albury, Shere, Abinger and Wotton abut the southern boundaries of the Clandons, Horsleys and Effingham, along the North Downs escarpment. Wotton, it will be noted, has an outlier plot on the Sussex border.

The longevity of these landholding patterns, is replicated in the sunken lanes of Surrey, which mainly run north-south, as one can note with satisfaction as one walks. These drove routes, or so-called driftways, probably date from the Iron Age, or perhaps earlier, the livestock being driven from and to settlements in the central valley. The reason that the lanes are so sunken is on account of the friability of the sand, easily worn away by countless trotters, hooves, feet and rainfall. The edges of the lanes are now usually stabilised with tree roots, often beech which seems particularly adept at holding steep banks.

AGRICULTURE

An expansion of agriculture and wood production between the years 1560 and 1640 occurred partly in response to the slow recovery of the population after the devastation of the Black Death (1349), and partly as a result of conscious attempts at improvement. Evelyn's *Sylva* (p.148) was an example of the attempt to set down methods of arboreal improvement. He had a shrewd eye regarding livestock breeding too. In the eighteenth century water meadows were introduced into the central valley, as a method of bringing on sheep.

Whereas the rest of agrarian England witnessed a tidal wave of enclosures in the eighteenth century, by 1800 Surrey was still a land of relatively smallholdings since much of the land was indifferent or poor. Agriculturally, Surrey was backward compared with its neighbours: Kent or Hampshire. Surrey's enclosures only occurred in Cobbett's time, around 1820. Where Cobbett regretted the changes to which he was a witness, however, William Stevenson, one of the growing breed of agricultural experts, was hungry for change to a whole new philosophy, with views that would appeal to the most ruthless modern entrepreneur:

> There are still to be found, especially in the Weald, and the more remote parts of the county, many of the old class of farmers; men who are shy and jealous in their communications; unwilling to adopt any new mode of husbandry; in short, with much of the ignorance and prejudice of former times, and with all its rigid and inflexible honesty – on whose bare word the utmost reliance may be placed, and who have so little of the *impartial* spirit of commerce, that they prefer selling their grain to an old customer at a lower price, to deserting him and accepting a higher offer from one with whom they have not been in the habit of dealing. The "round-frocked farmers" (for they pride themselves on frequenting the markets in the dress of their forefathers) are equal enemies to improvements in agriculture and relaxations in morals... those [farmers] in the Weald, and upon the smaller farms in the more remote parts of the county, consider it absolutely necessary for the management of their farms, that they

should work like their labourers; they have no idea of an active and comprehensive mind.

Thus, while farmers elsewhere were becoming hard-headed managers of farm improvements, capital and the labour of others, most Wealden farmers simply continued to work in the way they had always done. Looking back, it is difficult not to regret the eventual defeat of pre-capitalist values, of that 'inflexible honesty' and willingness to sell below market price to an old customer, an acknowledgement that there are more estimable things in life than making a financial profit.

By the time Stevenson was writing (1813) Britain had entered another period of adverse weather, which was to last for approximately 40 years, from 1780 to 1820. It is worth noting since today's weather pattern is also changing. He wrote:

> the *winter*, that is, the regular and continued frost, is much later than it used to be 40 or 50 years ago, and that season (November-December) which then was cold and dry is now rainy, and rather mild. In Surrey a continued and hard frost is seldom expected till after the new year.

This change in the weather depressed yields and the agrarian economy generally. It was followed by half a century of better weather, which coincided with significant improvements in agriculture, yields in the half-century 1820-70 increasing by 50 per cent. This was the result of better drainage, manuring, bone fertiliser and, from 1840, guano and thereafter superphosphates and for livestock, the use of oil-cake feed. These improvements, almost universal elsewhere, were very patchy in Surrey. This period came to an end with another economic depression in which rail and refrigerated ships allowed the British market to be flooded with cheaper wheat and frozen meat from the New World.

SURREY HOUSES

Until the sixteenth century, labourers had tended to live in manorial buildings or in their own hovels, covered with turf, heather or reed. The disintegration of the feudal system and the dissolution of the monasteries in the 1530s unleashed enormous social change and consequent building. A few timber-framed buildings with wattle and daub have survived. These had hazel rods wedged in grooves of the oak timber, a warp into which willow or hazel branches were woven. A daub of clay,

A lean-to Elstead cottage, typical of the more humble timber-framed and brick in-fill cottage.

chopped straw and animal hair was applied and given an outer crust of lime plaster. However by the 1580s, with the rapid growth of a new baked material, the vast majority of timber-framed buildings were filled in with brick, which was either left bare, sometimes in herring bone pattern, or covered with plaster render.

As elsewhere in the country, Tudor and Stuart dwellings were often not updated with Renaissance or later facades, except by those with money to splash around. Surrey builders on the whole retained simplicity, both in building method and appearance. A distinguishing mark of older dwellings is the use for a corner post of the up-ended butt of a tree, the spreading base carved into a rough corbel to carry a projecting storey above. Perhaps the best surviving example is the Crown Inn at Chiddingfold (p.46). External walls, particularly the west-facing walls, were often hung with tiles, to protect the brickwork from absorbing driving rain. Surrey roofs are distinctive: long hipped roofs which cover the main structure and often a lean-to as well. Roofs are either tiled or sometimes covered with Horsham slate.

Until the late nineteenth century the colouring of Surrey timber-framed cottages combined silvery weathered oak timbers and brick usually of a russet-pink hue, or plasterwork left a natural buff or ochre, or occasionally lime-washed off-white.

When the burgeoning professional classes chose to live in their rural idyll of Surrey, some commissioned architects to build mansions that would look like Surrey traditional cottages with cat-slide roofs, tile-hung walls, exaggerated chimneys and so forth. Pre-eminent among these architects were leading lights in the Arts & Crafts Movement like Philip Webb and C. F. A. Voysey. Two in particular, Edwin Lutyens (1869-1944) and his older gardening cousin, Gertrude Jekyll (1843-1932) created dream houses in the Surrey style. While they both had great sensitivity towards their subject, there were plenty of architects who did not.

Most farmhouses had their own brick oven which protruded out of the kitchen and was protected from the elements by a lean-to roof. Above one can see an old window, that was filled rather than glazed, but its original wooden mullions survive.

Disaster struck with the advent of London architects bent upon providing something romantic for their clients. The 'romantics', possibly inspired by Cheshire timber-framed houses, created the belief that the correct finished style should be blackened timber with whitewashed plaster or brickwork. It was not long before this became the popular treatment for older buildings, and then gave rise to the 'Jacobethan' semis of suburbia. There are still, however, examples of the traditional Surrey vernacular style to be found across the south-west part of the county.

Gertrude Jekyll also lamented the loss of the traditional contents of the old houses,

... the modern exchange for the solid furniture of pure material and excellent design... In the older days it was sufficient, strong, well-made, and beautiful of its kind. It gave a comfortable sense of satisfaction, in that it was absolutely suitable for its purpose. Many of the more solid pieces, oak tables, dressers, linen chests and cupboards, had come down from father to son from Tudor and Jacobean times.... Now, alas! this fine old furniture is rare in these country dwellings. It has been replaced by wretched stuff, shoddy and pretentious.... flimsy and meretricious.

The older pieces of furniture were either destroyed or became collector items for wealthier incoming classes. In such matters Surrey merely joined the rest of the country. Its traditions had lasted longer than many other districts.

SUBURBANISATION & THE GREEN BELT

The process of social and economic change has continued. Incomers first lived apart, in new 'Surrey-style' houses, then the next generation of incomers bought quaint old cottages. Village families moved to the periphery, often to public housing on the edges of villages or to local towns. Then supermarkets displaced village shops, and with them, what was left of community intimacy. Communities must now be self-consciously worked at. They are no longer natural. Until Cobbett's time the landlord farmer and his labourers were tied together, eating at the same table. Today many of the old farms no longer produce food. It is no longer worth it. Supermarkets 'source' their food from elsewhere, no longer locally. So, the owner of a farm might well keep horses instead, a register of the wealth of a society that no longer needs to grow food, but can import it. Today, like elsewhere, society is greatly atomised and largely consists of individuals, and nuclear or single-parent families. Work takes place elsewhere for most, as does shopping. Each of us has our own scale of gains and losses in this process.

After 1918 the urban rush to leafy country turned into a stampede. The North Downs were heavily built upon and, inspired by the enlightened example of Reginald Bray (see pp.171, 176), legislation was enacted to protect the countryside. In 1931, 1938 (Green Belt) and 1973 laws were enacted to protect effectively the whole county. In 2012 the government announced a loosening of planning restrictions which may undermine the protective purpose of legislation in the last century.

TREE HUSBANDRY

Until the advent of steel, petroleum products and fossil fuels, wood in its various forms was an irreplaceable material. Broadly speaking it came in two forms: timber, meaning loadbearing pieces of the tree, either the trunk or substantial branches, and underwood (or wood), which meant smaller pieces and branches. If you were a large landholder, you denuded the woodland at your peril.

Apart from writing *Sylva*, his great classic on arboriculture, John Evelyn also wrote briefly about managing the Wotton estate for his grandson's benefit in *Memoires for my Grandson* (1704), urging

> the Chiefe [improvement] would certainly rise by timely and most continual planting of woods and Timber to which the soil is so inclin'd.... Early and continual storing it [the estate] with Timber Trees, Oake, Ash and Elm, frequent Copses, which in few years will prove incredible Emoluments & Restore the Name of Wotton.

Timber. Trees were grown according to the species and appropriate growing methods to produce the kind of wood material required. Timber principally meant growing oak 'standards', trees protected from grazing and allowed to grow for up to 40 years. They were usually felled when about 250cm/10 inches in diameter. This would be strong enough for all loadbearing for domestic use, and would still be physically manageable. The tall oaks we see today, with a life of about 300 years, would have been a rarity of neglect in the Middle Ages as the trunks would have been too large to handle or to transport. Oaks were particularly favoured on account of their great strength and durability.

English or common oaks were also highly valued for their angularity, which arose from the tendency of their branches to abort terminal buds in favour of lateral ones. Since at least Saxon times, carpenters knew that naturally angled timber was infinitely stronger than man-made joints, however accurately the latter could fit the intended design. A carpenter would judge the angle he required for a particular purpose and then locate it on the living branch. The sessile, or durmast oak, the other British native oak was less inclined to angularity and consequently less popular with carpenters.

By the beginning of the nineteenth century a special Wealden method of regenerating oak stands had developed. A field would be mulched and ploughed in autumn, acorns would be planted into the soil and wheat sown. The wheat would be cropped the following summer, the shearing height of the sickle leaving an oak seedling unscathed but nicely protected from roaming livestock by the stubble all around it. It is difficult to say how widespread this method was, because Weald timber was also attracting criticism because it was insufficiently angular:

> the proprietors in the Weald are not so anxious to have their timber open and unencumbered as they are in other wood districts. Hence the timber, enclosed on all sides by the underwood, grows up tall and straight, unfit for any purpose in which knees or crooked timber is wanted.
>
> William Stevenson, *A General View of the Agriculture of Surrey* (1813)

By this stage, however, straight timber was probably increasingly in demand, and the need for angularity in decline as improved iron and steel began to substitute for timber. The decline of coppice at the close of the nineteenth century led to an increase in timber production. This has perhaps been less for economic considerations than for ornament, shelter of cultivated land, or for game.

Coppice. The other principal method of producing useful wood was by creating coppice, in which oak, ash, hazel and willow usually ruled supreme. Oak was used for poles, ash provided provided handles and shafts for hand tools, hazel produced hurdles or wattle, willow could be made into wattle or baskets. Almost any other tree species provided fuel. Unlike stands of timber standards which needed protection from livestock until the trees grew above the browse line, coppice required proper and permanent protection, with either hurdles or a livestock-proof hedgerow. Timber stands were often converted to coppice after the first 'fall' of timber, as Stevenson noted:

> After a fall of timber, the sapling shoots from the stools are the principal source of copse-wood... thus the undergrowth is continually increasing.

Coppice was established by routine cropping, usually about every 7-10 years, but dependent on the tree species, each periodic crop cut at ground level, leaving behind the 'stool', the base from which new growth would always shoot. Saplings of ash, willow and alder could be 'plashed', or half cut, and bent and pegged to the ground, to encourage re-rooting. After a couple of years, when the sapling had re-rooted, it would be separated from the parent stool.

Coppicing was economically more rewarding than timber production. It would produce the greater part of fuel, either simply as faggot 'cords' or bundles, known in Surrey dialect as 'bavins' of harvested wood, or more importantly in the form of charcoal (see pp.19-21).

Coppice and underwood production collapsed at the close of the nineteenth century in the face of metal mass production, the availability of cheap imported wood and a decline in the demand for hop poles. In just a few years the value of coppice declined from

A coppice-cutter, c.1900, making up a bavin, or 'cord' of faggots. Coppice or copse-cutting was a winter activity.

roughly £40 per acre to only £2 to £5 per acre. It never recovered, and landowners either allowed coppice to lapse or grubbed the stools out in favour of timber. In the first half of the twentieth century ash coppice was still bountiful around Chiddingfold, for the production of ash walking sticks. Today though, there is hardly any coppicing because we have cheaper alternatives for fencing (although chestnut is still coppiced for palings on galvanised wire), heating, containers and for the myriad other traditional uses of coppiced wood. There is plenty of lapsed coppice to be seen around as one walks.

Pollards and hedgerows. Finally, there was the question of harvesting what might grow in hedgerows. Here, oak trees in particular would be cropped, as in coppice, but above the browse-line, and the trunks would be protected either with wattle or with thorn to ensure they made it that far. After the first cut, the branches of these 'pollards' would be cropped every 10 years or so, to provide more useful wood, for fuel or as staves. Lapsed pollards, with their stout or squat trunks and angular branches, are wonders of man's symbiosis with nature, for they can easily outlive

A Weald collier living out in the woods in his makeshift canvas hut, c.1900. It is about this time that one Surrey writer observed: 'I used to visit a woodman one winter who slept in a hut he made in six hours one Boxing Day. With his billhook he cut the poles and the bean-sticks which formed the walls, padded with pea boughs. Bundles of faggots and bracken became his bedstead and mattress. The first time I visited him, snow held the entire great wood in the soft silence of death, not a single human footstep was visible leading to the snow-covered hut. A tripod, on which a pot was slung, stood by the door of the begrimed hut.'

standards and survive for over a thousand years. Indeed, if they had been routinely cropped until today, one thousand and perhaps even two thousand-year old pollards would be commonplace, able to outlive standards perhaps six-fold. The pollarding of hedgerow oaks fell into decline towards the end of the eighteenth century,

> … war has been declared against them; and already the work of extirpation has made considerable progress. The inconveniency of pollards, in rough coppice hedges, having been long experienced, the planters of young hedges appear to have carefully (yet improvidently perhaps) avoided the PLANTING OF HEDGEROW trees except the POPLAR, of late years partly or wholly by way of screens to hop grounds.
>
> William Marshall, *The Rural Economy of the Southern Counties, comprizing Kent, Surrey, Sussex, etc.* (1798)

Along streams and rivers willow pollards used to be a common sight, until labour costs rendered pollarding uneconomic.

Hedgerows were maintained by 'plashing'. By this method each year's growth was half cut and bent down to the ground so that it would re-root and thus thicken the lower part of the hedgerow. It is so labour intensive that no one can afford to do it any longer. An alternative method was to insert something akin to a wattle hurdle into a hedgebank. Stakes, preferably of chestnut would be driven into the bank, and rods of hazel or ash would be 'rostled' (another nice Surrey word) or woven between the uprights.

HOP CULTIVATION

Hops for turning ale into beer were introduced from the Low Countries in the early sixteenth century. Although Kent became England's principal hop region, all along the Holmsdale valley westwards from Westerham on the Kent border, past Reigate, Dorking, Guildford and the Hog's Back there was a thin string of hop gardens, sited mainly on the very fine line of Upper Greensand soil. Near the end of his life in 1704, John Evelyn, who knew a good thing, urged his young grandson at Wotton to 'By Hopps for which ye have some proper grounde.' And what was proper hop ground? Gilbert White, living just over the border in Hampshire, describes it as

> a kind of white land, neither chalk nor clay, neither fit for pasture nor for the plough, yet kindly for hops, which root deep into the freestone, and have their poles and wood for charcoal growing just at hand. This white soil produces the brightest crops.

It was at the western end of the formation, at Farnham, that by the eighteenth century the most desirable hops for popular pale beers were available.

William Marshall, the agriculturalist, visited west Surrey in 1791 and noted that 'the chalky lands of Farnham are wholly hopgrounds, and some of them old beyond memory.... the passion for hop grounds having then risen to a degree of rage.... At that time the hop grounds were surrounded by thorn hedges, and sometimes lime trees in close rows.' The latter must have served as windbreaks. By 1900 the Golding reigned supreme in Kent, but in Farnham Whitebine, a Golding variety, was 'the best but needs perfect soil'. Elsewhere in the strong soils of the Surrey Weald the delightfully named 'Fuggle' was the variety of choice, 'a hardy vigorous hop with large cones possessing pointed petals and good condition, though lacking the delicate flavour of Goldings.' By then, however, hop growing was already in steep decline. In 1885, still at its peak, Surrey hop growing accounted for 2,627 acres. By 1909 this figure had collapsed to 544 acres, the old gardens grubbed out to make way for houses for incoming city professionals or, in some cases, for gravel pits. Fuggle still grows in Surrey's last hop field, in Puttenham, (see p.139), the hop of choice for the Hog's Back Brewery.

From 1874 a sophisticated vinery system using wirework was introduced. Hop cultivation required deep pockets and great care, with only a narrow window – barely ten days - for harvesting, if one were to catch the hops at their best and thus secure the best price. Everyone was called upon to help. Village labour was insufficient and itinerants were also employed, principally landless squatters on the heathland and 'Egyptians', as Romany Travellers were often called. They would work from dawn to dusk, getting the hops down and picked. Completion of a successful hop harvest involved celebration (see p.139).

Drying in the kiln required care. The hops were dried on cloth laid on slatted a slatted floor above the kiln. Once dried in the kiln, the hops would be compressed into sacks, or 'pockets', marked with that year's Farnham mark, and hopefully sold at market by Michaelmas Day. Round kilns, characteristic of Kentish oasthouses, were a nineteenth century innovation. Previously they had been rectangular, or simply part of the hop barn. We should be glad that having fallen into disuse, so many kilns have been converted into dwellings, so we have not lost this remembrance of a past culture.

WOMEN'S WORK

Among the many things Gertrude Jekyll recorded was the way women used to work the fields at harvest time, an image redolent of Ruth gleaning in the fields of Boaz:

> Women, gleaning in the harvest-field – 'leasing' as they used to call it – are now no longer seen. The pitiless, grasping iron contrivances pick up the stray ears too closely... In the older days the wives and children of farm servants were allowed to glean or 'lease' on the fields of the farm where the father was employed, before the sheaves were carried. If others came who were not entitled to the privilege, they were roped off the field, where it was free of sheaves, by a rope stretched between two horses, and so carried down the field. After the corn was carried,

'Country methods of washing clothes have scarcely changed; the old coarse red-ware pan is always a convenient and favourite washing tub.' Gertrude Jekyll.

most farmers allowed anybody to glean. The children held the ears on the long stalks, in their hands close up to the heads, making neat bundles. The ears on short stems were dropped into an apron pocket.

Well into the twentieth century women's work was extremely hard. They were required to clothe and feed up five or six children in a two-up-two-down cottage, fetch all the water from the well, gather wood or turf fuel or purchase faggots, or possibly obtain coal. And they had to cook on a range or with a crane (or swee) over a fire, and heat the copper for the laundry over a fire too. With running water and electricity we no longer have any notion of what village domestic work was like only a century ago.

In the 1870s male labourers were paid 2 shillings per day [about £5 in modern currency], compared with women who received 10 pence [about £2 now]. With the agricultural depression from 1875 to 1910, it was unusual for women to be working regularly on farms. By 1904 they were not even employed to glean.

Making a day of it

ON THE NORTH DOWNS AND IN NORTH SURREY

Polesden Lacey, Great Bookham,
   (www.polesdenlacey@nationaltrust.org.uk)
Clandon Park, West Clandon
   (tel. 01483 222482, www.clandonpark@nationaltrust.org.uk)
Hatchlands Park, East Clandon
   (tel. 01483 222482, www.hatchlands@nationaltrust.org.uk)
RHS Wisley, just off A3 north of Ripley
   (tel. 01483 224234, www.rhs.wisley.org.uk)
Painshill, Portsmouth Rd, Cobham
   (tel. 01932 868113, www.painshill.co.uk)

ON THE WEST SIDE OF GUILDFORD

Farnham and the Farnham Museum, 38 West St, Farnham
   Open Tues-Sat, 1000-1700 (tel. 01252 715094,
   www.farnham.museum@waverley.gov.uk)
The Rural Life Centre, Reeds Road, Tilford
   Open Wed to Sun, mid-March–end October, 1000-1700, in winter
   Weds & Suns only, 1100-1600 (tel. 01252 795571,
   www.rural-life.org.uk)
The Watts Gallery, Compton
   (tel. 01483 810235, www.wattsgallery.org.uk)
Loseley Park, nr Compton
   (tel. 01483 304440, www.loseleypark.co.uk)

GUILDFORD AND EAST OF IT

Guildford Museum, and Castle Arch
   Open Mon-Sat, 1100-1700 (tel. 01483 444751,
   www.guildford.gov.uk/museum)
Guildford Cathedral
   (tel. 01483 547860, www.guildford-cathedral.org)
Dapdune Wharf, Wharf Road, Guildford
   (tel. 01483 561389, www.riverwey@nationaltrust.org.uk)

Shalford Mill, nr Guildford
(tel. 01483 561389, www.shalfordmill@nationaltrust.org.uk)
Shere Museum, Gomshall Lane
Open Jan-Dec weekends, bank holidays (except Christmas/New Year)
1-5pm, and April-Oct on Tuesdays and Thursdays (10am-3pm),
(tel. 01483 202769, www.sheremuseum.co.uk)
Oakhurst Cottage, Hambledon, nr Godalming
(tel. 01483 208936, www.oakhurstcottage@nationaltrust.org.uk)
Winkworth Arboretum, nr Godalming
(tel. 01483 208477,
www.winkwortharboretyum@nationaltrust.org.uk)

BEYOND SOUTH-WEST SURREY

Petworth House, West Sussex
(tel. 01798 343929, www.petworth@nationaltrust.org.uk)
Gilbert White's House, Selborne, Hants.
(tel. 01420 511275, www.gilbertwhiteshouse.org.uk)
Weald and Downland Open Air Museum, Singleton, West Sussex
(tel. 01243 811363, www.wealddown.co.uk)

Index

David McDowall has lived and worked in different parts
of the world: in Hong Kong, India, Iraq, the Lebanon and
Austria, serving in HM Forces, the British Council and the
United Nations. He has travelled widely in the Near East and
has written extensively on both British and Middle Eastern
history, in particular on the Palestine question, the Lebanese
conflict, and the Kurds of Iran, Iraq, Syria and Turkey. He
now writes walkers' guides to some of Britain's historic
landscapes. He is married to the writer Elizabeth Laird.